## Advance praise for Nick Tasler

"*The Impulse Factor* will force you to think—and rethink—how and why you make decisions. Nick Tasler's hip and hopeful approach entertains and educates in one fell swoop."

—Daniel H. Pink, author of *A Whole New Mind*

"If you thought you understood how people digest risk and spur innovation, think again. This should be required reading for any decision maker with concern for the future health of their organization, industry, or society."

—Priya Patel, assistant vice president of
revenue cycles, Advocate Health Care

"In today's business world, a company's competitive advantage is secured and sustained by the creative tension between its decision makers. This insightful and witty read is a playbook on how to leverage that healthy tension."

—Terry Barton, vice president of agencies, State Farm Insurance

"Nick Tasler is a beautiful writer who weaves his tale in such an engaging way that you can't help but hold a mirror up to yourself and ask how *The Impulse Factor* impacts your success and satisfaction."

—Beverly Kaye, CEO of Career Systems International
and author of *Love 'Em or Lose 'Em*

"Tasler's writing is as entertaining as his insights are useful. It's an exciting ride that is sure to make you see your choices in a whole new light. "

—Matt Olmstead, executive producer, *Prison Break* and *NYPD Blue*

"Weaving together research in genetics, psychology, politics, and Mother Nature's animal kingdom, this insightful work teaches powerful lessons                                      s, and how to start making                                      read it!"

—                                      Fleet Company

# THE
# IMPULSE
# FACTOR

Why Some of Us
Play It Safe and
Others Risk It All

## NICK TASLER

SIMON &
SCHUSTER

London · New York · Sydney · Toronto

This edition first published in Great Britain by
Simon & Schuster UK Ltd, 2009
A CBS COMPANY

Copyright © Nick Tasler, 2008

1 3 5 7 9 10 8 6 4 2

Simon & Schuster UK Ltd
1st Floor
222 Gray's Inn Road
London, WC1X 8HB

www.simonsays.co.uk

Simon & Schuster Australia
Sydney

A CIP catalogue record for this book
is available from the British Library

ISBN: 978-1-84737- 422-6

Designed by Jan Pisciotta
Printed in the UK by CPI Mackays, Chatham ME5 8TD

*To my wife, Alison*

# CONTENTS

# FOREWORD

F ew things in life can lead one to greatness or ruin as rapidly and decisively as impulsivity, which is why I find it strange that it's so poorly understood. We all know what impulsive people look like—they're pretty easy to spot. Most of us can even recall a time when the instincts of an otherwise rational person led them to act like a complete fool. But what made them do it? And why are some people so incredibly impulsive all of the time? There is knowledge of impulsivity floating around out there—in university studies, academic journals, and the like—but there's little, if any, real-world understanding of the powerful role it plays in our lives.

Until Nick Tasler came along.

Nick is the guy you'd want sitting next to you at a dinner party. He's witty, astute, and very inclusive, sharing his passion for the way people tick in a way that—flaws and all—makes you feel great about being alive. He will change the way you view the world. Then he will change the way you see yourself. Both will be the better for it.

In *The Impulse Factor*, he turns a once impenetrable concept into a dazzling exploration of how things work. Beginning with a newly discovered dopamine gene that mutated some fifty thousand years ago—right before humans migrated out of Africa and created music, art, and ultimately civilization—he takes us on an incredible, page-turning journey. Through riveting tales of a harrowing escape from a Canadian avalanche, Dutch tulip madness, and even why splitting dinner tabs always backfires, Tasler illuminates the role of impulses in every facet of our personal and professional lives. The mutant dopamine gene is still around today. It's seen in around one of every four people, including kids with ADD, alcoholics, and most anywhere we encounter the tricky side effects of impulsive behavior. But not all effects of the gene are negative. The same impulsive tendencies fuel superstar entrepreneurs, avant-garde musicians and artists, and most anyone who pushes us in bold, new directions.

What this book teaches you about the world around you will be trumped only by what it teaches you about yourself. The knowledge you'll gain is critical, as optimal performance is as much about perspective as it is about effort. My research has found that as self-awareness increases, people's satisfaction with life skyrockets, and they are more likely to reach their goals at work and at home. Building your self-awareness isn't about discovering deep dark secrets or unconscious motivations, but rather a straightforward and objective understanding of what makes you tick. In the workplace 83 percent of those high in self-awareness are top performers and just 2 percent of bottom performers are high in self-awareness. The impact of self-knowledge is so profound because it ensures we adequately recognize and utilize the situations and people that will make us successful. It also enables us to understand the limiting tendencies we can't avoid, which minimizes the damage they create.

The need for self-awareness has never been greater. In *The Emotional Intelligence Quick Book*, my coauthor and I exposed an emotional epidemic of massive proportions. We found that just 36 percent of people possess an adequate amount of self-awareness, and 70 percent of folks are ineffective at handling conflict and stress. The popularity of that book has helped to build awareness of the problem and bridge the gap to a degree, but more work needs to be done. We still live in a society that is driven by the mistaken notion that psychology deals exclusively with problems, falsely assuming that the only time to learn about ourselves is in the face of crisis. We tend to put on the blinders the moment something causes us distress. But it's really the whole picture that serves us. The more we understand the beauty and the blemishes, the more we can put them both to work to achieve our potential.

*The Impulse Factor* can heal the emotional epidemic we still face. It's the kind of book that you'll stay up late to finish and think about often once it's back on your shelf. While it may seem that impulsivity spurns us to act only in those moments where our fate hangs perilously in the balance, the reality is it's the hidden force behind all of the choices we make. Nick Tasler's phenomenal theory of conditional impulsivity illuminates just how it all works. Follow his suggestions and you'll make better decisions every day.

—Dr. Travis Bradberry
Coauthor of *The Emotional Intelligence Quick Book*

# Introduction:
## Thrill Riders

In February 1994 a snowmobile search-and-rescue team raced over the powdery hillsides outside of Pincher Creek, in western Canada. The experienced team was riding high on the success of a mission in which they had recovered a trio of adventurers stranded in the vast countryside of southern Alberta. George Barrington, Roger Taylor, and Ken Moriyama had failed to return home from a snowmobiling day-trip the night before, and the concerned families of the three men had alerted Brian Cusack, the rescue commander of nearby Westcastle Ski Hill. A gusty blizzard made conditions too dangerous for a rescue attempt that evening. The next morning Cusack's full-time staff had all it could handle with the avalanche threats at Westcastle, so Cusack called on a volunteer crew headed by Eric Bruder. Bruder quickly rounded up a local group of fourteen rescuers who tracked down the missing riders within just a few hours on the hunt. To celebrate another job well done, eight members of the rescue team split off from the group. Under a dreary midday sky, the playful bunch tore through the open plains at full throttle, kicking up the ten inches of new snow that had fallen over the weekend.

A little before noon, the eight riders stopped at an old well site at the foot of a hill. To avid snowmobilers, the flat approach leading up to a long incline makes for an irresistible invitation to play a game called "hammer-heading." Hammer-heading is like playing king of the mountain but on snowmobiles. The goal is to gather as much speed as you can muster on the flat approach, and then make it as far up the hillside as possible before the incline lets you know you've gone far enough. Then you turn around to watch and hope that nobody else makes it higher than you. Any snowmobiler will tell you that hammer-heading is a fun game. But in the presence of high avalanche danger, "fun" is draped in an unstable sheet of snow weighing upward of two million pounds.

Avalanches are one of nature's more temperamental disasters. Unlike other displays of wrath such as hurricanes, earthquakes, tornadoes, or floods, avalanches react to intrusions by humans in a very direct and destructive manner. Giant snow slabs are most likely to come unglued on slopes that have recently received a heavy snowfall, which creates a layer of snow that has not yet had time to bond with the preexisting layer beneath it. Skiers are fond of calling this unstable new snow a "fresh layer of powder." When it comes to powder, the general rule for skiers and snowboarders is that deeper is better. Avalanches agree. On a powder-drenched slope with just the right incline, it takes only one ill-advised move to set an avalanche in motion. This is a crucial point the Canadian rescuers would soon find out.

The tiny resort town of Pincher Creek sits on the tip of an especially deadly triangle. Perfect conditions and the surfeit of winter-sport enthusiasts make this treacherous little region stretching between Vancouver and southwestern Alberta the most dangerous in the country. It is no secret that nearly three-fourths of Canada's annual avalanche fatalities happen here, which means that members of a search-and-rescue team from Pincher Creek would almost certainly have a strong working knowledge of the conditions that set off a snow slide.

But rationally understanding the risks doesn't account for the fact that hammer-heading can be one hell of a good time. The hill that stood in front of these eight Canadian snowmobilers at Middle Kootenay Pass was neither too steep nor too flat. It was just right. And because hammer-heading is such a rare treat for the thrill-seeking snowmobiler, if you pass up one chance, you never know when you might get another. It didn't matter that another snowmobiler was laid to rest in a snowy grave on that same hill just four years earlier.

Rescue commander Brian Cusack was well aware of the temptation that might face the squad of rescuers that day. Before the team set out, he issued a specific order that "hammer-heading was out of the question." With that command swimming through their brains, all eight of the rescuers killed their machines at the hill's foot around 11:30 a.m. After a few moments, impulse overcame reason in one of the eight snowmobilers. Despite the direct order, according to Cusack, one of the other rescuers had dared or bet twenty-one-year-old Lane McGlynn that he couldn't make it to the top of the hill. McGlynn fired up his engine with one quick pull and took off toward the hill with reckless abandon. After climbing most of the way up the hillside, McGlynn's machine finally ground to a halt. Minutes later, the rider who dared McGlynn decided to try his luck. This was when things went terribly wrong.

In the middle of the second rider's ascent, the top layer of snow broke free. The other six riders were then forced to watch as the hill shed its 450-foot wide, three-foot thick cloak of snow. As the massive sheet picked up speed, it swept up more loose snow, eventually burying Lane McGlynn in nine feet of wet snow that might as well have been freshly poured concrete. The second rider reacted quickly, perhaps showing evidence that he might have known better than to be on the hill in the first place. Five of the six others at the bottom followed the second rider's lead and raced out of harm's way.

The eighth rescuer, Eric Bruder's brother, Kevin, was stuck in his tracks. Kevin had been dealing with a faulty kill switch that interfered with the quick-starting design of his snowmobile. Under other circumstances, the malfunctioning starter was nothing more than a nuisance. On that day in February 1994, this minor inconvenience trapped Kevin Bruder at the bottom of the hill pulling frantically, while staring straight into the eye of a level 3 avalanche bearing down on him. Kevin Bruder was unable to get his machine started and ended up sharing Lane McGlynn's fate.

Being a rescue team, the group was well equipped with avalanche recovery gear. One of the surviving members radioed for help immediately. The others frantically canvassed the hill's surface trying to track down the two buried riders. Using their radio locating devices, the team made quick progress in their search. At five minutes past noon, they dug out a near-lifeless Kevin Bruder. He was barely hanging on. While some of the survivors continued their desperate attempts to resuscitate Kevin, another rescuer uncovered Lane McGlynn's mangled body. "His body was mush, head was smashed, neck was broken. He was folded 180 degrees at the waist," Brian Cusack told me with a tone of marked pity and regret still clearly lingering thirteen years later. By this time a doctor had arrived on the scene. It took the doctor only one look at the unnatural jumble of body parts in front of him to pronounce McGlynn dead. At the bottom of the hill, after nearly an hour of exhaustive effort and an adrenaline shot to Kevin Bruder's heart, the team gave up CPR.

Avalanche experts Torsten Geldsetzer and Bruce Jamieson[1] described the ease with which the regrettable disaster could have been prevented had the rescuers heeded the wisdom that, on a fragile slope, "while one snowmobile and rider may be tolerable, any additional load will increase the chances of it avalanching." A traumatized survivor of the day's disastrous events summed up the confused sentiment of the group when he asked, "Why did they do it?" What was it that caused Lane McGlynn to abandon the group and disobey a direct order? What made the rescuer who dared McGlynn in the first place follow his lead and ultimately trigger the avalanche?

*The Impulse Factor* sets out to answer those questions.

## 1. The Cautious/Impulsive Ratio

Let's do a quick experiment. Imagine that I'm about to let you choose between two appealing options. All you'll have to do is tell me which you prefer. If you choose the first option, you will have a chance to win a three-week, all-expenses-paid trip through England, France, and Italy. I'll simply flip a coin, and if it turns up heads you win the trip, but if it turns up tails you get nothing. On the other hand, you can take what's behind door number two. If you decide to go with this second option, I'll give you a guaranteed one-week, all-expenses-paid trip to Italy, with no strings attached, no coin to be flipped. So there you have it—a fifty-percent chance for a free three-week vacation, or a guaranteed free one-week vacation. Which would you choose?

If you're like most people, you would take the safe bet. You would opt for the guaranteed one-week Italian excursion, and you would walk away feeling pretty pleased. Indeed, that's what about three-fourths of people do. But that isn't the choice everyone makes. About one-fourth of the population will let their luck ride. This smaller crowd will select the risky option just for the mere potential of a bigger payout, even though they may end up with no winnings at all. Daniel Kahneman, winner of the 2002 Nobel Prize in Economics, and his colleague Amos Tversky[2] first presented scenarios like this to students in the mid-1970s, along with a variety of other similar scenarios. Sometimes they asked people to choose between European vacations. Sometimes it was a choice between insurance plans, and still other times the choices were varying amounts of plain old cash. Since then, researchers all across the world have tested this idea using all sorts of prizes. And no matter where the experiment is conducted, the results are almost always the same. When any random group of people are given the choice between two good deals, the majority will play it safe, and the remainder will follow their impulse toward a riskier option. Because these studies have been repeated so often with so many different people from different backgrounds, researchers felt confident drawing a conclusion about how people make decisions. Specifically, they concluded that most people will usually choose the gain with a lesser value, just as long as they don't have to gamble for it.

But in those experiments there was always that small group of people who stubbornly refused to fall into line with the majority. Since Kahneman and Tversky's primary goal was only to learn something about the way that *most* people make decisions, this bolder minority received much less press. But if we give the studies a thorough once-over, it seems as though two different types of decision makers were involved. These two kinds of people view the world differently. More to the point, they view *decisions* differently. Decision researcher Lola Lopes[3] says there are "dispositional differences in the importance that different people attach to avoiding bad outcomes versus achieving good outcomes." Most people are stuck on their need to steer clear of sticky situations. Lopes calls these average, everyday people "security-minded." The cautious majority with a bent toward safety evaluate their choices in search of the option that offers them the most security. Their biggest concern is minimizing risk. The more impulsive people, on the other hand, are what Lopes labels "potential-minded." This exciting bunch is into getting the most bang for their buck. They usually set their sights on taking home the biggest prize, rather than running away from the biggest risks.

The fatal avalanche in Canada vividly illustrates the cautious/impulsive ratio. We would expect to find that, out of every eight people, one or two of them will tend to be impulsive. In fact, that is exactly what happened at Middle Kootenay Pass. Despite knowing better, one of the eight rescuers threw caution to the wind and followed his risky impulse. A second rider followed a few minutes later and set off the avalanche. But the remaining six rescuers kept their impulses on a tight leash.

So why is it that one person might be more prone to leaving well enough alone, while another person will continue pressing his or her luck?

## 2. Born to Be Impulsive

Genetics have a lot to say about it. All humans are born with an enzyme in their brain called monoamine oxidase (MAO), whose job it is to keep their impulses in check. Chief of the Laboratory of Clinical Science at the National Institute of Mental Health, Dennis Murphy,[4] discovered that some people have a shortage of this MAO enzyme, which makes them more willing to chase thrills. MAO acts like a well-intentioned parent as it regulates the brain's chemicals that control how much fun we have. One of these chemicals—dopamine— represents the kid in all of us. It's what makes us vibrant, sociable, and hungry for new experiences. In moderation these carefree chemicals are healthy, but too much or too little of them can be lethal.[5] The goal is to keep them balanced, which is also where we get the term *imbalanced* to describe people who seem a tad high-strung or moody. When MAO becomes too overbearing in our brains, it doesn't let us have enough of these fun chemicals and we can be real downers. We will get depressed and may rebel by hanging out with a hipper, more laid-back friend like Prozac. People with too much MAO can also be slow to respond to immediate threats or be too afraid to seize clearly advantageous opportunities.

In comparison, when MAO is in short supply in a person's brain, just the opposite happens. A shortage of MAO is akin to having parents who go out of town and leave their teenager home alone. Without MAO around to regulate it, dopamine is free to invite all its friends over for a wild party inside our brains. If the party grows big enough, it might encourage us to do stupid things that our parents told us not to—things like drive a snowmobile up a shifty hillside.

For the majority of people, impulses are like a backseat driver. We can hear impulse telling us to take a shortcut, but the MAO in our brains tells our impulses to put a cork in it. So most of us end up sticking to the safe, well-traveled paths. A relatively small fraction of daring souls, however, tends to let impulse take the wheel. Genetic researchers have recently uncovered a specific gene mutation that alters the way some people's brains handle dopamine, and it compels these people to seek out exciting adventures despite the risk. At their worst, impulsive people are exactly what nasty little stereotypes would predict. They are more likely to be sexaholics, dangerous drivers, bankrupt businesspeople, and the posthumous winners of the dubious Darwin Awards. But at their best, impulsive people have something of a secret weapon in their willingness to act quickly without letting fear of consequences break their stride. When opportunity knocks, impulsive people are more apt to welcome it in, while their more cautious neighbors peer apprehensively through the peephole until the opportunity moseys next door. Scientists now believe that this gene mutation may have been just the bold catalyst needed to uproot our prehistoric ancestors from Africa and ultimately secure modern humans' place in the world. The question now is whether this increasingly common genetic trait impacts our world for better or worse? The answer may surprise you.

## 3. Deciding Our Fate

*The Impulse Factor* tells the story of our decisions in two parts. Every decision that has ever been made in the history of humankind has two key elements that determine its outcome: the person and the situation. For far too long, we have been mystified by the process of our own decision making. Why are some of us so maddeningly indecisive? Why are others so uncontrollably rash? Can certain conditions cause us to behave clearly out of character? Why did Lane McGlynn climb that hill? Why did another rider follow him up the hill? Everyone seems to have their own speculations that they offer as answers. But these speculations usually fall short of convincing as they fail to take the relevant factors into consideration. A big part of our struggle to make sense of these questions has to do with our one-sided view of how people make choices. Many books shed light on general quirks of the human mind that cause all people to act in a certain way. Others cater to the unique specifications of individual types of people without much regard for the external influences on a situation. This book fuses these views into one formula for effective decision making.

The first part of *The Impulse Factor* shows you that our only hope for improving the quality of our decisions is to look at how people naturally differ from one another *and* how each situation can introduce its own set of influential conditions. Trying to understand a decision by looking at *only* the situation or at *only* the person is like trying to cook a gourmet meal with all the ingredients, but without a recipe. You will end up with something that looks like an answer, but it will leave you wanting.

Decisions are like avalanches in this way. Avalanches take into account certain conditions of the situation (the incline of the slope and the amount of snow buildup) and people (someone loosening up the snow pack). You could round up the most impulsive people on the planet for a snowmobile rally, but it isn't going to cause an avalanche unless the surface is at the right incline. On the other hand, one very cautious person treading ever so lightly on a perfectly sloped snow layer can (and does so multiple times every winter) trigger an avalanche.

Our patterns do not have to remain a mystery. We can each know our individual tendencies, as well as the conditions that determine how these tendencies result in a final decision. Our tendencies toward or away from impulsivity can have a profound effect on how we drive, how we vote, and whether our kids will take up delinquent behaviors. But these individual tendencies tell only some of the story.

The second part of this story is where the plot really thickens. It explains why an ordinarily cautious person will decide to uproot her whole life to follow a dream, or how having an artist's temperament can land someone in the captain's chair of a multinational corporation. *The Impulse Factor* explores the unique role that cautious and impulsive tendencies play in determining why it's so hard to beat Tiger Woods in golf, why we are such suckers for mudslinging political campaigns, what saints and sinners have in common, and why people bought stock in Webvan. It will also take you from the boardrooms of corporate America into the jungles of Venezuela to unearth the roots of these tendencies.

The most exciting thing about *The Impulse Factor* is that by knowing each of our specific decision-making tendencies, we can exercise control over them. Until now, we have been victims of our tendencies and circumstances. We have been given advice that is either too vague to be applied or too specific to apply to our different individual makeups and the different situations in which we find ourselves. Understanding your unique tendency and how it manifests itself in various situations is the only way to improve the choices you make. *The Impulse Factor* and its accompanying online test will reveal your tendency, and describe how to use it to make the kinds of choices you want in the situations you want. We will explore the edgy ways in which impulsive people attack their world, and stack those up against the approach of more cautious people hell bent on survival. Impulsive people can learn to balance the thrill of a heartbeat-skipping experience with the need to see another day. Indecisive people can learn to loosen up without the fear of losing it all. In doing so, we can spruce up our scorecards in golf, in business, in grocery shopping, and maybe even learn to live a fuller life. In the end, the goal is for us all to experience the joy of sailing across a snowy meadow without triggering an avalanche.

# CHAPTER ONE

# Origin of Seekers:

## From Cavemen to Cage Fighters

According to the official program, Nick Wernimont stands just under six feet tall and weighs 170 pounds. He looks like the kind of guy who, if you saw him walking down a dark alley . . . well, you would probably think he got lost looking for the VIP entrance to a night club. What's most striking about his appearance is how much he does *not* look like a ruffian compared to the other raw slabs of beef lumbering around inside the ring. Although he appears to treat his trips to the gym with due respect, Wernimont reminds you more of an underwear model than a cage fighter. Even from the cheap seats (which describes pretty much every seat in the house at an amateur boxing match), you can see Wernimont's sparkling rows of white teeth. He has a day or two's collection of stubble sprouting on his face, where an aspiring beard will have its hopes dashed by a razor as soon as tonight's fight is over. The shadow beard is presumably an attempt to draw attention away from his other metrosexual features, like the suspiciously perfect tan and what I can only guess are well-manicured nails. In truth, it just makes him look even more like Brad Pitt, but less like Pitt's demented character in the movie *Fight Club* and more like his dapper Dillinger role in *Ocean's Eleven*. Either way it's a thinly veiled effort to deceive, which probably fills his rough-looking opponent with confidence. Unfortunately for his foe, that confidence will prove to be painfully false. And then I start to think that maybe that has been Wernimont's strategy all along.

There is definitely more to this guy than meets the eye. Wernimont has been training with his boxing coach, his world champion Jiu-Jitsu coach, and his Muay Thai coach twice a day for six days a week for the last year, with just three exceptions. He took one week off to run with the bulls in Pamplona, Spain . . . on all five of the five days he spent there before returning home to Chicago. He spent a week in Florida in late December getting his skydiving certification. Then there was his trip to Brazil to experience the festival of sensory excess found nowhere else in the world except at *Carnivale*. Wernimont has no shortage of friends, but it seems right that the only person he could find to join him on his wild adventures should be a member of his own gene pool. His brother Chris's work schedule helps. He works two weeks on, two weeks off as a helicopter pilot carting roughnecks from their New Orleans homes out to drilling rigs in the Gulf of Mexico. But the average person would agree that spare time alone isn't a good enough reason to go on these types of adrenaline binges. Nick and Chris have far more than flexible schedules in common.

Tonight's boxing match was arranged as a warm-up bout before Wernimont's first full-contact cage fight in a few months. The arena is alive with murmurs of bloodthirsty fans hoping to see a pretty-boy pummeling. When the bell sounds, the pugilists dance around the ring for a few seconds and size each other up. Wernimont's face reveals what could best be described as a controlled ferocity—aggressive yet strategic. After a swing and a miss from his opponent, Wernimont makes his strike. A couple of hard blows reach their destination, and it isn't long before a cut opens up under his opponent's eye, causing a rivulet of blood to run down his cheek. The second round offers more of the same. The referee eventually intervenes, calling for a standing eight count to let Wernimont's opponent regain his composure. By the third round, the fight is all but over. Shortly after the bell sounds, the referee decides he's seen enough and the fight is called. Wernimont is officially one and oh in his fight career. His first full-contact fight is on the horizon.

Full-contact fighting (or mixed martial arts) is the closest thing America has to ancient Roman gladiators. Except for biting, hitting below the belt, and finger torquing, no violence is spared for the audience.

"Five wins and I can start making some money at this," he told me with a wink. Five wins on the sanctioned amateur full-contact circuit qualifies a fighter for a professional bout where they can actually get paid for doing something that most people would ransom their firstborn child to *avoid* doing. The real joke, however, is that Wernimont will have to become the world Ultimate Fighting champion before he begins to make the kind of money he does now at his day job. In this way he is like the rare few ancient gladiators who were not slaves, but free citizens who simply enjoyed the thrill of the games.

Wernimont's career, just like the rest of his life, is marked by short bursts of intense activity and radical changes. After graduating from the University of Iowa, he moved to Los Angeles, where stimulation is never in short supply. Once there, he spent his days at Morgan Stanley, clocking in as a financial analyst and earning their number-one new salesman award. He moonlighted as a bartender at the Saddle Ranch on the Sunset Strip. After narrowly missing final selection as one of the cast members for MTV's *The Real World: Chicago*, he decided to pack up and head to the Windy City on his own, leaving bartending and financial planning behind. Now he spends his days working as a successful sales manager for a dental implants manufacturer (an ironic selection for the future cage fighter) and buying real estate. His evenings are spent at the gym sparring with world-champion martial artists.

Getting to know Nick Wernimont only creates more questions. Of course, anyone who voluntarily chooses cage fighting as a hobby is a rather intriguing individual. But he is extraordinary even compared to his cage-fighting peers. This is what makes Wernimont's foray into full-contact fighting so compelling. He is not a former Olympic gold medalist who wants to make a living doing what he knows how to do best, nor is he a deluded dock worker who has seen one too many *Rocky* movies. His collar is as white as his teeth, and the only gold he owns is wrapped around his wrist and tells time with amazing accuracy. He lives each day in a waking, postmodern American Dream—young, smart, good looking, and financially successful, with no visible regrets about any of it. It just doesn't seem to make sense. With all of this going for him, why would he subject himself to the kind of punishment inherent in a crazy sport like full-contact fighting?

## 1. The Novelty-Seeking Gene

At the turn of the millennium, the world buzzed with anticipation about the possibilities and pitfalls in store for Y2K. Inside the walls of Jim Swanson's research lab at the University of California in Irvine, the level of anticipation was no exception. Two courses of fascinating research were about to collide in an unexpected way that would cause scientists from around the world to drop what they were doing and take note.

Jim Swanson is a humble man who insists that much of his

success as a scientist is owed to his "collaborations with other great scientists." Nevertheless, Swanson is still recognized as one of the world's foremost experts on child development. His research center in Irvine was one of the first seven labs chosen as a Vanguard Center for a very ambitious project called the National Children's Study that will stretch across the country with the aim of understanding the biggest problems facing American children.[1] Over the span of the next twenty years the centers will collaborate to study more than 100,000 children and their families. Swanson's recognition is due in large part to his groundbreaking work on the rising occurrence of attention deficit/hyperactivity disorder, or ADHD. Most people today recognize the disorder by its original name of just ADD, which first came into vogue in the 1980s after it was formally recognized as a psychological syndrome rather than a behavioral problem.[2] The term *ADD* has since infiltrated the everyday lingo that Americans use to describe kids who are unfocused or inattentive. Now psychologists have officially thrown hyperactivity's hat into the ring to describe the fidgety aspect of the disorder. As Swanson's team was about to discover, the hyperactive element of the syndrome is a key piece of the puzzle that may help explain a lot about ADHD, and also about human history.

Like many other mental illnesses, treatment of ADHD was very rudimentary once it was first recognized. But as the number of children diagnosed began to skyrocket, there was a need for treatment and understanding to catch up. From 1994 to 2004 the number of paid doctor visits for treatment of ADHD nearly tripled. This alarming increase has had many doctors and educators wondering how big the next wave of this possible epidemic might be. For researchers like Jim Swanson, the clock was ticking on finding some answers.

Early in 2000 Swanson's team sat a group of ADHD kids down to play a few brain-teaser games.[3] One of these games is called the Logan stop-signal test and resembles the popular children's game red light/green light. Each child was given a task such as watching a light or pressing a button on a computer keyboard. When instructed to do so, the child had to stop whatever action he or she was engaged in. Children with ADHD usually take much longer to complete this task than typical children, because they react more slowly to the stop signal. What Swanson's team found when they tallied the results surprised everyone, including Jim Swanson.

Before the experiment, Swanson's team had split the kids into two groups based on whether or not the children carried a specific variation of a gene called dopamine receptor gene D4.[4] The function of D4 is to tinker with the levels of dopamine in the child's brain. (As noted earlier, dopamine is the brain chemical that makes us feel happy and vibrant.) Every person has this gene in one variation or another, but we don't all have the exact same variation of it. This is standard practice in the world of genes. For example, we all have a gene that determines what color our eyes are, but we don't all have the same eye color gene. Some people have the blue eye gene, while others have the brown eye gene. The same is true about this dopamine receptor gene, D4. Everybody has it, but not everybody has the same variation. What separates the variations is how many times a segment of this gene repeats itself in the genetic sequence. Most people have a shorter variation of the gene that gets repeated four times. But some people have the longer variation that repeats seven times. This longer variation causes a less sensitive response to dopamine, which then creates a deficit in the amount of dopamine output to a person's brain. In other words, the dopamine that is present in the brain has to try a little harder. Such people have to round up even more of their chemical friends than the average person in order to get the dopamine party started and that requires extra-stimulating activities. In the mid-1990s scientist Richard

Ebstein[5] found that people with the longer variation were also likely to have a personality trait called "novelty seeking." Thanks to Ebstein's discovery, the longer variation of the D4 gene is commonly dubbed "the novelty-seeking gene."

As you might expect from the name, people with the novelty-seeking trait feel more compelled than the average person to seek out new and exciting experiences. The problem is that everybody's brain craves dopamine, so the people born with a natural shortage of dopamine output have to overcompensate. They find it hard to keep themselves satisfied with the ordinary, slow-moving pace of just about everything that happens in their lives. The normal acts of reading a book, sitting through a meeting, obeying traffic laws, and even a roll in the hay don't necessarily keep these people's attention. While most of us are happy and relatively satisfied doing most of these things, they quickly bore people with the novelty-seeking gene. That means these restless souls have to go looking for action anywhere they can find it in order to stir up some more dopamine just to feel "normal." They might drive fast. They might disregard instructions designed for safety. They might jump up in a cage with their fists cocked.

Heart-racing, dopamine-producing endeavors can also cause feelings of bliss in the ordinary person. But it's not all fun and games with dopamine. Too much of this good thing can easily turn excitement into fear and bliss into anxiety. What gives the carrier of the novelty-seeking gene an exciting rush is likely to do nothing for the ordinary person other than cause a panic.

Currently about one-quarter of people have the novelty-seeking gene, but more than half of people diagnosed with ADHD have it. Not surprisingly, Ebstein's discovery led many scientists to believe that the novelty-seeking gene may as well be nicknamed the "attention-deficit gene." Although not all kids with ADHD have the gene, researchers believed that the kids with the most severe cases of ADHD symptoms would carry the gene. The purpose of Jim Swanson's study was to verify that exact point. His Irvine research team expected to find that the kids *with* the novelty-seeking gene would do significantly worse on their brain-teaser tests than the ADHD kids *without* the gene.

After the experiment, Swanson's team tallied the results. The ADHD kids without the novelty-seeking gene performed just like run-of-the-mill kids with ADHD should. They made more mistakes than typical kids, and they were slower to respond. Their inability to pay attention caused their minds to drift, without giving their conscious reasoning a chance to catch them. Swanson's team reasoned that if ADHD kids with the normal version of the dopamine gene performed poorly on the test, then the kids with the novelty-seeking gene didn't have a prayer.

But they were wrong. When the numbers were crunched, they did find a difference between the kids with the novelty-seeking gene and those without it, but it wasn't the difference they had predicted. The novelty-seeking group did much *better* than expected. These kids ended up scoring the same as the kids with no symptoms of ADHD whatsoever. Furthermore, the novelty-seeking kids proved to be even quicker on the draw. Apparently, there was much more to this new gene than anyone had previously guessed.

Swanson believes that the kids classified as having ADHD who carried the novelty-seeking gene do not actually have the same version of ADHD as those without this gene. In the summary of their research for the *Proceedings of the National Academy of Sciences,* Swanson writes that this group only has a "partial syndrome characterized by behavioral excesses without cognitive deficits." So while these kids may behave a bit on the hyperactive side in the classroom, and have trouble settling down at home, there really isn't anything dysfunctional about the way they think. It is only those "behavioral excesses" that make these kids a handful for their parents and teachers. Swanson believes it is probably those same excessive quirks that can drive frustrated parents into their pediatrician's office to get a pharmaceutical fix.

This was a discovery that nobody saw coming. Whatever else they are, these kids are quick thinkers. Whether or not that is a good thing or a bad thing was the real question.

To find out, the Irvine researchers teamed up with another group of scientists and embarked on a journey back in time. In finding the novelty-seeking gene's roots, they hoped to shed some light on why this mutation lurks in so many of today's children.

## 2. Misguided Mutation or Misunderstood Gift?

Roughly 165,000 years ago modern humans (that is, *Homo sapiens*) debuted on planet Earth. Compared to their stocky and slightly older kin, the Neanderthals, our ancestors had long foreheads in order to accommodate bigger frontal and temporal lobes in their brains. They also were more gracile, with longer limbs and narrower hips. The two groups mostly kept to themselves, coexisting without much incident for the next 115,000 years. Then shortly before cave painting and music came into vogue, the short version of the dopamine gene D4, which had been around ever since *Homo sapiens* first appeared, spawned a lively mutation—the seven-repeat variation now commonly referred to as the novelty-seeking gene.

At this time in our prehistory (40,000–50,000 years ago), modern humans called the savannas of Africa home while Neanderthals dwelled mostly in the caves of Europe, the Middle East, and western Asia. Although the African continent was home to all of what we now regard as modern human civilization, hardly anything that existed then would fit our definition

of *civilized*. In the technical sense, there were people with physical attributes similar to those of the people of today. But they
were people with little to no symbolic behavior such as the
art and decorative objects that characterize our culture today.
They had no complex speech and no music. They hunted, they
gathered, and they died. They were not quite the homebodies
that Neanderthals were, but our ancestors were not exactly
circumnavigating the globe, either. Not yet, anyway.

Then all of a sudden, modern humans made a breakthrough.
Some restless souls embarked on a quest to see what they were
missing elsewhere in the world. Australian scientists David
Cameron and Colin Groves[6] explain in their book *Bones, Stones
and Molecules*, that "40,000 years ago, *Homo sapiens* began, for
whatever reason, spreading into the Neanderthal heartland of
Europe." That move signaled the beginning of the end for the
Neanderthals as they then became casualties of rapid extinction.
(The last Neanderthals died 27,000 years ago.) But it marked
the beginning of something big for modern humans. Their migration north was a bold move, considering the first map wasn't
drawn until just 800 years ago and they certainly didn't have
the luxury of Mapquest.com. Magellan and his troop of fellow
seafarers would not set sail for another fifty millennia. Moses
didn't hustle his people toward the exits of Egypt until less
than ten thousand years ago. These ancient people didn't know
the world was round, and they probably had no comprehen-
sion of what *round* as a concept even meant, given that the first
wheel wasn't rolled out until about five thousand years ago. Not
to mention that their slender physiques were not built for the
colder climate inhabited by the husky Neanderthals.

Trekking into unknown territory was a risky choice. Yet
humans did it anyway, and history's course was forever altered because of it. Not only did they become explorers, but
a kind of prehistoric Renaissance also began around this time.
Archaeologists found a flute in Germany dating back 36,000

years, and two others in France from 32,000 and 27,000 years ago. As early as 34,000 years ago people were carving animal figurines in Germany, and 32,000 years ago they were drawing pictures on cave walls in France and Spain. It's not that humans made no technological advances in terms of tools and hunting techniques since their inception in the preceding 120,000 years. They just had not made much headway in the kind of symbolic behavior that generally characterizes the emergence of modern humans. In *Bones, Stones and Molecules*, Cameron and Groves note that "compared to the later explosion in Europe there is little evidence for the widespread development of artistic or symbolic behavior within the earliest modern humans of Africa."

The question then is *why?*

## 3. Positive Selection

In 2002 a research team from the United States and China led by biologist Yuan-Chun Ding[7] at UC Irvine offered an answer to that question. In short, their answer was the novelty-seeking gene. Ding's team intended to find out where this peculiar gene variation came from and what it has been up to ever since then.

Determining the exact age of a gene is a complicated process. But if we indulge in just a moment of mental masochism, we can find an important clue about how humanity came to be where we are today. Biologists will look for two things when they "age" a gene. First, they want to see the size of a gene's family tree. If a gene has produced lots of branches on its family tree (that is, variations), then we can be pretty certain that it is an old gene. However, if the gene has only a few limbs on the family tree, then we know it is still young. Just like your grandparents are at the root of more branches on the family tree than you are, older genes will have more branches than younger ones. Second, geneticists know that if a gene is young, then it hasn't had much time to spread its seed, which means that not many people today will carry it.

As long as a particular gene or gene variation isn't too harmful—such as a gene that contributes to a disease—chances are that the gene will spread slowly but surely over a long period of time. This dispersal through the population is due mostly to chance. For example, having two webbed toes, like my son has, doesn't offer any huge advantages since our amphibious ancestors decided to shore up on dry land millions and millions of years ago. Unless we find ourselves in Kevin Costner's *Waterworld* soon, my son will just have to learn to live comfortably on the fringe of normal-toed society until the polar ice caps finish melting. At the same time, webbed toes are still genetically determined. Somewhere along either my or my wife's ancestry this recessive webbed-toe gene smuggled itself into our DNA and it continues to spread. But it is spreading only by the process of genetic drift, which essentially means it is spreading by chance. It doesn't offer any discernible advantage to its carriers, nor does it pose any kind of a threat. Even though having a pair of webbed toes is not typical, it isn't all that uncommon, either. The webbed-toe gene must have been around for quite a while to have spread to so many people simply by chance.

As a rule, genes mutate fairly regularly so that any single mutation is a rather lackluster event. A mutation needs to firmly stand the test of time before it can be considered something worth noting. After natural selection runs its course, the "good" mutations that offer an advantage—like opposable thumbs and sweat glands—end up sticking around. The not-so-good mutations get weeded out like bad fashion trends and ultimately become evolutionary casualties. The more neutral mutations, like webbed toes, loiter on the corners of our genetic sequences, simply because nothing has caused them to self-select out of the process. Since the novelty-seeking gene continues showing up disproportionately in an error-prone disorder like ADHD, the laws of selection would seem to give this gene very little staying power. After all, a mutation that might cause a person to leap without first looking is likely to disappear pretty quickly as the gene's carriers die off prematurely. But the novelty-seeking gene was spared the fate of other short-lived mutations. Somehow this gene with a strong connection to social problems—from chronic criminality to aggression to cocaine addiction—has made the improbable journey from mutation to mainstay. It is not only surviving; it is thriving.

That is why the novelty-seeking gene is a paradox. It has very few branches on its family tree, which means that it is still pretty young. However, lots of people around the world— about twenty-five percent—carry it. That isn't a majority, but twenty-five percent of six billion is still quite a few. This means that the novelty-seeking gene is not spreading randomly. If the novelty-seeking gene were like the gene for webbed toes, with no distinct advantage, then at this early stage in its life cycle, only a few people out of a hundred would carry it. If it caused kidney failure or cancer, then hardly anyone at all would still carry it. Look around you right now. Approximately one out of every four or five people sitting next to you is probably a ge-netic descendant of our ancient African seekers. At some time in the last 50,000 years, nature realized it had something good going with the novelty-seeking gene and elected to spread the good news. Despite being the bane of grammar school teach-ers dealing with attention deficit in the classroom, this gene must be offering an adaptive edge to those who have it.

It's fun to think that maybe the spunky guy or girl with the carefree spirit each of us knows—and all of us secretly envy from time to time—might have been responsible for the mass migration of our ancient ancestors. However, that claim is difficult to verify. The science of genetics is too complicated to tie any single gene's mutation to an entire human exodus. But as UC Irvine biologist Deborah Grady[8] pointed out, "the relationship of this gene to ADHD has been confirmed by so many research teams around the world . . . that it has stood as one of the most reliable genetic findings yet reported for the association of a gene with specific behavior." What we do have are some very significant historical human events (the migration out of Africa, art, and music) coinciding with the mutation of a very significant human gene (the D4 seven-repeat novelty-seeking gene). Yuan-Chun Ding's team suggests that

> It is tempting to speculate that the major expansion of humans that occurred at that time, the appearance of radical new technology . . . and/or the development of agriculture, could be related to the increase in DRD4-7 allele frequency. Perhaps individuals with personality traits such as novelty seeking, perseverance, etc. drove the expansion and partial replacement.

We can be certain that this mutation appears to have grown in influence faster than an average gene should. We know that for a trait to last, it has to be enduringly advantageous in some way. So what is it about the behaviors this gene seems to encourage that make it so sticky? In this case, the advantage may be the very same thing that was the deadly *disadvantage* at Pincher Creek.

## 4. Boundary Blind

September 11, 2001, is one of America's saddest days. Like many tragedies before it, the terrorist attacks of that day left

many victims, but it also produced a great number of courageous acts. Not the least of these displays of heroism was that
of firefighter Stephen Siller.[9] On the morning of September
11, Siller had just finished working an all-night shift at Brooklyn's Squad 1 firehouse. He was in his car on the way to meet
his four brothers for a morning round of golf at the Glenwood
Country Club when he heard news of the attacks on the
World Trade Center. Without hesitation, Siller headed toward
the Brooklyn Battery Tunnel leading into Manhattan. Always
considerate, he called his wife so that she could tell his brothers he would be a little late. Siller arrived at the tunnel only
to find that all traffic was being stopped by police. Again without hesitation, Siller grabbed his seventy pounds of gear and
took off on a three-mile jog toward the blazing inferno of the
World Trade Center. That was the last thing we know for sure
about Stephen Siller's actions that morning. He never made it
to meet his brothers for golf.

Most people regard Siller's determination that day as an
uncommon and inspiring act of bravery. He lost his life in the
impulsive decision to join his squad. His heroic trek is even
commemorated every September in the Tunnel to Towers 5K
charity run. What makes Siller's act remarkable is that the
average person might have decided to heed the call of duty
and pack his or her gear into the car with the goal of reaching
the Twin Towers. But when confronted with a roadblock three
miles from the destination, the average person probably would
have simply given up the effort to join the rescue. Someone
would still be applauded for trying, even if he or she ultimately
left the situation to the firefighters who were already on the
scene.

But Siller felt an undeniable impulse to do his duty, and he
acted on it despite the quite literal roadblocks in his way. Just
like the time in 1993, when he drove 2,000 miles from Brooklyn to Kansas City straight through, just to watch George

Brett's last home at-bat for the Kansas City Royals. Then he drove straight back to Brooklyn another 2,000 miles after the game to make it to work on time the next day. If that isn't impulsive, I'm not sure what is. Where the reasonable person saw boundaries, Siller saw an opportunity to be a part of history.

Most people are dumbfounded by the things that a guy like Stephen Siller does. But perhaps the late Lane McGlynn is one guy who would have understood perfectly. McGlynn's role in the Pincher Creek avalanche is an example of the tragic nature of impulsive decisions. Yet it is also symbolizes the tight relationship forged between tragedy and heroism. If we take another look at Lane McGlynn, we'll see that he and Stephen Siller were much more likely two of a kind than diametrically opposed. When you read about the Pincher Creek avalanche, you might have felt that McGlynn was responsible not only for his own death but also for that of his colleague Kevin Bruder. He blatantly disregarded an order when he charged up that hill. It was a tragic accident but one that might never have happened to begin with.

Before condemning McGlynn's character, we shouldn't forget why he was at the foot of that hill to begin with. He was part of a *volunteer rescue squad* whose mission was to brave the elements during a Canadian blizzard in order to find three complete strangers who were stranded. We also can't forget that McGlynn was just twenty-one years old. A twenty-one-year-old volunteer is a rarity, if not an oxymoron in today's "Generation Me." How many twenty-one-year-olds do you know who volunteer to do any work at all without pay, much less work that requires getting up at the crack of dawn to charge into the brutal conditions of a Canadian blizzard? Perhaps if McGlynn had thought more about it that morning when he woke up, he would have had some questions such as, *What if I get stranded out there, too? Aren't there enough people to help already?* Or maybe, *What's in it for me?* He could have conjured up a list of reasonable psychological boundaries. Fortunately, for the three stranded riders, Lane McGlynn didn't spend much time constructing obstacles in his mind. Instead, he hopped out of bed, threw on his snow gear, and took off to answer the call of distress—just like Stephen Siller did on September 11. Despite the risk and the consequences, both Siller and McGlynn went seeking. In the same way that humanity's ancestors crossed the boundary between Africa and the rest of the world, Siller and McGlynn crossed the boundary between security and vulnerability.

In spite of its prevalence in cage fighters, firefighters, and young snowmobilers too easily tempted by dares, such boundary blindness is not an extension of machismo. In fact, TalentSmart's research reveals no significant differences between the impulsivity scores of men and women. Former CEO of the Washington Post Company Katharine Graham famously said "once power was considered a masculine attribute. In fact power has no sex." The same can be said of impulsivity. Taking daring leaps into the unknown is not an exclusively masculine behavior. For example, it was this same sort of "damn the consequences" (or perhaps more appropriately, "what consequences?") approach that helped fuel the engine of the women's liberation movement. Joan Growe's rise through politics despite obvious barriers to entry illustrates the power of boundary blindness. When she was elected as the Minnesota secretary of state in 1974, Joan Growe became the first woman to hold a state office in Minnesota. She remained in office for the next twenty-four years. Her long political career began two years earlier—the same year that Katharine Graham became the first female Fortune 500 CEO—when Growe waged an almost accidental campaign for a district-level legislative seat. Her decision to enter the race came down to "if I can get a babysitter, I'll go to the local Democratic convention and try to get nominated." She later told Tom Brokaw,[10] "It

seemed like no big deal. I had no idea what I was getting into."
A more cautious decision maker might have spent more time,
or even some time, weighing the costs of jumping into local
politics. On the one hand, Growe was entering an uphill battle
that would rile old-fashioned male constituents in her conservative neighborhood. And her political career added strain to a
marriage that ultimately ended in divorce. On the other hand,
Joan Growe was carving out a little slice of history for herself
and contributing to the empowerment of women across the
country.

Of course, Growe was an intelligent woman with obvious
leadership qualities. But it is likely that a lot of other women
in her district possessed equal qualifications for the position.
Growe says that she wasn't even the most politically active
or vocally feminist in her group of friends—after all, she still
ironed her husband's shirts. Still, Growe is the woman who
entered the race, and she did so because she just happened
to find a babysitter on the day of the Democratic convention.
Growe's career proves that paying little attention to consequences is sometimes the only way to do the things that each
of us are really called to do, such as lead reform or save lives.
In the end, whether Joan Growe's personal sacrifices were
worth the reward of her long tenure as a public servant are
debatable. The voters who continued putting her in office
term after term were clearly thankful for Growe's choice.
Growe sometimes struggles with the question. She says that
during her youth "it never occurred to me that I would get
divorced or run for office." But she concludes that "if I had not
gone through that early trauma, I might not be where I am
today."

When we consider the lives of heroes like Stephen Siller or
Joan Growe, it becomes clearer why a gene like the novelty-
seeking gene has been on the rise since its mutation. When

people fail to observe boundaries, nothing stands in their way. This realization forces us to reexamine what it means to be impulsive. Maybe there is something more to people like Nick Wernimont than a predilection for cage fighting and skydiving. A little boundary blindness may be what set humanity on its course of rapid change. And a little more boundary blindness may also be just what we need to get us through it.

# CHAPTER TWO

# Impulsivity's Hidden Side:
## The Secret of Being Directionally Correct

I n early April 1951 in a small midtown Manhattan apartment, the newly published author Jack Kerouac hunched over his desk furiously pounding the keys on his Underwood typewriter. His first failed attempt at fame came in 1948 with his novel *The Town and The City*, which received a lukewarm reception from critics and readers alike. Even Kerouac felt that the book was too conventional and dull. But his new book was destined to be a drastic departure from convention. Sweating through multiple T-shirts each day and feasting on nothing but pea soup and Benzedrine for three weeks, Kerouac hammered out more than 86,000 words of the manuscript that eventually became the American literary classic *On the Road*. Only by using his free-flow style of "kickwriting" did Kerouac believe he could capture the vibrancy of the man that inspired the book, his friend Neal Cassady. To Kerouac, Neal Cassady was so much larger than life that traditional forms of writing simply would not do justice to the real person who was anything but conventional and dull. When Kerouac finally tapped into the hard-charging spirit of his hero, he released a masterpiece.[1]

Neal Cassady was allegedly born outside of Salt Lake City, Utah, in his parents' jalopy on a trip between Des Moines and Los Angeles. (In reality, his parents never owned a jalopy and Cassady was born in a hospital,[2] but the real story detracts from the legend's allure.) When Cassady was a little boy his parents split, and he lived with his alcoholic father on the streets of Denver where he spent most of his days carousing with "the old bums and beat cowboys of Larimer Street." By his teenage years, the charismatic young hustler had grown into a sort of modern-day cowboy in both his rugged appearance and his restless soul. Although various chapters of Cassady's life were shared with the world in the poetry of Allen Ginsberg, the journalism of Hunter S. Thompson, and the music of the Grateful Dead, Cassady is still best known as the inspiration for the semifictional protagonist, Dean Moriarty, in *On the Road*. Kerouac's telling description painted Cassady as "a young Gene Autry—trim, thin-hipped, blue-eyed, with a real Oklahoma accent—a sideburned hero of the snowy West."

However, as cowboy comparisons go, Cassady was probably more like the Marlboro Man. He was a rugged individualist who could be the life of one party and the scourge of the next—rather than the perpetual good guy that Autry was. His unquenchable thirst for joyriding stolen cars landed him in juvenile detention centers as a teenager. Oddly, it was locked away as a "jailkid" in Denver that Cassady buried himself in classical literature and philosophy, and crafted his writing style. Kerouac would later claim that one of the finest pieces of American literature was a long letter Cassady had written him detailing his sexual escapades with a girl he called Cherry Mary. Paradoxes like these established Cassady as a lovable outlaw and folk hero to some people, and as a careless conman to others. Fueled by jazz music, spiritual wanderlust, and an

Iggy Pop-ish lust for all things alive, Cassady became the archetypal hero of the Beat Generation. Whether this infamous character offered more virtue than vice remains the subject of great debate. Despite all the labels and whatever else he might have been, Neal Cassady was undoubtedly impulsive.

When most people hear the term *impulsive* used to describe someone, they conjure up an image of an eternal wild child like Neal Cassady. Research on impulsivity supports that collective image. For example, a prominent feature of highly impulsive people is their penchant for risky driving—something Cassady showed a passion for throughout his life. On Kerouac and Cassady's road trips across the United States, Neal genuinely professes his love to multiple women and steals countless cars, which he drives until neither he nor the car can physically endure any more. *On the Road* is a fascinating joyride that millions of people continue to enjoy reading. For most people, however, this is where the celebration of impulsivity ends. Cassady's life is one that the rest of the world views as being sort of cool for artsy types but of little practical value beyond the idealist confines of bohemia. Even the kind of fame that Cassady achieved is something that the average citizen would be quite content living without. But what if there was more to impulsivity than beat heroes and reckless driving? What if impulsivity could have a real impact on our success?

## 1. Risky Business

Another high-risk driver entered the world in 1955 in Seattle, Washington, the same year that *On the Road* was published. Unlike the jazzy coolness that signified the beat artists, however, this high-risk driver is far better known as the antithesis of cool. His hiked-up high-water pants and laughably large glasses defined the style of an entirely new generation of heroes we now call "nerds." Trey, as his family called him because of the third slot he held in the line of William Gateses, also found excitement in testing the limits of legality and speed. As a teenager, Bill Gates bootlegged free computer time in the early 1970s, before his dream of computers gracing every desktop became our world's reality. While "Microsoft's Mogul" never stole any cars, he did spend the summer of 1977 "borrowing" bulldozers from a New Mexico road construction site. Much like Cassady, Gates had no intention of employing the machinery for anything more than a thrill at friendly midnight "dozing" sessions with a pal. But bulldozers were much too slow to keep Gates's attention for long. He had a hunger for risky driving that was every bit as insatiable as Neal Cassady's. A twenty-year-old Gates once complained to a mechanic that his used, dark green Porsche was supposed to hit a top speed of 126 miles per hour, but he could only get it up to 121. In their biography Gates,[3] Stephen Manes and Paul Andrews relate how Gates treated every trip to the airport to pick up potential Microsoft customers as an opportunity to stretch the limits of his car's handling and power "leading an early Japanese customer, shivering and pale, to ask Paul Allen. 'Mr. Gates—he always drive this fast?' Bill's driving skills, with drag strip starts and panic traffic-light stops (and sometimes no stops at all), so stupefied some passengers that they refused to ride with him ever again."

Gates's signature risky behavior spilled over into his steering of Microsoft. In the early years, when Microsoft was little more than a young and brash David, Gates hungered to take on the Goliaths of the industry like IBM and Apple. With the overnight successes of many high-tech companies in the 1990s and 2000s, it is easy to assume that Microsoft was destined to succeed from conception. But Gates's decision to drop out of Harvard and run Microsoft full time was far from a no-brainer, or a safe bet. In 1976 the personal computer had not yet taken hold of the public's imagination. Microsoft was a niche business catering to a relatively small network of supernerdy customers. Even in this small sector, Microsoft was a long, long way from dominating the market. In those early years in New Mexico, most of the staff—including Bill Gates and Paul Allen—shared a single apartment. Despite concerns from his family, Gates put it all on the line, anyway, to follow an impulse. He dropped out of Harvard and triggered a revolution that has been devouring market share for three decades.

While we don't know whether Bill Gates, Nick Wernimont, or the other daring characters previously mentioned carry the novelty-seeking gene, their impulsive behavior is certainly in line with what we know about the gene.

So what is it about impulsivity that makes it such an explosive success factor?

## 2. Standing Out

Imagine yourself sitting in a small room, seated at a table next to six strangers. Nobody is saying much to one another, so you can feel reasonably safe assuming that all six of the strangers are unknown to one another as well. That makes sense to you given that you are there because you signed up to participate in a research study. You give each of the participants a quick once-over glance and maybe flash an obligatory tight-lipped smile when your eyes accidentally meet. At the front of the room, a researcher sits next to a stack of cue cards. After a few minutes the researcher clears his throat, welcomes everyone, and thanks you all for participating in the study. He tells you that he is going to be showing you pairs of white cards with black solid lines on them just like the cards in the figure on the next page. The first card has one solid black line on it. The second card has three solid black lines on it.

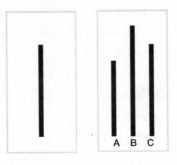

Your job as a participant in the experiment is to tell the researcher which of the three lines on the second card is the same length as the line on the first card.

The researcher begins by holding up both cards next to each other. It is clear to you that line A on the second card is shorter and that line B is longer than the line on the first card. Line C is obviously the right answer. It's almost too easy. You assume that this must be a warm-up question designed to get you in the right frame of mind for the *real* test. You are a good sport, so you play along. The first person is instructed to give a response. Much to your surprise, the first participant says that line A—the short line—is the same length as the line on the first card. Now, you assume this is a screening round to weed out any incompetent participants. You conclude that this guy must need glasses and he won't be joining you in the later rounds of the experiment. What you don't know is that everyone in the room except for you is in cahoots with the researchers. The people sitting next to you are acting. They were all told ahead of time to give the same wrong answer just to see what you will do. So the second participant gives the same incorrect answer as the first participant. Now you start to get a little confused and probably question your initial judgment. You ask yourself, *Did I misunderstand the instructions?* Pretty soon it is your turn, and you have watched all five of the people before you choose the same wrong answer. You rub your eyes, or maybe give your glasses a quick wipe on your shirttail, and then refocus. No change. It still looks to you that line C, and not line A, is clearly the same length as the line on the first card, despite what all five of the seemingly normal people in front of you have said. Which answer do you give?

Psychologist Solomon Asch[4] conducted this experiment in the early 1950s, while Kerouac and Cassady were making their legendary trips across the country. In Asch's experiment, three-fourths of the people in the study knowingly gave the wrong answer in order to conform to the other people in the group. After each experiment, Asch's team interviewed the study's subjects. All of those who gave the wrong answer confessed that they knew full well which line was the same length, but they consciously chose to give the wrong answer. Why? Because that is what everyone else did. Asch's study proved that an overwhelming majority of people—three-fourths of us—are not willing to take the social risks necessary to decide for ourselves in a group setting. We have a powerful urge to remain in good standing with the group, and we believe that we can keep our good standing by agreeing.

The belief that disagreeing will lead to falling out of favor with a group is not a paranoid delusion or undue social anxiety. In later studies Asch turned things around so that only one person in the group was an actor, and the other six people were legitimate subjects. This time Asch's actor was instructed to give wrong answers in order to find out how the rest of the people would treat the nonconformist. Just as all of our instinctive social phobias would predict, the rest of the people in the room treated the actor like an outcast. They even went so far as to laugh at the nonconforming actor when he gave an incorrect answer. At the end of the study the subjects said flat-out that they did not like the nonconforming actors. It was plain evidence that when a person chooses not to conform, that person pays a hefty social price. The study proved that, for most of us, being correct is trumped by the need to remain in the group. Asch found his results alarming, commenting "that we have found the tendency to conformity in our society so strong that reasonably intelligent and well-meaning young people are willing to call white black. . . . It raises questions about our ways of education and about the values that guide our conduct."

The widespread contagion of conformity alarmed a lot of people beyond just Solomon Asch. Asch's results came on the heels of a world war that saw normal people incinerating their neighbors for no good reason beyond the fact that everyone else was doing it. It scared people to think that the same kind of blind conformity might exist in our culture as well. However, another interesting finding in that study often gets overlooked. One-fourth of the people held firm to their own judgments. This group gave the right answer despite any possible repercussions. Just as we saw in Kahneman and Tversky's studies, only about one-fourth of people followed their own impulse and took the risky option while everyone else selected the safe route. There is clearly something unique about this quarter of the population. The novelty-seeking gene might provide a genetic clue about the roots of nonconformity even in the face of unfavorable consequences. But beyond quick thinking and the courage to stand alone, another advantageous trait guides the impulsive person's behavior.

Impulsive people do not just make different decisions or arrive at different conclusions than cautious people. Impulsive people actually see the decision itself from a different angle. It is not necessarily that they choose risk over safety. It is more that they are naturally predisposed to pay little attention to risk because their mind is consumed by the potential reward. When we look at impulsive people's decisions from this perspective, it is no surprise then that an impulsive snowmobiler would charge up a hill despite the warnings, because the warnings do not speak to his particularly impulsive mindset. Nor is it surprising that some people will take the chance of winning no trip at all because they are too focused on the opportunity for a three-week trip. Telling Lane McGlynn that there was a "high avalanche danger" was an appeal to his sense of risk avoidance and security, instead of to his drive for potential.

Sometimes that deep focus on potential pays off. Other times it's a death blow. That contradiction is what makes impulsivity such a slippery trait. Free thinking, risk taking and potential seeking are all double-edged swords. So that raises the question, is impulsiveness good, or is it bad?

## 3. Directionally Correct

At TalentSmart, an applied psychological research firm, we wrestled with that question for months. Our team at TalentSmart is no stranger to scrutinizing anomalies in human behavior and then learning everything we can about these discrepancies until we can emerge with an applicable answer. Our curiosity encourages the search, and our clients have come to expect it. But finding the answer about what makes impulsivity "work" just isn't that simple. To get to the bottom of how we behave as individuals and as groups, we created a short scale to measure impulsivity. The higher your score on the scale, the more impulsive you are. We collected data from more than 2,000 people and compared the impulsivity scores to a set of success indicators such as the number of promotions test-takers received, their annual incomes, and their overall job performance. We also looked at something we call the Quality of Life Index, which includes how satisfied people are with their jobs and their lives and how much purpose they feel their lives have. In each of our comparisons, when we plotted the scores on a graph, a tight trend began to emerge. At the bottom end of the scale, we saw that people who were the most cautious received the fewest numbers of promotions, reported the lowest job performance, made the least amount of money, and reported the lowest quality of life. It seemed to be that as impulsivity increased, so did personal and professional success, and satisfaction.

In research, when one factor increases proportionally with another such as the way success seemed to increase with impulsivity scores, it is called a linear trend. Linear trends are all around us. For example, the more people exercise, the healthier they usually are. So we say that the relationship between exercise and health is a linear one. Just as the more profit a company makes, the higher its stock price usually goes. So being impulsive appears to be a good thing then, right?

Well, sort of.

There was a point about three-fourths of the way along the impulsivity scale, where the success indicators stopped following the neat linear trend. Our nice straight line started bouncing up and down once it reached the impulsive people on the far right side of the scale, or the most impulsive of the group. Some of these impulsive types were climbing toward the pinnacle of achievement. But for every impulsive person who was getting rich and enjoying personal satisfaction, another impulsive person was flat-lining at the bottom of the success scale, so our trend fell apart. It became clear that impulsive people's daring acts could yield priceless payoffs or costly consequences. It turns out that the trouble with going for broke is that *you just may end up going broke*. For most impulsive readers, the glass is still half full because half of the impulsive crowd in our research did in fact achieve their high potential. This in spite of the fact that behind every big win lurks a big loss just waiting for the right moment to strike.

The ambiguous conclusion—some impulsive people benefited while others did not—wasn't enough for us to close the case. Our research team at TalentSmart wondered if there was some way to tap into the stand-out success made possible by impulsivity, without having to bet the farm on a series of whims. After months of studying our data, poring over related research and applying our discovery to real-world situations, we finally uncovered the hidden side of impulsivity.

## 4. Binary Like Bill

Bill Gates is known in some circles by the nickname Binary Bill. The clever moniker derives from the computer programming method known as binary. Binary systems operate on a lengthy series of digits that essentially act as a collection of on and off switches. For example, if you hit the spacebar on your keyboard, the action flips a switch that takes you over a space. Because the coding system had only two switches—on and off—rather than a whole alphabet, it was called binary. Gates cut his teeth on binary programming, so he had an obvious connection to the early system. But he was given the nickname for an altogether different reason. Binary Bill represented his two modes of thinking. On the one hand, Gates is the definition of impulsive. He could probably wallpaper Microsoft's boardroom with his traffic tickets. On the other hand—especially when it came to business—Gates tempered his inclination to take risks with a legendary pessimism. For most people, pessimism is not a good thing. But then again, most people are not naturally impulsive.

In 2001 customer research firm Miller-Williams surveyed more than 1,600 executives to determine their decision-making styles, and they concluded that Bill Gates was a perfect example of a risk-averse decision maker.[5] Remembering Gates's earlier proclivity for taking chances, that sounds a little hard to believe. Risk averse is probably not how you would classify a Porsche-driving college dropout who made a career out of jumping from one big idea to the next in a single bound.

But Miller-Williams's classification of Gates is in fact correct. It taps into Gates's other side. It represents the Bill Gates who would not let any idea—even his own—leave his office without first running it by his patented skepticism and intense scrutiny. In the early 1980s, Gates preached the impending demise of a fledgling spreadsheet program the world now knows as Microsoft Excel. Throughout the 1980s, Gates suffered sleepless nights dreading the total annihilation of a little operating system called Windows. In the wiring of Bill Gates's brain, it is as if there is a bright collection of ones that always switch on for potential, but then there is another gloomy cluster of digits that zeroes in on calamity.

This binary thinking was made clear to me by another group of business big shots on a muggy summer day a few months after we conducted TalentSmart's initial research. I was conducting the first in a series of global decision-making workshops with the brightest up and comers in one of the most respected Fortune 100 corporations. The group's decision-making styles broke down just as you might expect, with most of the leaders leaning toward a more calculating style, while a quarter of them made a career by tempting their impulse. The impulsive thinkers were deep in discussion about the ways in which their style of thinking could be effective when one of the members of the group blurted out, "directionally correct." When the group pitched that revelation to the room at large, I saw a sea of heads nodding yes, but eyes that were squinting with uncertainty and confusion. Intuitively, everyone seemed to understand what directionally correct meant, but nobody knew exactly why it made sense. When pushed to explain, the group struggled. They suggested that following an impulse is only good when that impulse is taking you in the right direction. It seemed rather obvious that in any case, for any person, you want to be headed in the right direction. But there is something special about being directionally correct for impulsive people. What the group had stumbled onto was the secret to being successfully impulsive.

It turns out that all impulsivity is not created equal. In the 1990s Scott Dickman,[6] a clinical psychologist at the University of Texas, discovered a distinction between what he labeled as "functional impulsivity" and "dysfunctional impulsivity." There is a difference between a good kind of impulsive that is helpful and adaptive, and a bad kind that is destructive and gets people into trouble. Functional impulsivity is of the mischievous, Eddie Haskell variety. It makes people willing and able to take risks when it might be appropriate, and also sometimes when it might not be so appropriate by conventional standards. But as a rule, functional impulsivity doesn't cause serious harm. Recently, psychologists in Estonia determined that people with functional impulsivity are far more likely to get a lot of speeding tickets than the average person.[7] However, functional impulsivity alone is not very likely to spawn drunk drivers, and the difference between lead-footed drivers and habitual drunk drivers is huge in terms of the damage they can cause. In 2004 alcohol was involved in seven percent of car crashes in the United States but was responsible for nearly thirty-eight percent of traffic deaths.[8] Whereas high-risk drivers have some sense of what risks are acceptable, drunk drivers' sense of what is acceptable is, well, impaired. It is dysfunctional impulsivity that is likely to encourage people to get behind the wheel after a wild night of tequila shooters without any regard for the negative consequences that might be prowling around the corner.

The same scenarios play out with all kinds of antisocial behavior. Functionally impulsive people are quick and decisive thinkers, and that makes them more likely to engage in the kind of activity that society frowns on, like petty thievery and vandalism. But here again there is a difference. A group of Spanish researchers tracked a group of 1,200 adolescents in Madrid who were all guilty of some kind of delinquent behavior.[9] But the kids varied on the level of delinquency. Some just broke minor rules at school, and others broke windows around their neighborhood. All of the kids possessed the quick-thinking side of the impulsive trait. But the ones who graduated to the hard-core crime also scored high on the dysfunctional kinds of impulsivity. Functionally impulsive people are generally only antisocial to the extent that they aren't afraid to stand alone, as we saw in Asch's conformity studies. They aren't very likely to turn into major criminals, at least any more than the average person is. But that decisive trait becomes dysfunctional when quick thinking is accompanied by a lack of planning and a complete disregard for consequences.

Becoming functionally impulsive requires that a person be binary like Bill Gates. Harnessing the power of an impulsive instinct is about taking risks while maintaining a clear focus on being directionally correct. Functionally impulsive people are better at reminding themselves that a correct path exists and that they may not currently be traveling down that path. By acknowledging the importance of being directionally correct, functionally impulsive people acknowledge the limitations of their judgments. This allows them to trust their impulsive judgments, while at the same time reevaluating whether their judgments remain correct. Functionally impulsive people won't blindly follow impulses to the ends of the earth without stopping to examine the course. It is the delicate combination of trust and questioning that keeps impulsive thinking useful. On the other hand, people with dysfunctional impulsivity are generally not concerned with any path other than the one they are currently traveling on, and that is what makes them so dangerously dysfunctional.

Everyone knows what happened to Bill Gates. He became the richest man in the world and continues to push the envelope in the realms of business and technology.[10] He recently graduated to new challenges like fighting world hunger and disease in the developing world.

But what about Neal Cassady? His legacy is a mixed one. His impulsive lifestyle single-handedly inspired the enduring success of his friends like Jack Kerouac and Allen Ginsberg. Yet Cassady was never able to reel in that kind of personal success. Kerouac reached the pinnacle of his profession. He is still celebrated by literary critics across the world for the high-intensity kickwriting style inspired by Cassady, even though Cassady himself isn't credited with the style. That isn't for lack of trying, either. Cassady had always wanted to be a writer. Despite the fact that many thought Cassady a brilliant writer, he never saw any of his works published (his memoir, *The First Third*, was published posthumously).

What is most ironic (and tragic) is that Cassady's madness to live was largely to blame for his abbreviated life. On a cold and rainy night in 1968, Cassady, just shy of age forty-two, decided to leave a wedding party by himself in San Miguel de Allende, Mexico, to take a fifteen-mile stroll down a set of railroad tracks wearing nothing but a T-shirt and jeans. He passed out drunk next to the tracks and died of pneumonia the next day. A few months before his premature death, Cassady seemed to recognize the self-defeating patterns that resulted from his unchecked impulsivity. He told his ex-wife, Carolyn, "I don't know where else to go. I'm a danger to everyone—to myself most of all." Perhaps Cassady had finally recognized the importance of being directionally correct, but it was too little, too late.

# CHAPTER THREE

# Eat or Be Eaten:

## What Politicians Have Learned from Primates

One of the most precious benefits of being human has to be our ability to roll out of bed each morning without the imminent threat of a jaguar darting through the patio door, intent on using our hollowed-out rib cage as a breakfast platter. Not all of our cousins in the primate world are quite so lucky. For capuchin monkeys in the rain forests of Venezuela, every day is a balancing act, toeing a tight rope between life and death. Capuchins are cute little things wearing a coat of brown fur that snuggles around their pale faces. Weighing in at only about 10 pounds, their size makes them little match for a beefy 200-pound jaguar. Yet capuchins have little to fear most of the time. They have made the treetops their home, which generally keeps them out of reach of their ground-dwelling predators. But during the jungle's seasonal dry months, food and water are scarce in the treetops. These little fellows have to shinny down from the jungle canopy in order to find nourishment. That's just the opportunity that predators like jaguars and snakes have been waiting for.[1]

Fortunately for the capuchins, they are a social bunch. There might be as many as fifty monkeys in one troop. This social structure gives them a number of advantages. For one, they aren't forced to breed with a sibling. It also means that every now and then they can outnumber a much larger predator and actually send the big cat running for the hills. Other times in the smaller groups, the entire bunch will just stay put, or "freeze," until the hungry beast gives up and moves on to another opportunity. Anthropologist and author of *Eat or Be Eaten*, Lynne Miller[2] says that these monkeys "are so nervous that they don't even bother to come to the ground. It becomes a choice of eat or be eaten and they would rather forgo eating to forgo being eaten." In either defensive tactic, the first crucial step always requires identifying the threat. At least one monkey in the group has to spot the approaching predator. Once the predator makes its way into the line of sight of one of the capuchins, the vigilant monkey broadcasts the headline news from the treetop. Almost immediately a few other monkeys hear the distress call and just like that, in a matter of seconds, the treetops light up like the phone lines at the Jerry Lewis MDA Telethon.

The biggest reason why our furry little friends choose to remain in troops is because fifty pairs of eyes cover more ground than one pair. The bigger the group, the more chance each monkey will be alerted to a threat. For this security system to work, capuchins must be sensitive to calls of impending danger and they need to trust their news sources. It's not hard to imagine how long a rebellious monkey would survive in that environment. The impulsive capuchin who ignores a warning call in favor of hunting down just one last fruit will soon find itself the tasty treat. For capuchins who prefer not to die a gruesome death, it seems best to err on the side of caution, which most monkeys do.

Greg Vicino is the primatologist at the San Diego Zoo,

where he oversees the zoo's world-famous Monkey Trails. Despite Vicino's tall and slender build, touring the Monkey Trails with him is about as close as you could come to being guided by an actual monkey who happens to speak very articulate English. His passion for, and understanding of, primates is evident not just in his descriptions but also in the way the monkeys respond to him, running up to the glass to make silly faces and playfully plaster their hindquarters against the glass. (I like to think that was out of their love for Vicino, rather than their disapproval of me.) In the various groups of monkeys, females outnumber males by an average of about five to one, because three out of every four males die before reaching sexual maturity. The gender disproportion has something to do with why females call the shots in monkey societies, and is reminiscent of Katharine Graham's wise words of "in fact power has no sex." The cause of death for oh so many of these young lads, Vicino says, is typically "gambling, drinking, and motorcycles . . . exactly like us." The ones that make poor choices simply don't survive, and unfortunately for the males they fall victim to impulsive choices much more regularly than the females.

As a researcher at the California National Primate Research Center in Davis, California, prior to being recruited for his position at the zoo, Vicino had ample opportunity to observe monkeys in a natural setting. Vicino says matter-of-factly that in dangerous situations, whether at the research center or in the wild, "the impulsive monkeys get smoked." In experiments when monkeys are introduced to a novel object, the impulsive monkeys are the first to go check it out. When the novel object turns out to be a predator, the curious monkey "is severely punished for his impulsivity." Vicino does mention that if the object happens to be a nutrient-rich food source, like a cantaloupe, which can be all the food he needs for days, it is the impulsive monkey who earns the last laugh. But the majority of monkeys hold the possible threat in much higher esteem than the possible gain.

So that's great for jungle monkeys, but what does the social structure of capuchins in Venezuela and monkeys at the zoo have to do with people? Thousands of years ago humans may have had to engage in this eat or be eaten song and dance just like the capuchins still do. But not now in the civilized world, right?

Well, yes and no. It is true that most people today don't have to worry much about the threat of being mauled by a tiger, but we still have our fair share of predators to contend with. Most immediately, we have cell-phone-wielding, text-messaging, radio-blasting drivers behind the wheels of the cars whizzing by us every time we stroll down the street. Most of us face the threat of financial peril with every new shift in the economy, or in our careers. Then there is the unyielding threat of disease, terrorist attacks, and any number of hurricanes, tornadoes, earthquakes, and avalanches. The point here is that threats have never disappeared. They have just evolved, which is why the majority of people still are born equipped with an acute sensitivity to threats to their well being. Preservation of our resources and of our lives is still a long way from guaranteed, even in our civilized world.

So far, *The Impulse Factor* has focused almost exclusively on the impulsive minority—those boat-rocking few who brazenly cross boundaries with one eye fixed on the horizon looking for the next big cantaloupe. Sometimes these impulsive seekers blaze the path to new and prosperous frontiers, and other times they push nothing other than the limits of good judgment. We'll return to them later, but right now we are going to shift gears and take a look at the rest of the population— the cautious majority. As the capuchin monkeys make clear, an eye for safety is a key to achieving the most basic survival goals. But this universal need to pay special attention to danger, although protective, has led to some unintended side effects. In some cases the apparent threat is nothing more than our mind playing tricks on us. There are certain times when our uncanny ability to spot danger causes us to overlook opportunity. What we want to determine is at what point does that keen attention to threat transform into an obsession with safety, and ultimately a liability in our decision making.

## 1. The Election of 1828

The 1820s was a turbulent decade in American political history, but you never would have guessed that judging by the way the decade began. In 1820 James Monroe was welcomed back into the White House for his second term by what seemed like the entire U.S. population in the only uncontested U.S. presidential election. The only dissenting electoral vote he received was allegedly cast on purpose to pay homage to George Washington so that "His Excellency" could remain the only unanimously elected president in U.S. history. The truth of the dissenting elector's motivation is up for debate (and who did he vote for, since Monroe had no opponent?), but nonetheless Monroe won an overwhelming majority of the votes.

Back then, congressmen were free to sit on whichever side of the aisle they preferred, as the Democratic-Republican Party was the only organized show in town. James Monroe was the party's leader and the last remaining Founding Father still able and willing to assume the role of commander in chief. And what better man for the job than the guy who would officially get Daddy Europe off America's back with the signing of the Monroe Doctrine. Finally, America was free to kick whomever's butt had the misfortune of getting in its way. Despite the ongoing slave trade and those pesky Indian uprisings, things were so sweepingly peachy in Washington that one New England journalist dubbed the time under Monroe's unified leadership the "Era of Good Feelings."[3]

Even though it appeared warm and fuzzy to outsiders, Washington was crumbling from the inside out. Everyone— including members of Monroe's cabinet—started pushing their own agenda.[4] The division of parties across the aisle from each other in the House of Representatives would soon be instituted as the nation said good-bye to the Era of Good Feelings and ushered in the Era of Hurt Feelings. In 1824 the Democratic-Republican Party did what it seemed destined to do ever since the two-headed monster was given its name: It split. Neither of the two competing camps had a clear leader, which made the next election anybody's race. In total, there were four candidates for president in 1824. For the first and only time in U.S. history, not one of the candidates could be named as a victor based on the popular vote *or* the electoral vote. (It would be nearly two centuries before we would have the "sophistication" to track down ambiguously punched ballot chads for a recount.) The newly partitioned House of Representatives intervened and John Quincy Adams squeaked into office.

Adams's most able opponent, Andrew Jackson, never stopped crying foul over his defeat. Adams had struck a back-room deal with the third runner-up, Congressman Henry Clay. When Clay saw that he wasn't one of the top two candidates, he backed out of the race and threw his support to Adams, which gave Adams the edge he needed in Congress. Adams and Clay weren't exactly bosom buddies, but Clay hated Jackson more than he disapproved of Adams. So like most voters do today, with the exception of the few unwavering Ralph Nader supporters, Clay opted for the pragmatic choice and sided with the candidate he least despised who also actually had a chance to win. In exchange for Clay's loyalty, Adams appointed Clay secretary of state. Jackson called the deal between Clay and Adams a "corrupt bargain." It was indeed a bargain, but whether it was corrupt is debatable. In any event, even though he didn't win a majority of the votes in either case, Jackson won more votes than any of the other candidates. So it really did stink to be Andrew Jackson in 1824, and the whole ordeal left him rightfully sour. But Jackson would have bittersweet revenge four years later.[5]

The election of 1828 is now widely regarded as the birth of mudslinging in American politics. Exactly which side cast the first clump is hard to say. The disregard for the lines between political and personal issues by both parties was so rampant it would make today's paparazzi blush. You could argue that Andrew Jackson had been muddying the waters of the Potomac ever since 1824, with his relentless claims of the "corrupt bargain" struck between his opponents, Adams and Clay. But it didn't take Adams's camp long to start firing shots of their own, and Jackson's history provided them with ample fodder. The tenacious Indian fighter and hero of the War of 1812 never left anyone guessing about where he stood on any issue. And when anyone aimed an insulting finger at him, he wasn't afraid to challenge them. And the challenge that Jackson offered wasn't one of op-eds or debates, it was the kind of challenge replete with twenty paces, two loaded guns, and two questionably sane "gentlemen" facing off against each other. In his lifetime, Jackson participated in a whopping 103 duels. That number doesn't even count the informal duels like the time when, as a thirteen-year-old prisoner of war in the American fight for independence, Jackson was nearly killed by a British soldier after he refused to clean the Redcoat's boots. Even though dueling was a pretty standard practice in the late 1700s (just ask the face staring back at you on the ten-dollar bill, Alexander Hamilton), by 1828 it was frowned upon. The Adams camp didn't hesitate to remind people of Jackson's history with those sordid standoffs.

But Jackson's dueling past was just the tip of the iceberg for Adams's critiques. Jackson was most sensitive about attacks on his beloved wife of thirty-seven years, Rachel. One reputable duelist, Charles Dickinson, paid the ultimate price in a duel with Jackson after Dickinson made an allusion to Rachel's alleged extramarital affairs. The dead-eye marksman, Dickinson, took the first shot and hit Jackson just above the heart. Unmoved by the bullet, Jackson raised his gun and returned one shot that killed Dickinson. All because of a disrespectful comment about Mrs. Jackson.

Rachel Donelson Robards Jackson earned her Scarlet Letter back in 1791 when she wed Andrew Jackson. At the time, Rachel was separated from her first husband, Captain Lewis Robards. She believed that her divorce from Robards was final, but that did not turn out to be the case. Legally Robards had only been granted *permission* to file divorce but had not yet filed for divorce. So when she and Jackson tied the knot, it made Rachel a bona fide adulteress in the courtrooms of eighteen-century Tennessee. In truth, it was little more than a clerical oversight. But thirty-some years later, Adams's supporters didn't hesitate to make the incident public. In an attempt to goad Jackson into self-destructing, they made the couple's personal life so public that it would probably horrify the TomKats and Brangelinas of today's tabloids. Before all was said and done, they painted a picture of the portly Mrs. Jackson akin to the real-life incarnation of Hester Prynne. This ugly battle is regarded as one of the first in the birth of modern politics and political campaigns.

Not to be outdone, Jackson's camp fired back with accusations that Adams was a pimp for child prostitutes. Their claim? That while doing a stint as the U.S. ambassador to Russia, Adams had let his Russian "John," the Czar, have his way with an American servant girl. And in a claim slightly closer to the truth and more relevant to political issues, they alleged that during Adams's first term as president he was skimming off the top to feed his gambling habit. What they apparently meant was that Adams had purchased a chess board and a pool table for the White House. This was not exactly a national security issue.

But a little spin never hurt anyone, right? Nobody that is, except for Rachel Jackson. She had been dealing with a bad ticker all throughout the election, and it finally did her in two weeks after her husband was elected. Andrew Jackson went to his grave believing that it was the verbal attacks on Rachel by the corrupt bargainers—Adams and Clay—that pushed her weak heart beyond its limits.

## 2. The Lesser of Two Evils

Today, politicians from all parties still sling mud. Sex still makes headlines. What's new?

What remains important about the election of 1828 is not so much that the candidates got personal with each other. But that election was remarkable because the candidates shifted the focus almost entirely away from what they themselves were doing *right*. They instead focused on what was *wrong* with the other candidate. It was the precursor to the common practice of today's political ads. You know the attack ad where you watch the entire commercial without knowing who the advertisers actually want you to support, because it focuses solely on the shortcomings of another candidate. Only in the last few seconds of such an ad are we clued in to whom we are supposed to vote for when we hear the mandatory "paid for by supporters of . . ." The Jackson versus Adams campaign was the first in a long line of campaign trails in which both candidates promoted who they were *not*, and what they would *not* do. In the heat of the 2004 presidential campaign, author and NPR commentator Kenneth C. Davis[6] commented that "pseudo news stokes the endless appetite of our 24/7 media. The real losers are not the candidates, but we, the people." The success of this campaign tactic reveals something more fundamental about the rest of us than it does about politicians.

It is worth taking a closer look at exactly why politicians are so determined to fling insults at each other. Is it that they are by nature a slimy, name-calling bunch who never graduated morally from kindergarten? Is there something special about politics that attracts a certain kind of disingenuous, disrespectful personality? Both options are possible and are probably true of some politicians, but *all* of them? Should we really believe that the slimiest one percent of Americans are somehow successfully getting elected to fill every political position in the land? Or maybe modern Americans truly are as morally bankrupt as some domestic and international pundits would like to believe, and politicians are just a representation of that culture. However, another explanation is worth exploring.

Above all else, politicians need to get elected. Maybe they want to get elected so that they can make the world a better place, or merely because they are on a power trip and want to do nothing but promote their own agendas. Or maybe, they just want a job that requires them to work even less time each year than a writer. Whatever it is that they want to accomplish in office, the first step is always to get elected. This is the one incentive common to politicians, regardless of their ultimate intentions. So how do they get elected? Or maybe the better question is *who* elects them? The answer of course is that *we do*. Whether we know it or not—and whether we want to acknowledge it or not—mudslinging has a powerful appeal to our psyches. Psychologists have found that, just like capuchins, we are far more sensitive to bad news than we are to equally good news.

For example, imagine a situation in which I asked you to choose between two presidential candidates. Jane Candidate promises that her Super-Duper economic policy will cut the national inflation rate nearly in half. This reduction will make a buck go a lot further than it does now in the grocery store and in the housing market. With any luck the new Super-Duper economy might enable you to buy German beer and French wine without losing two bucks for every Euro in the exchange. But there is a cost to decreased inflation. In order to cut inflation, Jane's Super-Duper policy is going to require a trade-off with jobs. She is going to have to raise the unemployment rate by about a quarter more than what it is now. So unemployment goes up by twenty-five percent in exchange for inflation being cut by half.

Jane's opponent is Mary Nominee. Mary Nominee's platform is based on her "Let Sleeping Dogs Lie" policy. Mary doesn't like the high inflation rate either, but more than anything, she doesn't want to cut inflation at the expense of unemployment rates. Mary intends to leave the inflation and unemployment rates right where they are because she doesn't want to slash the jobs of her hard-working constituents like her opponent, Jane, does.

All else being equal, would you vote for Jane Candidate and her Super-Duper policy or Mary and her Sleeping Dogs policy?

If you're like the majority of people, you'll probably choose the second candidate.[7] You aren't happy with the inflation rate, but you would rather leave well enough alone. After all, who wants more unemployment? Never mind that inflation will be improved twice as much as employment will be cut. The fact that Jane's policy is going to eliminate even a small number of jobs is all that many people need to hear before dismissing Jane from consideration. For most people, the danger call is sounding too loud to hear the sound of opportunity knocking. Their brain tells them that Jane is a predator who is threatening to eat their economic well-being with her increased unemployment rates. So they forget about feasting on cuts to inflation and instead dwell on the standard rations of unemployment.

What's most important to recognize is that, in situations like this, the majority of voters pay more attention to bad news than good news. In effect, politicians are sending out danger calls, trying to warn people that their opponent is a predator who voters should fear. Most of us listen to that call. Consciously or subconsciously, we think "safety first." However, we tend to believe that when presented with two options, we will simply choose the better one. Deep down, we are not really looking for what is better. In fact, we are just looking at which option is *not worse*. Politicians know that. They know that they are all being compared to the impossible prototype of perfect politicians from the past. They know that, unlike George Washington, they are indeed capable of telling a lie. So why bother with the uphill battle of trying to measure up to the myths of the forefathers, when all you really need to do is make your opponent appear to be even further from that ideal statesman. The alternative, of course, is for the politician to spend her time showing the voters where the nutrient-rich sources of opportunity are, and asking voters to follow her there. But when it comes right down to it, voters are far less concerned with *eating* than they are with *being eaten*, and that makes them much more attentive to danger calls than to dinner bells.

For our capuchin cousins, always having one ear cocked for danger can be highly beneficial. For humans it also can be very beneficial, except for one little point. The key difference between us and monkeys—aside from the fact that we sling mud and they throw poop—is that capuchins have no incentive to beguile one another. Crying wolf doesn't advance a monkey's agenda or improve its chance of reelection. So they have no reason not to trust one another. Politicians, on the other hand, have a built-in reward for manipulating the tendencies of their voting constituents.

I am admittedly not a chemist, but I think my humble roots as a mud-pie-making child do establish me as somewhat of an expert on the formula required. From my best recollection, no mud can exist without a delicate combination of dirt and moisture. In politics, politicians and the machines that do their heavy lifting need to dig up dirt on their rivals. But dirt alone is basically useless without that key ingredient of moisture. The dirt turns to mud only when a significant portion of the population (that is, voters) salivates all over that dirt. When our mouths do inevitably start to water, *voilà!* The entire country becomes a political mud-wrestling pit. But the politicians are only responding to the rules of the game set forth by the voters, thanks to our instinctual focus on bad news. So to borrow a verse from modern hip-hop parlance, "don't hate the player, hate the game." The politicians are simply catering to the desires of those who put them into office. Instead of spending the lion's share of their campaign dollars telling us about what they can do to *help* us, politicians tell us about what their opponent will do to *hurt* us. They let out a piercing danger call that the cautious decision maker can't help but pay attention to.

## 3. Fear of a Smaller Prize

As we saw previously, Lola Lopes calls the cautious majority "security-minded." Lopes spent the better part of her career studying how and why people make the choices they do, and she concluded that a tendency to be security-minded is not in any way irrational or illogical. It simply is what it is. In one study, Lopes offered people two different versions of a cash-payout lottery.[8] Both lotteries had a potential payout of between $0 and $200. In the even-odds lottery, she offered the same number of tickets for every dollar amount, which meant that people had the same small chance to win $0, as to win $10, $100, or $200. The other lottery was "peaked" near the middle. The peaked version contained very few tickets at the extremes near $0 and $200. Gradually the number of tickets in the peaked lottery increased toward the middle range of dollar amounts. As one of her more cautious subjects commented, "the odds [in the peaked lottery] indicate an excellent chance of winning an amount between $80 and $119." For the cautious decision maker, it was a no-brainer. The peaked lottery offered a good chance of a reasonable gain, even though it offered only a minuscule chance of the larger gain.

Just as Lopes suspected, most of the people in her study opted for the secure choice of the peaked lottery. In perhaps an even more telling statement, one subject pointed out that the odds in the even lottery gave "too many chances of getting a lower prize," compared to those in the peaked lottery. The statement speaks volumes about the tendencies of cautious people. This person did not mention anything about the peaked lottery offering *better* chances to get a good prize. His reasoning was based solely on determining which lottery appeared to have a *lower* payout, and then choosing the other alternative. When forced to make a decision, cautious people often tend to define the outcome that they *don't* want and then let that conclusion guide their choice. The same comment could be applied to voting. Many people find themselves voting for a candidate they only somewhat approve of, because voting for the opposing candidate offers "too many chances of a lower prize." So if you're a campaign strategist, wouldn't it be wise to spend your time making the opposing candidate appear to be the lower prize? The alternative is to make your candidate appear to be the higher prize, but most people simply don't care as much about that. The other key point to notice is that the subject paid no attention to the fact that while the even lottery had more chances to get a lower prize, it also offered more chances at a higher prize. That reasoning never factored in to his decision. His odds of winning a higher prize were equally as strong as the odds of being stuck with the lower prize, but that didn't matter. Once again the inclination to *avoid an undesirable outcome* trumped the motivation to *obtain a desirable outcome*.

Objectively, there really is no right answer to Lopes's lottery choice. If you averaged the dollar amounts available in both lotteries, you would end up with an average of $100 in both cases. So which lottery you choose is simply a reflection of your natural tendency, rather than proof of your skill in making decisions. This is also a pretty accurate reflection of the decisions that confront people in real life. The criterion for a "good" decision is often different depending on the preferences of the decision maker. Choosing a more certain gain over a less likely chance to grab a bigger gain is not necessarily a bad choice, even if probability refutes it. That's because mathematics is not very good at accounting for peace of mind. To many people, the ability to rest easy at night with a small but guaranteed gain is much more valuable than the anxiety attached to a higher stakes gamble *even if they win*. For cautious decision makers, the pursuit of safety is often one and the same with the pursuit of happiness.

Being cautious certainly has its benefits. First and foremost it helps to keep people alive, which is why most people are indeed prone to err on the side of caution, as the old adage informs us: It is indeed better to be safe than sorry. It is why for every Pincher Creek avalanche, six out of eight people are going to think long and hard about the explicit warning they were given before deciding to speed up the treacherous slope. Even in the absence of a life-threatening situation, it can be helpful.

This point was driven home a few years ago with another group of corporate leaders I was working with. While the smaller group was off in one corner singing the praises of their own impulsive disposition, the larger group was on the other side of the room analyzing why careful analysis is effective. When asked why a more calculating decision style works, they came up with a number of thoughtful answers. One of those responses in particular summed it up better than anything I could write. They told me that a tendency toward caution quite simply "keeps us out of jail." It's hard to argue with that logic. Not surprisingly, this particular point came from a representative of the risk management department, which makes a cogent argument for the existence of a certain time and a certain place where a calculating style is not only welcome, but essential. Under these specific circumstances, we really have to question the value of the ardent potential seeker. Calculation is necessary, because what's true of the rules in the jungles of Venezuela is also true of the campaign trails of America, on the snowy hillsides of Canada, and inside the corporate conference rooms of the world's most successful businesses. So maybe it makes sense on a basic, primal level that we are more focused on the bad news brought to us by a plausible threat than on the good news regarding a potential gain. If most of us were not programmed to be hyperattentive to threats, with one eye always peeled for impending danger, we would be far more vulnerable to hungry predators of all industries and political affiliations, both foreign and domestic.

# CHAPTER FOUR

# Bubblology:

## The Plague of the $76,000 Flower

In 1559 in the hilly Bavarian city of Augsburg, an even-tempered scientist named Conrad Gessner sauntered through a private garden. A long gray beard framed his weathered face like a lion's mane as his gaze danced across the spread of exotic plants rare to the gardens of sixteenth-century Germans. For the passionate naturalist now regarded as the father of modern zoology, the experience had to be every bit as personally fulfilling as it was professionally interesting. Among the plants he observed that day, one blossom in particular caught his eye. Gessner was smitten by the rare specimen as he could not recall ever encountering such a beauty. Like a child on Christmas morning, Gessner hurried over to quiz the garden's owner about the flower's origins. His flattered host, the well-to-do Councilor Herwart, was more than happy to indulge his distinguished guest's curiosity. Proudly relaying tales of his travels, Herwart explained that he had the flower shipped to him all the way from the capital of the flourishing Ottoman Empire, Constantinople. He called the delicate, bell-shaped bulb a "tulip." Still basking in the glow of Gessner's admiration, Herwart continued, recalling that the tulip derived its name from the Turkish headwear it resembled, known in English as a turban.

Gessner immediately began touting the merits of the frail but radiant colored tulip bulbs. Before long the elite of Western Europe were having bulbs shipped to them from Constantinople just like Councilor Herwart had done. Less than a decade later the tulip had become the absolute must-have garden fixture of every wealthy person in Germany, Holland, England, and France. For the next five years, Gessner watched his prized discovery paint itself into the landscape of prosperous European life. At the same time, the proud father, Gessner, was awarded a position as a distinguished lecturer in his hometown of Zurich, Switzerland. Gessner's career appeared to have soared to a new height, but his fortune quickly bottomed out. In the winter of 1565, just one year after his appointment, Gessner came down with a fever accompanied by a throbbing headache and severe nausea. Days later, he was dead. A small outbreak of the bubonic plague had swept into Zurich and robbed Gessner of his twilight years. Although his beloved tulips were just beginning to reach full blossom in high society, Gessner's fatal bout with the Black Death was an eerie sign of things to come for his cherished tulip.[1]

Europe's obsessive love affair with tulip bulbs grew until 1634, when a phenomenon known as "tulip-mania" had officially overtaken the international markets of Amsterdam.[2] Tulip-mania was the perfect product of economics' most fundamental principle—the law of supply and demand. The appeal of the tulip was tied directly to its fragility. The color of its petals becomes more appealing to the eye as the flower begins to die. This quaint feature gave tulips the perfect combination of scarcity (low supply) and beauty (high demand). At the peak of tulip-mania, people were reported to have paid as much as the equivalent of U.S. $76,000[3] for a single tulip bulb—all for a flower whose most enduring quality was its dying beauty.

If the tulip craze had been contained to only the wealthiest few among Amsterdam's high society, it would have been nothing more than a bizarre obsession popular in small circles of eccentric speculators. In that case, it would be easy for us to dismiss the outrageous expense as something that a level-headed person would never incur. But the mania didn't stop there. It spread through Amsterdam from nobles to chimney sweeps. People from all classes found a way to get in on the action by putting anything they owned—including their homes and their property—up as collateral against a loan for tulip bulbs. They then hoped to sell the bulbs again in the way that today's real estate investors flip houses. In his classic nineteenth-century book *Extraordinary Popular Delusions and the Madness of Crowds*, British historian Charles Mackay described the beginning of the end: "At last, however, the more prudent began to see that this folly could not last for ever. Rich people no longer bought the flowers to keep them in their gardens, but to sell them again at cent per cent [*sic*] profit. It was seen that somebody must lose fearfully in the end. As this conviction spread, prices fell, and never rose again." The tulip market began a landslide that wiped out the Dutch economy on its way down.

## 1. Losin' It

While relatively unknown to the world in the early 1970s, Daniel Kahneman and Amos Tversky were on their way to fame and/or infamy depending on whom you talk to. In his autobiography, the Nobel laureate Kahneman writes that his partnership with Tversky (they were known to their peers as the "dynamic duo") was an exercise in contrasts.[4] Tversky, a witty man with an athletic build and a magnetic personality, was often described as being as funny as he was smart. Kahneman is an astute researcher who in his own words "grew up intellectually precocious and physically inept." As a platoon commander in the Israeli army at the age of twenty, Tversky was awarded a bravery citation after risking his life to save one of his young soldiers. Kahneman, on the other hand, fell short of the honor roll in eighth grade due only to his lackluster performance in gym class. Despite their differences, however, they clicked immediately as colleagues. As Tversky was a night owl and Kahneman a morning person, they settled on common ground for lunch and long afternoon work sessions. Although both were Israeli, they spent 1971 and 1972 in Eugene, Oregon. It was there, at the Oregon Research Institute, that they concocted the simple choice scenarios discussed earlier, such as whether you would prefer to bask in the cloud-drenched English countryside for a week, or take a longer three-week excursion across more of Western Europe. They then presented these scenarios to see which options their subjects preferred. What they found shattered the beliefs on which much of our political, economic, and social systems are based, and would later earn Kahneman a Nobel Prize.

For virtually the entire twentieth century, most of the world's brightest scientists and thinkers believed that people generally avoided risky propositions when possible. The average person heeded the wisdom that it is better to err on the side of caution. But something about that conclusion didn't ring completely true for Kahneman and Tversky. Like other researchers, Kahneman and Tversky found that under certain conditions a small percentage of people will knowingly make a risky choice. However, that told only half of the story. There were different situations in which the majority of people stepped out of their cautious mindset. When Kahneman and

Tversky presented people with the same scenarios, except flipped the situation upside down, the results were exactly opposite. When subjects were asked whether they would prefer to take $500 free and clear, or take a fifty-fifty chance of wining $1,000, most took the sure thing. But when the same people were presented with a fifty-fifty chance of *losing* $1,000, or accepting a guaranteed *loss* of $500, most of them decided to take the gamble. Rather than accepting a known amount as a loss, they rolled the dice and risked losing double that amount just for the chance to break even.[5]

That second part of Kahneman and Tversky's study was as brilliant as it was simple. Their study showed that people— even the cautious majority—are indeed very capable of making decisions that appear to be impulsive. In 2005 Japanese psychologists Hiroyuki Sasaki and Michihiko Kanachi[6] revisited Kahneman and Tversky's research. Sasaki and Kanachi tested whether or not their subjects at Tohoku University were impulsive and then gave each of them gambling scenarios. When they asked the subjects to choose between gaining a lot with a risky gamble, or gaining a smaller amount with a sure bet, they noticed a distinct difference. Impulsive people took the riskier gamble, and cautious people took the sure bet. However, all that changed when the researchers gave people choices between a gamble for a risky loss and a smaller, more certain loss. In the loss scenario, the difference between the cautious and impulsive people vanished. It seems that maintaining good sense is relatively easy for cautious people when the choice is between a guaranteed good choice and a riskier but potentially higher paying choice.

But people's good sense becomes muddled when faced with the decision to accept a sure *loss* or take a big gamble in hopes of returning to even. In fact, cautious individuals will predictably make risky decisions whenever they believe they have fallen below some self-set reference point. They might take a perfectly good investment in something like a home, and then refinance to transfer that investment into an unstable tulip market. In gambling and business, it is what is commonly referred to as "throwing good money after bad." People may dig an even deeper hole for themselves by attempting to claw their way back to the surface. When we take this aspect of human nature into consideration, the mystery of tulip-mania begins to unfold.

Deciding to put your home on the line to invest in absurdly overpriced tulip bulbs has the distinct flavor of impulsivity to it. It sounds just like what a brazen, cage-fighting entrepreneur might do if the market for dental equipment should suddenly be knocked out. But presuming that the entire city of Amsterdam somehow had a remarkably high concentration of impulsive people is not a very satisfying explanation. It is even less satisfying when we consider that a similar mania took hold in Paris and London shortly after it ended in Amsterdam. Something else was happening with the tulip craze that caused calculating people to seemingly lose their minds. They were acting out the phenomenon of *conditional impulsivity*.

## 2. I'll Have What He's Having

Let's forget about tulips for a second. Think about the last time you and a group of friends went out for a relaxing dinner. You wash down your food with a few drinks, have a few laughs, and then it comes time to pay the tab. This leads to a tense divvying-up of the check, during which you try to figure out exactly what each person ordered, inevitably coming up short on the tip because half of the people forgot to add on sales tax to their fajitas. (Ever wonder why an automatic gratuity is tacked on to parties of six or more?) To avoid this awkward postmeal hassle, many of us just decide to split the bill evenly. But economists have good reason to question the efficiency of splitting a bill. While at the University of Chicago, economist Uri Gneezy[7] now at the University of California at San Diego, discovered that when people split the bill even-steven, the total bill ends up being considerably higher. Here's why: Assume that you are going out to dinner with a group, and you know ahead of time that everyone will be paying the same. You also know that your buddy at the other end of the table has a bad habit of impulsive spending. Without a doubt, you know that guy is going to order the most expensive entree on the menu. Under normal conditions, or when eating by yourself, you would be content with something along the lines of a club sandwich. But now you'll feel gypped if that guy orders the forty-dollar lobster and you only order the twelve-dollar club sandwich. You may even really enjoy club sandwiches, but with every crunch and crack of that guy's expensive little seafloor dweller, you will be reminded that you and the lobster guy are both going to pay the same portion of the bill for two very different meals.

Well, you're no dummy. You order the lobster so that guy at the end of the table doesn't one-up you. Far from feeling impulsive, you feel like you've actually protected yourself by maximizing the value of your dollar. Since everybody's individual split should end up being around 20 bucks, you will pay $20 for a $40 lobster plate. It's a tasty deal unless you aren't the only one to have this revelation. The other people in your party may also decide to treat themselves, not necessarily because they are lobster lovers either, but because they don't want to feel like you two are getting ahead of them. Now everyone orders lobster. Everyone is now "treating themselves" to a dinner bill twice as high as anyone had originally anticipated. The individual split on the bill is now $40 (without drinks or desserts) instead of $20. Of course, nobody's taste buds changed just because of the payment structure. The only thing that changed was how you determined what would be your fair share. It felt like you would lose out on the same opportunity to enjoy a lobster feast on the cheap that your dinner partners were cashing in on.

Multiply this dinner group by a few hundred thousand people and substitute club sandwiches and lobster with modest wages and tulip bulb profits, respectively, and it is easy to see how tulip-mania became all the rage in Amsterdam. It was conditional impulsivity on a grand scale. When left to their own devices, cautious people won't usually choose to order lobster, or put their homes on the line for a tulip bulb. These are things we expect only an impulsive person to do. Unlike their impulsive counterparts, cautious people weigh their options in units of security. For the cautious majority, security from possible harm is the foremost concern. Merely believing that a tulip bulb investment could offer the possibility of reward is probably not going to light a fire under cautious decision makers. Instead, these anxious individuals will be motivated to invest when, and only when, they see it as a bigger risk *not* to invest—when the situation begins to look like one in which only a soon-to-be-sorry sucker would not invest.

In our very own made-in-America edition of tulip-mania, the dot-com bubble of the 1990s, the same mindset took hold of the country.[8] At the high point of the bubble, Internet stock analyst Henry Blodget[9] epitomized the condition when he said that the possibility of losing a little money buying an overvalued stock wasn't nearly as risky as "missing the much bigger upside." In other words, the perception was that an investment in dot-com stocks was as good as money in your pocket, and *not* to invest would be akin to losing that money. It is at that moment—directly in the face of a potential threat to our security and comfort—when conditional impulsivity kicks in.

When people see their neighbors ordering lobster on their dime or moving on up the social ladder because of a tulip investment, their frame of reference changes. Suddenly the situation is no longer about the chance to feast like a king, but instead it is the risk of "missing the much bigger upside." In their need for security, people are not so concerned with getting ahead, but they absolutely dread falling behind. So people decide to order the lobster. They decide to risk everything they have to buy the absurdly priced tulips. If time allows, they may even decide to chase a more daring friend up a temperamental slab of snow.

Poor investment decisions are hardly criminal. But we can learn something about our decision to buy lobster from other people's decision to steal it. Psychologists have long known that antisocial, criminal behavior is actually a very social activity. Just like you learned watching after-school specials, it truly is the influence of peers, above all other variables, that inspires criminal behavior. In a 1993 study, Marvin Zuckerman, renowned psychologist at the University of Delaware, teamed up with researcher Paula Horvath[10] and found that the likelihood of an individual's shoplifting increased threefold when his buddies did. This negative impact occurs whether or not a person is naturally inclined to impulsive behavior. Certainly a part of this is the human desire to belong to the group, just as our earlier comparison experiment proved. But it's hard to imagine how buying lobster or investing in tulips paves a direct path to social acceptance. It seems just as likely that people are encouraged to invest because they simply don't want to get stuck holding the short end of the stick.

A team of researchers at Princeton University found that the individual need to get a fair share is hardwired into our brains. The team, led by cognitive psychologist Alan Sanfey,[11] resurrected a classic experiment known as the "ultimatum game," in which researchers put two people together and ask them to split a sum of money. One player gets to determine what the split is and the second player gets to determine whether he wants to accept the split or reject it. The catch is that if the second player rejects the split, then neither player gets any money. If the first player is logical, then she is supposed to recognize her advantage and offer an extremely lopsided split in her favor. This is supposed to be the smart move because the second player is expected to accept the uneven split regardless of how unfair it might be, because he will logically conclude that any amount of money is better than nothing. *Who cares if it is unfair?* he is supposed to reason. In truth, nearly everyone cares. That is why most people who play the ultimatum game end up offering a fifty-fifty split to the second player.

But some players do try to cash in on their perceived advantage and offer the lopsided split. Guess what the second player does when offered an uneven split? He rejects it, knowing full well that both players will walk away empty-handed. It may not be logical, but it feels like the right thing to do.

Sanfey's team took this classic game into the modern era. They used the space-aged functional MRI machine to watch what happens inside people's brains when they play the game. What they found was that when people are offered an unfair split, a part of their brain known as the anterior insula lights up. The anterior insula is a primal part of the brain not exactly known for deep thinking, which is why it is often ground zero for impulsive explosions of anger and disgust. When offered an unfair split, the second player's brain tells him that something is not right. The anterior insula lets him know that the first player is trying to get ahead. His brain sends down the danger signal on which he bases his decision to reject the split. That's why it is so hard not to covet thy neighbor's goods. When thy neighbor orders lobster on a split bill, thy anterior insula lights up like a Roman candle. It doesn't matter that rejecting the split—no matter how unfair—is a poor financial decision. Psychologically, you feel better off knowing that you finished the game even with the first player, rather than letting that creep get ahead. You may not have won, but more important, you didn't lose.

In Kahneman and Tversky's experiments, people used the amount of money in their purse at the beginning as the reference point to determine whether they gained or lost. In the real world, our reference point is much less personal. Being the social animals that we are, our reference point usually rests firmly on other people. Our perception of how attractive or how smart we are depends mostly on how attractive or how smart we think other people are. Even our perception of how nonconforming we are is based on how *conforming* other people are. In a variation on the experiment, Sanfey's team pitted a person against a computer rather than another person. When the computer offered an unfair split, it didn't elicit the same strong response in the anterior insula as that elicited by the actions of a person. Of course, nobody enjoyed the unfair split whether given by a computer or a person. But the most intense reactions to the unfair split were only those that resulted from another person's taking more. Falling behind a nonhuman object just doesn't matter as much as falling behind thy neighbor. That's because it isn't the money alone that drives us. It is how much money everyone else has that pushes us to make out-of-character decisions. But the results of the ultimatum game show us that most people are not actually trying to get ahead. The vast majority of first players offer the supremely fair fifty-fifty split. When those few opportunists do try to get ahead, their efforts are thwarted by the bitter second players who prove that misery really does love company.

Cautious people don't behave impulsively to distance themselves from the group. They behave impulsively to keep up with the group. Staying in step with the group is often the safest bet we can make . . . except when it isn't. The problem is that the safe choice is not always as clear as it may have first appeared.

## 3. Security Traps

I have an uncle who likes to tell a somewhat morbid joke in which he says, "Nobody has ever died from falling off a building."

"How do you figure?" you ask skeptically.

"Well, you see, it isn't the fall that kills you," he says wryly. "It's the sudden stop at the bottom that'll getchya."

The joke, of course, is that the sudden stop is the inevitable conclusion to the long fall so there really isn't much difference between the two. The long fall and the sudden stop invariably go hand in hand. However, technically my uncle is right. It is indeed the abrupt stop on the pavement that forces an early retirement from life.

The same clever logic applies to bubbles built on the fundamentals of conditional impulsivity. As a bubble builds, nobody gets hurt. In fact, it is quite the opposite. Nearly every investor involved in the building of a bubble accumulates more money, at least on paper. Those first-come investors who get in early and sneak out early end up cashing in on their early-bird status with a Grade A nest egg in hand. One look at the dramatic increase in housing prices near Silicon Valley is proof that not quite everybody went belly-up following the busting of the tech stock bubble in early 2000. There was still plenty of dot-com money available to build a housing bubble. The people who really pay the price in a bubble are the latecomers. It is the average Joes and Janes who didn't know much at all about what was happening in the stock market until they began hearing wild stories of quick riches while huddled around the office water cooler, or at their neighbor's backyard barbecue next to the brand new gas grill courtesy of a tantalizing three-week run on E*Trade. Prior to that point in the bubble, investing in high-risk/high-growth tech stocks was restricted to a smaller group of inherently potential-seeking professional investors and their clients called "growth investors." For the growth investor, it pays to have a wave of investors jump in to the market and drive prices up. The problem arose when the "get in before it's too late" virus swept into the mindset of the average Janes and Joes of the world. By this point, investing in temperamental tech stocks was not a risky move intended to get ahead. Instead it was seen as necessary to keep up with the neighbors and the guy in the next cube. Latecomers were looking out for their own security by trying not to miss out on the group's move.

Once this next wave of novice investors entered the market, things became doubly dangerous. It was more troublesome not only because the bubble had reached critical mass due to this huge influx of investors, but also because the new breed of investor had entered the unstable market. Risky investments might be okay for those early adopters who are used to living on the edge, but it becomes a real problem for the others who are not so comfortable in uncertain situations. When the good-times train appears to be running out of steam and some of those darling investments—tech stocks, tulips, or townhouses—start losing value, the cautious person's brain registers the call loud and clear: *predator!*

It is at this point in a bubble where the cautious conglomerate of investors freeze. They are uncertain of exactly how to proceed. They don't want to sell their stocks at a loss because that would turn a paper loss into a tangible, real-world loss. Some of these investors won't do anything, and others might buy more in a desperate attempt to get back to even. It is right about here when the rising bubble reaches the top floor, from which there is only one direction to go. When Charles McKay's words prove their timelessness and "the more prudent realize that this folly could not last for ever"—the sell-off begins. And what happens when everybody stops buying and starts selling? The fall begins, followed by the inevitable splatter at the bottom.

The fall happens fairly quickly because the average person doesn't have much of a stomach for high-stress, risky situations. Risky situations are awfully scary for most of us. One of the basic reasons that cautious people aren't comfortable with risky situations is that they just don't have much experience with them. When you don't have a learned response to a situation, your better judgment goes on cruise control. Your brain can't recall a pattern of behavior for being cool and calm in a certain scenario, so it acts on pure reflex—pure impulse. And the resulting behavior does bear a striking resemblance to impulsiveness. In other words, most people aren't that good at dealing with high-risk situations because they have been too good at avoiding those situations in the past. Unfortunately, at these times it is usually the dysfunctional impulsiveness that rears its ugly head, rather than the quick-thinking functional kind. The potential seeker might be better able to dismiss the danger call as ordinary, and nothing to get too excited about, simply because they have been there before. They stand a better chance of reacting with a functional decision. However, for the ordinarily cautious person, danger is danger. Some may make a desperate attempt to escape by buying more stock "at a discount" in the vain hope that this is just a temporary dip in the market. Others won't buy or sell, and will simply freeze. Both will get trapped under the weight of the falling bubble and ride it into the ground. The lucky, "more prudent" ones will have given in to their flight impulse and sold off at a more manageable loss.

This phenomenon of investors buying an overpriced gem, and then subsequently scrambling for the exits when the gem reveals a blemish, is so common that researchers in the investment community have given it a name: the overreaction hypothesis. As the name implies, people tend to react to news about their prized holdings much more than they should. When a good company's stock is on the rise and consistently performs above the market, it acquires a certain mystique that makes it appear as though this company can do no wrong. It appears to be a safe, virtually guaranteed money-maker. The first comers get in halfway up the rise. Then the cautious people, who usually don't like to take big chances, see the rising stock price and suddenly feel confident about setting their nest egg inside that company's impenetrable fortress. Unfortunately, all companies are composed of mere mortals, and they are always one-quarter's earnings away from a slip. The seemingly safe investment is, in fact, a security trap.

Take Dell Computer. Dell arrived on the stock exchange in the late 1980s and then took off in the mid 1990s. Their new system of selling directly to consumers without any middleman distributors or retail shops proved to be a profit-making machine in the exploding personal computer industry. The investment world paid close attention. Dell's stock price soared off the charts from 1997 to 1999. After all, what could be better than a stock on the rise based on an unquestionably good idea being carried out by highly competent management? It was almost too good to be true. The problem was that Dell's stock had soared to unreasonable heights with expectations that went far beyond what any company could achieve. Dell's sales were indeed growing at a healthy fifty percent each year, but the company's stock price was simultaneously increasing that much every few weeks or even days. Fifty-percent growth of sales was small potatoes compared to the growth in stock price. Then in 1999, Dell's sales—while still growing—didn't grow quite as much as analysts expected. That one piece of unexpected news pushed Dell's stock price toward the ledge, where it teetered for a few more months before taking a free fall. Over half a decade later, despite a whole generation of young dudes being assured that they were getting a Dell, the highly successful computer manufacturer's stock still had not bounced back to its high in 2000.

Dell is just one of countless examples. People continued buying stock in companies like Yahoo! at prices that estimated its worth at a billion dollars even though it was earning only a million dollars a year. The folly can't last forever because the sirens in the most primal corners of sometime-investors' minds will eventually sound. Those high-rising stocks that everyone so eagerly let into their henhouses soon shed their sheepish outerwear and exposed themselves as the over-inflated gambles that they truly were. And when people start selling a stock, that stock's price drops even further, which scares still more people into selling. From that point, it isn't very long until the plummeting prices reach terminal velocity, leaving many investors no time to get out before hitting bottom.

But there is hope. There are some investors who slowly and steadily scoop up earnings from the rubble of collapsed stock prices. David Dreman is one of those investors. As the author of *Contrarian Investment Strategies*, Dreman[12] was one of the first investors back in the late 1970s to recognize the predictability of the overreaction hypothesis. Back then, the idea was dismissed by most of the investment world. Economists believed that people were unwavering in their cautious choices, just as the stock market was unwavering in its efficiency. So Dreman and his dreary suggestion that people don't react appropriately were dismissed as unwelcome poopers at the efficient markets party. Though perhaps Dreman was finally vindicated by the tech stock bubble rise and fall, his resentment is still very evident in the tone of *Contrarian Investment Strategies*.

Dreman's contrarian strategy is basic. He adheres to the most generic of all investment advice, which recommends that we "buy low, sell high." Though it is the oldest advice in the proverbial book, Dreman has found that a striking number of investors choose to ignore it. The majority of us tend to buy a stock or a home when the price is near its peak, and then sell when that price starts to drop—directly contradicting the age-old wisdom. Most of us use little quips of rationalization to justify these purchases like "I was afraid if we didn't get into the market now, we would never get in." The implication of such a suggestion is that everyone else is already "in" and will continue driving prices up for eternity, and I will be left behind penniless, homeless, and/or lobster-less.

Dreman, however, has used his naturally calculating nature to create a highly effective counterstrategy. Through extensive study, he has found that when a company with an inflated stock price receives good news, not a whole lot usually happens to it, except that maybe a few more Johnny-come-lately investors will jump in. But when it receives even a little bad news, the price plummets. The same is true in the case of companies with deflated stock prices. More bad news doesn't usually affect a low-priced stock much, but a little good news can send it soaring. Reading this now, I'm guessing this sounds logical. But too many people in the thick of an investment don't view it that way. They see a good company as a good investment regardless of the price. *You get what you pay for,* we reason. And how do we know that we are getting something good? *Well, just look at how much the stock price has been rising lately, and besides, everyone is talking about it.* We reason that it is a good investment because the stock price is rising, so we buy it, and the stock price continues to rise because everyone else is buying it. But it isn't rising because it's a great company anymore. It is rising because everyone is buying it. It is that kind of circular reasoning that gets most of us into trouble and makes Dreman a rich man. What we are really saying is that a stock on the rise is *safe*. It's a proven winner, whereas a stock that is on the decline must have been beaten down for a reason. This line of thinking is a security trap.

This is not a critique of the security-minded investor. Naturally impulsive decision makers almost certainly have a hand in creating bubbles, so the solution in this case is not simply for the more cautious person to become impulsive. Indeed, cautious consumers under threat of a security breach show a strong willingness to behave impulsively, and it obviously doesn't help. Investors must recognize when the intense need for security drives them to make poor decisions, which then pushes them further from their goal of security.

Dreman is not the shoot-from-the-hip, quick-gain growth investor who jumps in and out of the market trying to capitalize on momentary swings. In fact, he is outspoken about his dislike for that kind of investing. What is important to learn about his style is that he, too, tends toward the cautious style of decision making. He, too, pays attention to risk and—more important—he pays attention to minimizing risk. He doesn't concern himself with quick gains that more often than not are indeed too good to be true or, at least, too good to last. But unlike some of his colleagues in the investment community, he has recognized that people predictably overreact to negative news about their darling investments. He has spotted a pattern and has responded accordingly in spite of the criticism from his peers.

This is a tell-tale difference between the run-of-the-mill cautious decision maker and the more intentional, systematic calculating decision maker. Both have the same essential goal, which is to maintain their security and possibly achieve measured growth when the risk is low and the probability of a gain is high. However, the overtly cautious choice too often leads people to overreact to threats and err significantly and detrimentally on the side of caution whenever they feel as though their security is being threatened. Essentially, they throw all of their cautious hard work to the wind. They then play the impulsive role and end up fulfilling their fearful prophecies about committing a financial blunder. On the other hand, calculating decision makers are prepared, which doesn't give their anterior insula a chance to get fired up and cloud their judgment. They study the pattern of the situation and take into account the long-term consequences without being sucked into a bout of conditional impulsivity brought on by the fear of falling behind their peers. These "more prudent" decision makers that Charles McKay wrote about study the situation before defaulting to what appears to be the safety of the group's movement. Through calculation, they are able to maneuver around security traps instead of falling into them.

# CHAPTER FIVE

# Common Sense of Ownership

E very year in the hours before the National Football League draft kicks off, an anxious energy connects football fans and players across the United States. During the draft, owners of professional football teams gather to pick the best college players for their teams for the following season. Although a bit more sophisticated (and with much higher stakes), it's a lot like picking teams for a grammar-school pickup game. The earlier you get to pick, the more options you have to choose from. The team that gets the first pick can choose any college player it wants, which naturally gives that team a distinct advantage. To keep the balance of talent somewhat even in the NFL, the order of picks is set in reverse order of the previous season's league standings so that last year's league champion is theoretically handicapped with the last draft pick. If you finished last in the league the year before, then you get first pick in the following year's draft as your consolation prize.

In the 2004 NFL draft, an uncommon tension settled over its observers. All-American and Heisman Trophy runner-up Ole Miss quarterback Eli Manning was at the center of that tension. The San Diego Chargers—who just happened to be in the market to fill their quarterback slot—were awarded first pick in 2004 as they had finished dead last in the league in 2003. For most college football players, the prospect of being selected first in the NFL draft is quite an honor. Not only does it mean that you are just a few signatures away from a multimillion-dollar contract, it also says a lot about how the general managers of the greatest athletes in your sport think your talent stacks up. It should have been a fairy-tale ending to Manning's storied amateur career. But the 6'5", 260-pound Manning wasn't most college football players, and he didn't want to play for the Chargers any more than his father, former NFL quarterback Archie Manning, wanted him to. The elder Manning believed that the Chargers were destined to lose for years to come, and he made his opinion known publicly. He even went as far as to have Eli's agent specifically call the general manager of the Chargers to tell him that Manning was, well, less than thrilled about suiting up in Charger blue. Despite the objections from father Archie, the Chargers drafted Eli anyway.

At this point, Manning took a page from other unfavorable drafts in history and opted out. However, draft dodgers in the NFL don't go to Canada (not by choice, anyway). They go to "law school." Minutes after reluctantly posing behind a Charger's jersey with sad eyes under a perfectly parted blond tuft—looking more like an abnormally large six-year-old whose birthday cake had just toppled to the floor than a pro football player—Manning announced that he would be pursuing a law degree instead of playing for the Chargers. For the viewers at home, you can translate that publicity-speak as: *I would rather move in with my mom and dad than accept millions of dollars to play for your hopeless football team.* Minutes later the Chargers orchestrated an uncommonly rare draft-day trade with the New York Giants, in which they gave Manning to the Giants in exchange for the Giants' first pick, Philip Rivers, as well as two draft picks in the later rounds of that draft.

The most striking thing about the Chargers' first-round trade is that such trades are strikingly rare occurrences. Economically, the smartest thing for a team to do is to pick the player that is worth the most to another team—regardless of whether or not he fills an open position on your own team. It is a very basic tenet of a cash economy. You should acquire whatever goods (players) people are willing to pay the most for, and then trade them for what goods (players) that you need the most. To illustrate, pretend that you are sitting at your desk right around lunchtime listening to your stomach growling. You inevitably decide it's time to go get a sandwich. Outside of the sandwich shop, someone stops you and offers you a choice between a sandwich and a $20 bill. Which would you take? You may really want that sandwich right now to curb your craving, but it is still a no-brainer. Of course, you are going to choose the $20 bill because you know that you can then march right into the sandwich shop with your $20, buy *two* sandwiches and still have enough left over to buy a drink and maybe even a bag of chips. It's the same concept with the NFL draft. You should take the highest valued player even if he doesn't satisfy your immediate hunger because you know that you'll be able to trade him to another team for a different player that also satisfies your hunger and some additional draft picks for an overall better team. You might still have enough room in your salary cap to get all that and another bag of chips.

So if picking and subsequently trading is usually the best choice a team can make, then why did the Chargers do it only begrudgingly after they were practically forced to? After all, if there is one thing that most NFL football team owners know even better than how to make a good football team, it is how to most economically make a buck. Yet draft-day trades hardly ever happen. Could it really be true that the managers of the multibillion-dollar professional football industry make logical decisions only *by accident?*

## 1. Endowment Effect

Renowned economist Richard Thaler[1] believes the lack of trading on or immediately following draft day has something to do with what he calls the "endowment effect." The interesting thing about the endowment effect is that it has more to do with the decisions of the fans than the owners. The endowment effect says that once we take possession of something—once it becomes part of our endowment—we hate giving it up. We hate it so much that we might even act impulsively when that cherished thing appears to be slipping away from us. Even if giving up our endowment will make our cash stretch further, we still would prefer to hold on to it. In the case of the NFL draft, the endowment is the star college player your team just drafted. Thaler believes that "when a player is drafted he becomes part of the fans' endowment. If he is sold or traded, this will be treated by the fans as a loss." What he means is that fans won't look at the trade as a strategic move designed to create a better overall team. They will instead see it as a boneheaded move that cuts loose a favorite player. From there the math for the team's management is pretty simple. Losing their endowment makes fans unhappy (even more so when the notification of their loss comes part and parcel with an insulting appraisal of their favorite team's future prospects). Unhappy fans don't buy as many tickets as satisfied fans. Owners need fans to buy tickets in order to keep making money. Hence, owners try to keep fans happy by holding on to their endowed draft picks. As it turns out then, NFL owners may be making the most economically sensible decision after all. It is actually the fans' impulsive response to losing their endowment that forces the irrational play.

This idea of the endowment effect was illustrated by a study at the University of Victoria in Canada led by Jack Knetsch (now at Simon Fraser University).[2] A group of students were given a new coffee mug branded with the university's name and logo. The subjects were then asked if they wanted to trade in that mug for a pound of delicious, neatly wrapped Swiss chocolate. Guess how many took the chocolate and ran? Only eleven percent chose to give up their new coffee mug for that scrumptious chocolate bar. But that didn't necessarily prove anything. Sure, eighty-nine percent is an overwhelming majority of people who chose to hang on to their newly bestowed coffee mug. But what if the researchers just happened to have a bunch of calorie-counting kids or coffee addicts at the University of Victoria? Maybe the students don't even like chocolate, much less a belly-aching pound of it. To give those doubts a fair shake, the researchers gathered another group and turned the tables on them. They gave the second group the chocolate bars first, and then gave them a few moments to gape at the candy and imagine drifting away down a Wonka-esque chocolate river before unveiling the highly coveted coffee mug—the same coffee mug that eighty-nine percent of the previous students chose to hang on to. Then they offered the trade, asking the students who wanted to swap the candy bar for the coffee mug. This time a paltry ten percent elected to give up their chocolate for the coffee mug. The first time nine out of ten students were not willing to swap the mug for the candy, and the second time nine in ten were not willing to give up the candy for the mug. There is obviously more at work here than a fondness for coffee or chocolate. It seems that whether it's a chocolate bar, a coffee mug or a quarterback, people simply prefer to hold on to what they have been given regardless of its "true" value.

Giving the Chargers the benefit of the doubt, they may never have intended for Eli Manning to spend even a day in a Chargers uniform. To the applause of economists everywhere, the Chargers may have simply chosen the player that they knew the New York Giants would pay dearly for—which they did. And because Manning had made his feelings about the

Chargers so public, the Chargers' owners didn't have to worry about losing ticket sales by trading Manning. The backlash from the fans would all be directed with laser-like precision at Eli Manning. This was like a get-out-of-jail-free card for the Chargers' owners. Without the possibility of upsetting the fans, the owners were finally freed to make the value-maximizing decision without potential fan fallout. And what happens when management is free to make the most economical choices? You get a more modern fairy-tale ending, along the line of a *Shrek* movie. Just two seasons after this scandalous draft, the storied prince, Eli Manning, found himself in the midst of some serious performance issues. The Chargers ended the 2006 season with the best record in the league, led by Manning's replacement pick, Philip Rivers. The following year, Manning went on to lead the New York Giants to an improbable Super Bowl victory while the Chargers were eliminated in the league championship. I'm sure many Chargers fans still feel the burn of Manning's departure and to this day believe that Super Bowl title should have been theirs. But the fact is, Manning never wanted to play for the Chargers and never donned their uniform. But as far as his playing skills, maybe his quarterbacking, like his public relations, just needed some time to mature.

Even though the Chargers' owners were able to dodge the endowment bullet, that doesn't mean the resentment described above didn't need to find an outlet someplace. And indeed, San Diego Chargers fans were predictably aggrieved at having to give up Manning. Sure Manning's substitute, Philip Rivers, was no slouch, and he certainly proved that with his all-pro performance in only his second year with the team. But Chargers fans could not have known how good Rivers would turn out to be, and at the time of the draft, they could not have cared either. They remained focused on the fact that they had to give up their endowment, Eli Manning, and that really ticked them off. However, even Richard Thaler or the University of Victoria researchers might not have predicted the widespread outrage expressed by fans all across the country—not just among the hometown fans that Manning dissed. The fans of other teams apparently felt that, all rivalries aside, Manning had done an injustice to the Chargers.

A week after the draft, *Sports Illustrated* writer Phil Taylor[3] noted that "it's hard to understand why quarterback Eli Manning . . . was widely criticized as the biggest diva since Diana Ross after forcing San Diego, which took him with the No. 1 pick, to trade him to the New York Giants last Saturday." In Taylor's opinion, "Charger fans are the only ones that have the right to be peeved. . . ." But right or not, fans everywhere were rubbed the wrong way by the Manning trade. Taylor made an appeal to fans to get off Manning's case based on the fact that what happened with the 2004 draft is exactly what *should* happen. "If they're smart . . . the Chargers will use their return on the Manning trade to improve themselves, and the draft will have worked the way it's supposed to work. . . ." And, in fact, the Chargers did just that.

## 2. Universal Law

The average fan, however, just doesn't see things the way a seasoned economist or sports writer does. The public outrage by fans of other NFL teams who had no real personal interest in seeing the Chargers succeed speaks volumes about just how deeply ingrained this notion of endowment or rightful ownership is. People hold this concept so dearly that it shapes their belief in the natural order of the world, even when it doesn't impact them personally. Fans outside of San Diego cared that Eli Manning stripped himself from the Chargers because the fans felt like a universal law had been broken. In essence, those fans were exactly right. Our laws—almost universally—are indeed based on the concept of ownership. Specifically, ownership or possession is said to be "nine-tenths of the law." At the University of Victoria, this single concept—the sense of ownership—determined nine-tenths of the trading activity that went on with coffee mugs and chocolate bars.

But for the sporting world's most devout parishioners, resentment over Eli Manning's lack of loyalty is the real culprit in the case. Certainly Manning's inflated sense of his own worth didn't help soothe their sore feelings. But if you remain unconvinced about the role that perceived ownership played, allow me a further illustration from the world of sports that began two years earlier and a few hundred miles up the California coast. In the last baseball game of the 2001 season, controversial San Francisco Giants slugger Barry Bonds cracked his seventy-third home run. With that, Bonds broke the all-time single-season Major League home run record. Of all the madness and mayhem that ensued after the ball left his bat, perhaps the most shocking event was that, for once, the ensuing legal controversy did not cast Bonds in the leading role. Instead, the courtroom melodrama starred two previously anonymous fans. One was Alex Popov, who momentarily touched greatness when he caught Bonds's ball, only to immediately lose it in the melee of leather mitts and frenzied fans in the right field stands of Pac Bell Park. The other was Patrick Hayashi, the lucky spectator who eventually came up with the prized piece of history.

Not surprisingly, Popov sued Hayashi. Both fans claimed their rightful ownership of the ball. While you might see a baseball as something to pick up for a few bucks at the local sporting goods store, anyone who follows the world of sports memorabilia knows that a record-setting ball like this would be valued into the hundreds of thousands of dollars. In fact, the media quickly took to calling it the "million-dollar" ball.

Popov's case rested on the complex premise that the early bird does in fact *deserve* the worm even when said bird does not *get* the worm. Hayashi countered with a devastating finders keepers, losers weepers line of reasoning. For Judge Patrick McCarthy, it was a call as tough as any big league umpire would ever have to make (move over *Plessy v. Ferguson*). In the absence of a clear owner, the uncharacteristically benevolent Bonds came forward with a suggested compromise. Judge McCarthy took Bonds's recommendation and auctioned off the ball, splitting the proceeds evenly between Popov and Hayashi. McCarthy's decision once again showed that rightful ownership is one of the touchiest topics decision makers have to contend with.

In fact, the right of ownership dates back to the legal tenets of Ancient Rome, and it is still fully supported by modern American law. One of the most significant shapers of our current legal system, the honorable Oliver Wendell Holmes,[4] offered his highly influential support for the concept when in an 1897 essay he wrote for the *Harvard Law Review:*

> It is the nature of man's mind. A thing which you have enjoyed and used as your own for a long time, whether property or an opinion, takes root in your being and cannot be torn away without your resenting the act and trying to defend yourself, however you came by it. The law can ask no better justification than the deepest instincts of man.

Think about something that you have in your possession. Maybe it's a certain love interest, or your favorite player on your favorite team, or maybe it's just your favorite ink pen. Imagine what it looks like and feels like to know that it is yours. Got it? Okay, now think about your love interest falling into the arms of a dark stranger, or your Montblanc in the hands of that crafty cubicle farm-mate whom you never trusted. We all know what it feels like to have lost something. It can range from mild annoyance to heart-wrenching agony. Although the feeling may vary in intensity, almost without fail your stomach ties itself in knots, your throat tightens, and the tiniest of tears may even well up in the toughest among us— including professional football players. We know that feeling, and we don't like it much. As Holmes so aptly pointed out and codified, it is a fact of human nature that most people will go to great lengths—and occasionally make careless and impulsive decisions—to avoid the toxic feeling of losing what they have or *think* they have.

In 2005 Keith Chen,[5] of Yale School of Management, created a clever study to see just how universal this sense of ownership was. Except in this study Chen's participants were not subject to the principles of human nature because they weren't even human. Chen and his team set up a free-market economy in which monkeys were able to take possession of certain assets and then trade them just like people trade money for goods in shopping malls and grocery stores. First the researchers introduced small metal discs to the monkeys that had no real functional value, much like paper money has no functional value to people outside of what those bills can be traded for. Through repeated trials, the monkeys eventually learned that Chen's team of researchers valued these small metal discs so much that they were willing to trade fruit and jelly for the useless pieces of metal. And just like that, the formerly worthless discs took on a trading value just like our cotton-made cash.

In the study's second phase, two researchers acting as salespeople introduced themselves to the monkeys by peddling apple chunks. The first salesperson (we'll call her Kathy) dangled two pieces of apple in front of the monkeys to entice a trade for their discs. But half of the time when she offered a trade, Kathy would play a bait-and-switch trick. After the monkeys had already offered up a disc to trade, Kathy took back one of the apple chunks and only gave the monkey one chunk instead of the promised two. The other salesperson (we'll call her Andrea) was instructed to take the honest approach. Andrea offered only one piece of apple for a trade. However, in half of the trades, after the monkeys accepted the offer, Andrea would throw in an extra apple chunk as a bonus. Initially the monkeys preferred to trade with Kathy because she appeared to be giving them two apple chunks for the price of one. Eventually, however, the monkeys picked up on Kathy's little game. They realized that they would only get that second apple chunk in about half of the trades, despite the fact that Kathy implicitly promised them the second chunk *every* time.

As the experiment continued, the monkeys grew to prefer Andrea over Kathy. Keep in mind that the total outcome of the trades with both Kathy and Andrea were identical—the monkeys received two apple chunks in half of all trades. The only difference was that Kathy started out offering two apple chunks, leading the monkeys to believe that they were entitled to two chunks if they made the trade. The monkeys felt like they owned both chunks as long as Kathy came through on her offer. In effect, Kathy raised the bar on the monkeys' expectations. When Kathy took the second chunk back, it seemed to the monkeys like they were being robbed of a second chunk, even though they never actually had it in their possession. They must have felt in their monkey hearts that they were missing out on what should have been theirs.

Andrea played it differently. By offering the monkeys only one apple slice, she set their reference point at one instead of two. When she then threw in a second chunk, it was seen as a treat, not an expected outcome that had already been factored into their thinking. She under-promised and over-delivered. Ultimately, Andrea did not really sweeten the deal for her primate pals any more so than Kathy tricked them. All that Andrea did was to sweeten the *feel* of that deal, whereas Kathy left the monkeys with the bitter aftertaste of bad faith.

Keith Chen concluded that monkeys—just like people—are often remarkably cautious when they sense they might be losing out on the bigger piece of the pie. There is a psychological cost to the feeling of disappointment that comes with losing expected ownership. The cautious majority prefer more bang for their buck only when that bang is guaranteed. But if the bonus is not certain, and they have to risk that feeling of loss, they would rather not get their hopes up to begin with. Chen's experiment also shows us the malleable nature of ownership. What exactly people and monkeys see as rightfully theirs is really a matter of perception. Of course, when something that is yours is taken away, the action is condemned in courts of law, in public opinion, in offices, and among friends. In legal jargon, it is called "theft," and you'd be hard pressed to find someone outside of the aforementioned *Ocean's Eleven* films willing to speak in its defense.

But ownership is not always that cut and dried. Things that we only *expect* to own can take hold of our imagination as powerfully as things we already own. Both Alex Popov and Patrick Hayashi went to the San Francisco Giants' last game of the 2001 season with the hope of seeing a good ballgame and maybe witnessing a historic swing if they were lucky. Yet as soon as the idea of possessing Barry Bonds's coveted and quite valuable seventy-third home-run baseball entered their consciousness, neither was able to uproot it.

Oliver Wendell Holmes was one of our country's greatest minds and a seminal figure in our legal history. But exercising the power of twenty-twenty hindsight, we need to make two modifications to his statement. As Keith Chen's study showed, it is the nature of more than just *man's* mind to feel slighted and resentful when something we expect to own is taken from us. The same also appears to be true among our close relations in the primate world. Echoing Jack Knetsch's observation, Holmes might also have wanted to adjust the time restriction he placed on ownership. Specifically, it doesn't seem like we even need to use or enjoy something for "a long time" for us to resent its loss. As witnessed at the University of Victoria and in Eli Manning's ever-so-brief tenure with the San Diego Chargers, people claim ownership awfully quickly. The almost comical epilogue to the *Popov v. Hayashi* dispute only serves to drive this point home. Even the great King Solomon, who once proposed dividing a baby in half to settle a dispute between two women claiming maternal rights, would have scratched his crowned head at this one.

Not to be outdone by his client, Alex Popov's attorney, Martin Triano, also seemed to acquire a sense of ownership for the perceived value of the ball. The so-called million-dollar ball brought only a measly $450,000 at auction, which gave Popov and Hayashi $225,000 each. Triano then sued his former client, Popov, for legal bills totaling $473,530.32—just under half the million-dollar sum everyone felt the ball *should* have received at auction. Adding further insult to Popov's injured sense of ownership was the fact that Patrick Hayashi had offered to take Bonds's suggestion of splitting auction proceeds before the trial began. In this real-life rendition of the ultimatum game, Popov rejected the pretrial split offered by Hayashi. Had he accepted the split before going to trial, Popov would have saved himself the exorbitant legal fees and could have pocketed a six-figure sum for doing little else than holding on to a baseball for a measly six-tenths of a second. But apparently, his amygdala and powerful sense of ownership could not bear the thought of losing the full promise of the "million-dollar ball." Popov's inability to let go of his perceived endowment came at a steep financial cost. He not only lost the million-dollar payout, but had to fight another legal battle just to keep from going into the hole.

The case of the million-dollar ball is a somewhat outlandish example of how perceived ownership impacts the choices we make. Despite his involvement in the high-profile circumstances of this case, Alex Popov is not much different than the rest of us. People can get bent out of shape after losing something they feel like they've owned for about the same duration as it takes them to say the word *mine*. In fact, people just like you and me require no real ownership at all before being driven to acts of uncharacteristic impulsiveness aimed at protecting that thing which has "taken root in our being."

## 3. Playing Mine Games

Expected ownership is largely made possible by the process of what Harvard psychologist Daniel Gilbert[6] calls "pre-feeling." In his book *Stumbling on Happiness*, Gilbert describes pre-feeling as our ability not only to imagine future events, but also to experience now how we might feel in the future. It is like emotional fortune-telling. Our brain uses experience from both our past and our present to create current emotions about what we believe might actually happen. When you think about getting that promotion or finally making that elusive beauty at the corner coffee shop your partner, your heart picks up the pace and the hair on your skin starts to prickle. Never mind that those things are not yet truly yours. The fantasy feels all too real. It is exciting to imagine the things you can finally purchase with your new raise, the people you'll no longer have to take orders from, or the sense of accomplishment you'll finally claim as "mine" once your boss pats you on the shoulder and prepares the company-wide memo. The more you think about this possible future outcome, the more real it becomes in your mind's eye, especially for your feelings.

Our feelings are undeniably powerful, but they are not

very good at distinguishing the difference between reality and illusion. As far as our emotions are concerned, imagining possession can be every bit as real and almost as intense as actually possessing that thing. However, with the exception of a select group of artists and the clinically delusional, most of our adult imaginations can't just spin imagined experiences from whole cloth. Even if we succeed in allowing a fantasy to sweep through our senses, the rational part of our brain quickly and efficiently reels us back in. For example, if I asked you to imagine riding on a unicorn, I am sure that you could probably create that vision in your mind. But even if you envision it, the image isn't going to flood you with intense feelings. It won't feel all that real because you know that your chance of saddling up a unicorn is about as good as your chance of sliding down a rainbow into a bowl of Lucky Charms. Your logical brain understands that and is quick to remind your feelings. But that could all change one day if you looked out your window and saw your neighbor guiding his brand new unicorn into an empty bay of his two-car garage. What was a fantastic unreality just days, or minutes, before will have suddenly become a real possibility right before your very eyes. Now there is a basis in experience to your fantasy, and the flood of emotions that follow will have you calculating annual hay expenditures and wondering if the FAA needs to be contacted for unicorn takeoffs and landings.

Our ability to mentally reach into the future, take ownership of something and then enjoy the feelings that come with that ownership is what makes the process so dangerously powerful. If you feel that a certain thing is "as good as yours," then your feelings may take the liberty of claiming ownership. It is the job of your rational thinking to keep those feelings in check. But all that your rational brain needs is a little convincing to get caught up in the fun and climb on board the unicorn your feelings are already grooming. Being able to mentally walk through potential events is certainly a wonderful part of our human imagination (and, as we've seen, perhaps our primate cousins even fantasize promotions from their troop leader). Without the power to want feelings we've imagined to manifest themselves in reality, we might not put in that extra hour to make a PowerPoint presentation that much better. And it can break the routine of our day to day to enjoy the positive feelings associated with acquiring something we've always wanted.

But the downside to the unparalleled power of imagination is the risk of feeling like you've lost something you never had. If we can trick our feelings into thinking that we are really experiencing something, then it is really going to sting when we rob our feelings of that thing. Have you ever thought about why car dealers want you to test drive a car? Customer test drives take up more of the salesperson's time. They add miles to the car. They burn gas that the dealers will then have to replace on their own dime. There is a much higher risk to damaging the car than there would be if it just sat empty in the lot. Still, dealers would love for you to take the car for a test drive. If you are cruising down the road in that car, adjusting the temperature, switching on your favorite radio station, and yelling at illusory kids in the backseat, you are going to have a much clearer vision of what it will be like to really own that car. The dealer likes that reaction because it makes it much more difficult for you to leave the car lot without the keys to your new hot rod in your hot little hand. You will have really *felt* what it is like to own the car. So if you then decide *not* to buy the car, you are deciding to trade in that feeling of ownership for the empty feeling of a lost opportunity.

*The Impulse Factor* began with a look at the two determinants in every decision: the individual and the situation in which that individual acts. We explored the two kinds of decision makers: the majority of risk managers who tend to exercise caution and listen to that internal authority figure telling them to take it slowly, and that one-quarter of us who are potential seekers, the ones who stood up at the tribal meeting and pointed to the mountains, suggesting that just beyond there might be a land of milk and honey.

We saw that, no matter what kind of decision maker we might be, the external factors of our situation have immense power to influence us in ways we might not readily perceive. Splitting a check might make us order a dish we never wanted as the waiter stands over us. We might execute a trade that we would have shunned days before, because we heard that our high school nemesis just put a pool in her backyard paid for by a soaring stock. Or we might walk away from a reasonable profit because we think the other guy is taking advantage of us. At the conclusion of *The Impulse Factor*, we'll look to the future of the science behind decision making and the external factors that shape its future. But before we go further, you are probably asking yourself: *So what kind of decision maker am I, anyway?* Let's find out.

CHAPTER SIX

---

# Factoring *You* Into Your Decisions

A t some time during our tumultuous junior high school
years, we are taught the right way to make decisions.
Up until that point, nearly all of our decisions are made for
us—where to go to school, what to eat for lunch, which kids
are approved for play dates, and the like. Only during these
difficult adolescent years do we begin facing the onslaught
of choices that fill our minds from that day forward. At this
time we are given one or another generic strategies for making
decisions and solving problems. These processes are usually
values-based strategies that masquerade as decision-making
strategies. They are designed largely to teach us to study and
not to indulge in drinking and drugs, eat junk food, break the
law, or hang out with the bad crowd. While they are not without merit, this introduction to the art and science of decision
making can be turned on its head by most tweens and teens
and used to determine the best bad crowd to hang with, the
most outrageous rules to break, and so on. While these strategies might not always have had the desired outcome, we had
to start learning about decisions somehow. And the easiest

way to start is to learn to see the world as black and white, right or wrong, good or bad.

Now, however, it is time that we graduate to a more specialized approach to decision making. This approach takes into account the fact that meaningful differences between us exist. We know that we are not all starting from the same place when we make a decision, that the distinction between us is not merely one of good kids versus troublemakers, and that not every situation has a clear-cut right and wrong. There are many shades of gray in the world of adults and their problems. The differences that we find are ones in perspective due in part to genetics and in part to life experiences. But rest assured that there is a difference, and any generic approach to decision making that overlooks individual differences is severely limited in its ability to improve the quality of our decisions.

A simple formula for decision making looks like this:

Decision Maker x Situation = Decision

Theoretically, if we know the tendencies of the decision maker and the relevant variables of the situation, then there is a good chance that we can predict or improve upon the outcome. Unfortunately many situations are in a state of flux. Trying to analyze a situation correctly requires constant recalibration as the environment changes. To be sure, the science of psychology has made astonishing progress in helping us see how situations can sometimes be much more complicated to understand than we originally assumed. Our earlier examples of politics, bill splitting, and assumed endowment show how situations like these can produce outcomes we wouldn't have imagined. But even identifying those variables beyond a few common situations is tricky business. Outside of a controlled laboratory setting, other factors can influence the process in countless ways. What was accurately defined as the situation today stands a very good chance of being replaced by an altogether new situation tomorrow. Looking at the preceding equation, we have to assume the situation will always be a variable with an infinite number of possible values.

We, the decision makers, however, are not necessarily so mysterious. Each of our tendencies follows a rather predictable pattern. You might fancy yourself as unpredictable, but even your self-proclaimed unpredictability makes you all too predictable. And that's okay. In fact, that's great because algebra gets exponentially easier the more known values we introduce into an equation. The predictability of our individual tendencies makes each of us a potentially known value in our decision equation.

With that premise in mind, TalentSmart designed the Impulse Factor test. We wanted to give people the opportunity to identify their decision-making tendencies and then benefit from that knowledge. Because decision making is such a pervasive part of human functioning, it touches and is touched by a vast array of other psychological concepts. So, to get an adequately encompassing view of human decision makers, we combed through our existing database of the hundreds of thousands of test scores, opinions, ratings, and general comments we have received at TalentSmart covering topics as diverse as general leadership prowess, emotional intelligence, influencing skills, and personality. We looked at the numbers in a variety of ways in order to see what patterns emerged. Sometimes we looked more closely at how people rated themselves and other times at how they commented on the people around them. Still other times we analyzed ways in which people saw the challenges around them. Then we took what we found and matched it up with the discoveries of leading researchers from fields as diverse as molecular biology, neuroscience, ecology, and the social sciences. The Impulse Factor test is the result of that effort.

## 1. The Test

The Impulse Factor test is not graded, at least not in the traditional sense of As, Bs, Cs, and such. The test is designed to make you a known value in your decision-making equation by identifying your tendency. As we've discussed, there are two basic types of decision-making tendencies: The majority of us are risk managers, while approximately one-fourth of us are potential seekers who are more inclined to impulsivity. The test and this book will help you identify and apply your style to the decision-making process for the best possible outcome. In short, it quantifies your Impulse Factor and tells you how to use it effectively.

Do not be misled by the term *value*. One tendency is not more or less *valuable* than the other. If there is one thing that should be abundantly clear by now, it is that there is a time and a place for both risk-managing and potential-seeking tendencies. Even the determination of the appropriate time and place for a decision is a largely subjective one. In an identical situation the "right" decision will often vary depending on the individual decision maker. This truth makes it even more essential to know each of our tendencies.

To discover your Impulse Factor, take your book's dust jacket off and lay it flat on the table with the blank side up, facing you. In the bottom right-hand corner, there is a unique nine-digit code. Log on to www.TheImpulseFactor.com and type in that eight-digit code to take the test. Your results are for your eyes only. After you have completed the test, you will use this same code to go back online whenever you wish to review your results.

So dog-ear this page, and go now to www.TheImpulseFactor.com. Come back here when you get your results.

## 2. Your Impulse Factor

The Impulse Factor test provides you with feedback on your impulsive tendency, as well as on the overall effectiveness of the decisions you make. Your tendency has to do with how impulsively you typically approach decisions. The less impulsive decision maker takes a risk-managing approach. A risk-managing approach focuses more on probabilities and long-term consequences. Or you might be the kind of person on the more impulsive side who tends to focus on opportunities for bigger, or more immediate, gains. All people are capable of occasionally playing both roles, but our research shows that people are usually squarely in one camp or the other. Within each of the two categories, a spectrum of styles range from the mild to the intense.

Your intensity is captured by two subscales that combine to make up your Impulse Factor. The first subscale is called hastiness. High scores on the hastiness subscale mean quite simply that you tend to be hastier than the average person when making your decisions. Low scores mean that you tend to take your time when making decisions, compared to other people. The second subscale is labeled risk. Your risk score is a reflection of your propensity to take chances for a bigger gain even when there is a less risky alternative. The subscales provide a deeper look at your overall tendency. The more extreme your scores on the subscales, the more intense you can assume is your risk-managing or potential-seeking tendency. If your scores were closer to average on the subscales, then you have a more moderate risk-managing or potential-seeking tendency.

No two people can be expected to react to a situation or an environment in exactly the same way, even if their styles fall within the same grouping. But we will find ourselves in one of these two core categories. An analogous classification exists in politics. For example, there are both liberal Democrats and moderate Democrats, just as there are conservative Republicans and moderate Republicans. Yet the subgroups within each party are both registered as members of the larger faction because they are similar enough in their perspectives when compared to the alternative.

At this point you might be wondering which is the better kind of decision maker?

Without a doubt, the clear and irrefutable answers to that question are "both," "neither," and "it depends." Either type can be the better decision maker. What constitutes the better decision often depends on who is asking the question and on any decision's unpredictable outcome. One person's correct choice is often another person's boneheaded move. In fact, one person's correct choice in one situation could be that exact same person's boneheaded move in another. People often arrive at different decisions simply because they make decisions in service to different masters—one master commands that they protect what they have while the other commands them to get the biggest prize. In other words, some people are in pursuit of peace of mind, while others tend to search for a bigger piece of the pie. Combining those people and their opposing perspectives creates a healthy balance. So, as we will explore later in the book, once you have identified your own style, learning to maximize your connection to people with an opposing style is an essential factor for overall success. This synergy is called "connectedness."

The second part of the Impulse Factor test addresses how effectively you use this tendency to make decisions. Effectiveness ratings account for two different kinds of ability. There is objective effectiveness, which is usually viewed as a measure of a decision's basis in the "rational." Objective effectiveness is the kind of efficiency at which computers excel. It accounts for probabilities and maximizes the return on some kind of investment of effort or resources. Outcome is king when measuring objective effectiveness. It is a compelling guideline in ultimately determining whether impulsivity is functional or dysfunctional.

Subjective effectiveness, on the other hand, considers factors like conscience and emotions. It weighs the process you took to arrive at a decision as well as how that decision made you feel, regardless of the objective outcome. For instance, a decision that maximizes your financial investment gets a high rating on objective effectiveness. But if it prevented you from sleeping and ate a hole in your stomach while you waited for that return to materialize, then that same decision rates low on subjective effectiveness. Your boss or your organization isn't always so concerned about subjective effectiveness, and it isn't really their job to be, but you will probably want to pay close attention to it.

## 3. Your Tendency

The names for the two core categories—risk managing and potential seeking—are designed to serve as archetypes or ideals to strive for, as much as they are labels or descriptors. As opposed to describing you as only high or low on the impulsive scale and leaving it at that, the terms *risk managing* and *potential seeking* add another layer of clarity to your tendency. In a broader sense, *impulsive* can describe any person who frequently acts on impulse. *The Impulse Factor's* definition of impulsive certainly includes that description. However, an impulse can be a feeling or an instinct that tells you to avoid danger. You read about such impulses in the chapters discussing our voting and investing habits. Although impulsive people are on average more likely to find themselves in riskier situations than are cautious people, an impulse does not necessarily lead to dangerous or uncertain endeavors. Theoretically, an impulse could be a cautious impulse telling you to avoid a perceived danger. So, to make your Impulse Factor test results the most effective in helping you to make better decisions, we have defined not only *how much* you tend to act on impulse, but also *which kind* of impulses tend to drive you. So, think of your tendency—risk managing or potential seeking—both as a measure of how impulsive you are and as a description of the kind of impulses on which you tend to act. People with an average or lower level of impulsivity are at their best when they refine their ability to manage risk while still pursuing suitable opportunities, whereas people with higher impulsivity scores are at their best when they polish their potential-seeking skills. We do not encourage the two groups to try to be more like the other. Risk managers should not seek out their inner potential seeker (and vice versa). Instead, each group should maximize the strengths inherent in each style.

## Risk Managing

Approximately three-fourths of all people have a risk-managing tendency. They pay special attention not just to the outcome itself, but to the likelihood that a given outcome will happen. From a subjective perspective, they concern themselves with achieving peace of mind. The refined risk managers are usually viewed as deliberative decision makers because of the more thorough approach they take. Their tendency to look before they leap keeps them comfortable and safe in most situations, yet they will usually act when it is necessary to do so.

The risk-managing tendency is marked by measured progress as opposed to big jumps into the unknown. Risk managers challenge the status quo when necessary but are unlikely to make a radical departure from it in the short term. However, over the course of time and following a series of well-thought-out decisions, they might find themselves a long way from the status quo of yesteryear. Risk managers look for steady, continual gains that have a high probability for return and expose them to only the degree of risk that is absolutely necessary. Getting rich quick is something they will gladly let others do because they believe that the path to quick riches is just as likely to lead to a dead-end bankruptcy.

When accounting for other people when making a decision, the risk manager must be on guard against the possibility of being led by other people's opinions, or by the fear of getting left behind by others' apparent advancement. Highly effective risk managers will treat others' opinions like a piece of data—giving the information due consideration but not allowing themselves to be victimized by conditional impulsivity.

Indecision is perhaps the risk manager's biggest challenge. The fear of making the wrong decision can easily become a hindrance that leads to indecision. Indecision is not necessarily a problem as long as you are at complete peace with the way things are, and as long as it is possible to keep things that way. But most situations in our day-to-day lives require some decision that simply will not allow things to remain as they are—situations in which not choosing is not an option. It is in these moments when indecision sabotages both your subjective and objective effectiveness. When you deny yourself permission to make a choice in a timely manner, hoping that somehow the decision will get made for you, you become especially vulnerable to security traps. For example, a risk manager might have to make a decision about bringing a new product to market that capitalizes on a newly developed technology. The kind of money that will need to be spent on a proper launch warrants market analysis. But the market is all too often a moving target. So if the risk manager waits for the perfect analysis that proves that this product will be a slam dunk, the market may very well have already shifted. Perhaps competitors have already staked a claim and consumers are already establishing favorites. Now the risk manager might be kicking himself or herself for waiting so long and letting the opportunity pass by. But instead of cutting his or her losses and moving, there will be a powerful temptation to go for the launch, anyway, so that all of the prep work and analysis was not for naught, or simply in order to catch up with the early-launching competitors. The most effective risk managers maintain their emphasis on safe decisions, while being decisive and thorough in their actions.

## Potential Seeking

The potential-seeking tendency influences a smaller percentage of people. These people score high on both the hastiness and the risk subscales. Successful potential seeking involves mastering the art of functional impulsivity. Potential seekers are innately drawn to choices that offer an improvement to the status quo. They are willing to trek into the unknown quickly, but their experience—specifically, their reflection on past experience—has taught them when to fend off an impulse that could cause damage.

Decisiveness can be a clear strength for potential seekers. This assured style is very effective as long as potential seekers understand their limitations. It is easy for them to become intoxicated with the special brand of freedom that comes from acting with little regard to risk. That impulsive action can spur new ways of thinking, but it can also be dangerous. Whereas risk managers may tend to redundantly review their tracks, potential seekers can fail to evaluate their course often enough.

Opportunity costs occupy a prominent position in the potential seekers' list of considerations when making a decision.

Potential seekers can be viewed as visionary because of their relentless focus on the way things *could be*. Paradoxically, they can also be very short sighted because of their occasional failure to see that a particular short-term gain can create a long-term debt.

In a group setting, potential seekers are not always aware of the impact their decisions will have on other people. Whereas risk managers can occasionally be too focused on what other people are doing or thinking, potential seekers have a tendency to be too focused on immediate gain and not enough on other people. That is why impulsivity can sometimes cause potential seekers to appear as though they have a lack of empathy. In their defense, it isn't so much a lack of empathy as it is a lack of consideration for anything beyond their impulse. They are not choosing to disregard how other people feel; they are disregarding virtually all other considerations. Other people's feelings and opinions just happen to be among those considerations. Rarely, however, can we make a decision that won't affect other people. This goes without saying in a group context—whether the group is a family, a team, a business, a church, or a club. From time to time, impulsive decision makers can get so wrapped up in pursuit of the next opportunity that they lose sight of the effects their choices will have on others. In the pursuit of future gains, effective potential seekers take other people into account in order to realize the highest reward that the situation has to offer.

Risky choices can be the cornerstone of the potential seeker's daily diet, but potential seekers are not drawn to risk for risk's sake. Potential seekers don't particularly enjoy risk or failure any more than anyone else. A risky choice, however, is often the one that offers the most reward when realized successfully. The potential opens impulsive decision makers up to all sorts of new possibilities. However, when its direction goes unchecked, potential seeking poses a strong danger of becoming dysfunctional. Potential seekers' impulsive tendency can be counterproductive if it is pointed in the wrong direction. In these instances, instead of being freed by their impulses, potential seekers are held captive by them.

For some people the impulsive tendency is a lifestyle choice as much as it is a genetic predisposition. Living in the moment can be fun. But we need to bear in mind that moments have a strange way of stringing themselves together, one right after another on into eternity. So living without any regard for future moments while, say, driving 110 miles per hour down a winding mountain road in this particular moment is a good way to ensure that you won't have many more moments to worry about. Focusing on potential more than safety can be a perfectly healthy way to make decisions. Impulsivity becomes dysfunctional only when it consistently prevents people from reaching the potential they sought in the first place.

## 4. Deciding Your Fate

Decision making will always be a complex task laced with uncertainty. As I've said, black and white answers are rarely found in the adult world. Generic advice aimed at the all-encompassing "human decision maker" is based on the questionable assumption that there is a single best method for making decisions. *Think more. Trust your gut more. Listen to your heart. Control your impulses.* All of that advice has its place, but it will be ill used if it is given everywhere to everyone. If it exists at all, I would like to humbly suggest that the universally correct way to make a decision is a moving target that will forever be one to two steps ahead of us. If we are going to increase our chance of making more satisfactory decisions, we cannot forget *who* is making the decision, and then tailor our strategy to that style.

So the question of which is the better kind of decision maker is really the wrong question to pose. The relevant questions are (1) *Which kind of decision makers are you and the people that surround you?* and (2) *What is each of you doing to capitalize on your natural tendencies?*

Your Impulse Factor answers the first question. The information included in this book, and the learning techniques included in the test, are designed to help you begin crafting your answer to the second question.

Now that you've taken the test and have your style in hand, I hope you will think about some of the recent—or some of the more memorable—decisions you've made, whether they were personal or professional. Can you see how your personal style affected the outcome? Do you feel like you've harnessed your impulsivity in a mostly functional way or a dysfunctional way? How would you approach future decisions differently knowing what you do now? These are just some of the questions we ask ourselves and that we ask our clients at TalentSmart.

In the coming chapters, we will focus first on the potential-seeking style and then on the risk-managing style before offering an overall look at the state of decision making and what the future holds. Just because you are a risk manager does not mean you should skip the chapter on potential seeking, and vice versa. As we've touched on briefly and will explore further, it is the connectedness between the two styles that can offer the solution to the best possible decision making by either style. So having insight into your impulsive brethren, or better understanding your cautious cubicle mate, will serve you well in the days and years to come. But since we've already established that they perhaps have the shorter attention span, let us turn first to the minority of you who are potential seekers.

# CHAPTER SEVEN

# Potential Seekers:

## Exploring the Connection between Sinners, Saints, Barbies, and Farmers

In the summer of 1216, French historian Jacques de Vitry traveled to Italy. As a prominent figure in the Roman Catholic Church, Vitry spent much of his trip observing first hand the cardinals and the recently appointed Pope Honorius III. In general, Vitry was not impressed. He wrote plainly in a letter that most of what he witnessed "was repugnant to me. The church leadership was so occupied with worldly affairs, with rulers and kingdoms, with lawsuits and litigation that they hardly let anyone speak of spiritual things." Vitry's words spoke not just to the ever more contemptible corruption that many Roman Catholics saw among their church's leaders, but also to the paralyzing bureaucracy that had developed within their ranks.

But a new group of servants within the church known as the Lesser Brothers and Lesser Sisters gave Vitry a sense of hope before he left Italy that summer. "During the day they go into the cities and villages giving themselves over to the active life;

at night, however, they return to their hermitage or solitary places to devote themselves to contemplation. The women dwell together near the cities in various hospices, accepting nothing, but living by the work of their hands." Not only did they live in accordance with the idealistic precepts of the original church, but Vitry noted that they were also incredibly good at spreading their holy message by providing labor and compassionate service wherever they went. Vitry believed their success was due in no small part to the fact that the Lesser Brothers and Lesser Sisters acted on genuine concern for the personal hardships of the people around them, while simultaneously spreading a message of joy and hope instead of doom and damnation. These "simple and poor" men and women were achieving the true goals of the church—idealistically *and* pragmatically—in a way that the appointed leaders were not.

The revolutionary movement witnessed by Vitry sprung from the actions of a man named Francis Bernadone. For the first twenty-three years of his life, Francis appeared to be a highly unlikely candidate for spiritual work. The immensely popular French-Italian boy—always clad in the finest garments from his father's shop—played best the role of *rex convivii* in his cadre of like-minded upper middle class friends. Together, they saw no better way to pass through their young adulthood than by squandering it. *Rex convivii* was an ancient Latin label meaning "king of banquets." The title was bestowed upon whichever noble soul bankrolled the biggest and the best parties. Being labeled the *rex convivii* was quite an honor if your role model was Caligula. But after Francis's stint as a prisoner of war thanks to an overly ambitious attack on a neighboring town, a failed attempt to join the Fourth Crusade as a knight a few years later, and a growing disillusionment with his family's pursuit of material wealth, Francis began regarding the "honor" as dubious if not downright insulting.

On a windy day in March 1206 in the Bishop of Assisi's

courtyard, the twenty-three-year-old Francis renounced all ties to the Bernadone family's wealth and influence following a public dispute with his father. In a scene now regarded as St. Francis of Assisi's holy debut, he voluntarily replaced all of his worldly security with a lifelong vow of extreme poverty and service to the downtrodden. The crowd on hand that day was awestruck. As biographer Donald Spoto[1] points out, "[I]n 1206, to have nothing meant literally to have nothing, not simply less." Here was this enormously popular and privileged young man choosing to give up not only his wealth and material comforts, but also forgoing any means of acquiring even the basic necessities of life. In spiritual terms, one's decision to give up security and comfort is usually referred to as an act of uncommon faith. At the risk of downplaying the spiritual import of the occasion, psychology calls those decisions "impulsive."

Francis of Assisi's choices both before and after his conversion illuminate the true essence (you might even say "the soul") of a potential seeker. Having given up his worldly goods and exhibiting no sign of industry up until that point, things could have gone either way for Francis. In some ways he had provided himself with a clean slate—no responsibilities, no expectations to live up to, no possessions to worry about losing. But in the process, he had also introduced himself to far more basic responsibilities such as how not to starve or freeze to death. Had he failed to adjust to his new lifestyle, history might never have heard more from this wayward son. But Francis pulled his act together. Over the course of months he was able to take command of his impulsive tendencies instead of continuing to be a victim of them. He is a symbol of the kind of transformation from dysfunctional to functional impulsivity made possible by a focus on direction. His work shows that the apparent chasm between the indulgent youth and ruthless fighter he was and the compassionate saint he became might not be as wide as it appears. In fact, the careless king of banquets and the ambitious soldier existed within the exact same person as did the humble servant. Where he had once impetuously pursued worldly pleasures and personal glory, Francis redirected himself toward the passionate pursuit of simplicity and service. Had Neal Cassady been an iconic thirteenth-century figure, instead of hailing from the twenti-eth, he and the young Francis Bernadone might very well have hit the road the way Cassady and Kerouac did 700 years later. But unlike Cassady, Francis redirected his impulsive desires before they overtook and destroyed him. Francis's accomplish-ments are important to note because, as much as we might discuss the petty criminal nature of the impulsive minority, neither potential seekers nor risk managers hold a monopoly on the spiritual high ground. There is no limit, except the self-imposed, to the moral or spiritual heights to which members from either group can rise.

In finding the directionally correct path, Francis became an agent of profound change in the struggling institution of the church. He also became a beacon of hope for society's most needy. And he did all of this while being regarded as one of the most remarkably jolly figures in history.

In our research at TalentSmart, we discovered that the same impulsive tendencies ascribed to the patron saint of both merchants and ecologists still exist all around us in today's po-tential seekers—both the strengths and the weaknesses. If we look closely we can see how the principles that guided Francis nearly 800 years ago can be applied to the decisions of today's seekers.

## 1. Decision, Then Reflection

Many of the most notable tales about Francis highlight a cen-tral theme of potential seekers: Action precedes contemplation.

In one telling instance, shortly after he turned his life over to poverty, Francis encountered a leper on a road north of Rome. During the Middle Ages, leprosy was considered so contagious that even the kindest of travelers would only throw food scraps to lepers from a safe distance. Leprosy was believed to be caused by extreme sin and therefore just as contagious spiritually as physically. Lepers were required by Roman law to ring a bell any time they came near a town so that people could have ample warning. Actually touching a leper was a boundary people in the Middle Ages simply did not cross.

True to form, Francis failed to heed the convention. Having no money or food to offer the sickly group, Francis threw himself at the feet of one of the most severely afflicted among them, and then embraced him. Only *after* hugging the man did Francis reflect on what he had done. He concluded that fearing the supposed dangers of consorting with lepers was neither true, nor in line with the life of unconditional compassion he had chosen. His commitment to that compassion was so strong that it allowed him to overcome the faulty "knowledge" of that day and age. Today we know that lepers need not be quarantined and most people now view the practice as entirely unethical. Francis cared for lepers for the remainder of his life.

Francis's habit of impulsively compassionate action, while paying little attention to his personal safety (physically, at least), would continue, and it proved highly successful in bringing him the sense of spiritual accomplishment and freedom he sought. Indeed the act now, think later principle worked magnificently for the thirteenth-century Italian monk whose stated objectives were to lead a life of humility and poverty. But can that Franciscan strategy work as well today? Can it be applied also to the pursuit of more worldly success?

My work at TalentSmart takes me around the world, where I have had the opportunity to explore that question within global Fortune 100 companies. A couple of years ago I had the opportunity to work with a group of talented potential seekers in Australia who offered a valid answer. You might not expect a group on the fast track in the financial services division of a multinational corporation to apply the same radical principles as a humble friar from centuries before, yet that was exactly what I found. While St. Francis's actions are an extreme example of acting impulsively without thinking first, the same style manifests itself in our home and office life today. This group of financial potential seekers candidly revealed an inclination to first decide and act, and then reflect later. "It's easier to say sorry, rather than please," they told me in a breakout session following their own self-analysis with the Impulse Factor test. A remark like that sounds like these impulsive mavericks might be prone to insubordination, carelessness, or worse in their daily operations. Are you eager to work with colleagues who would rather apologize than come to you first for your input? After more discussion, however, they pointed out that this element of their mode of operation applied specifically to ambiguous situations in which conventional wisdom does not jibe with their strategic direction. In the absence of a clear right answer or under time pressure, our Australian potential seekers make the decision that appears to take them toward a desirable outcome. Later, they deal with the repercussions, if any. It's not about disobeying rules. Rather it is about being decisive when the situation calls for action. That action-oriented principle can open doors that—only because of fear or hesitation—have remained closed.

But it is the second element of the corporate "shoot first, apologize later" tactic that really makes it useful. Failing to say "please" works only if you remember to say "sorry." The act of apologizing is obviously a good gesture that goes a long way toward maintaining solid relationships with the people around you. Just as important, however, being mindful of the possible need to apologize mandates reflection. In order to recognize your error, you must first subject your decision to open and critical examination. That examination ensures that you remain directionally correct. As noted in Chapter 6, the goal of potential seekers is not to adhere to the caution of risk managers, which we'll explore in the next chapter. Potential seekers have a gut instinct compelling them toward the pursuit of gain, and they should exercise it judiciously.

In his encounter with the lepers, Francis looked within and confirmed that his direction was correct. So he committed himself to caring for them. However, in other situations he was forced to alter his course after finding that he'd strayed into untenable territory. In an early manifestation of the Franciscan vow of simplicity, he encouraged extreme fasting among his followers. This was an ascetic practice commonly employed by many religions throughout the world and was intended to let the spirit, not the body, flourish. After a particularly harsh winter, Francis saw this practice had led his group astray. He realized that the decision to invoke extreme hunger did little to advance their primary objective of love and service (a conclusion also reached by Siddhartha Gautama on his path to becoming the Buddha). Francis continued advocating simplicity and warned against becoming dependent on rich foods. But he realigned the vow within the greater direction of spreading love and peace.

My Australian colleagues' practice of saying "sorry" instead of "please" also contains the implicit admission that decisions may very well lead to a dead end. Acknowledging that they may find themselves apologizing for a decision down the road keeps them fully aware that failure is always one possible outcome no matter the power of the conviction behind the action. But this acknowledgment does not prevent them from acting in the first place. They understand that, no matter how prepared we think we might be, chance—specifically the chance of failure—is unavoidable. They accept failure without ignoring or dismissing it. Every decision carries consequences, and the more important the decision (the more people it impacts, the more business it carries), the greater the consequences. If potential seekers are going to seize an opportunity, they also have to grab hold of the realization that there is a tomorrow and that they will have to watch the dominoes fall after they have acted.

Potential seekers are natural experimenters. They are energized by trying new things, which is the catalyst for any experiment. After all, it is not much of an experiment if the outcome is already tried and true. But darting off into unfamiliar territory is the easy part. Constantly reflecting on the decisions already made is another matter that requires more effort. It is that sometimes challenging practice of reflection that creates the distinction between functional and dysfunctional impulsivity. You have to examine where that experimental course has taken you. If you like where you ended up, then you should keep going in that direction. If the results are not especially pleasing, then it might be time to change directions or scratch the experiment entirely.

Harvard psychiatrists and experts on adult ADD Edward Hallowell and John Ratey[2] highlight this point in their book *Delivered from Distraction*. Hallowell and Ratey offer adults with ADD two clear and connected directional suggestions: "Don't stop doing what worked before" and its corollary, "don't repeat the same failed strategy." Reflection is required to determine the difference between the two. Hallowell and Ratey suggest that the distinction should be fairly obvious if you give it just a little thought: "Instead of taking the same kind of job over and over, and quitting or getting fired each time, try a new field. Or instead of dating or marrying the same kind of person over and over and breaking up or getting divorced each time, try going out with someone totally different. Or instead of inviting the same friend or relative into your life over and over, only to have him hurt and disappoint you over and over, try saying no the next time." If it works, then go for it. If it constantly leads to a dead end, then recalibrate your compass.

Impulsive leaders tell me that, if leveraged, their quick mode of decision making provides them with the unique advantage to backtrack when necessary. In a fast-paced environment, speedy decisions often put them far enough ahead of the game so that there is still time to reverse when a direction proves faulty. Spending more time calculating on the front end reduces the time available for redirection on the back end. Of course you could argue that more planning on the front end reduces the need to backtrack. But preplanning is simply not potential seekers' strong point. They will be fighting a steep—and largely unnecessary—uphill battle to incorporate more preplanning into their naturally quick decisions.

The successful potential seekers readily admit that their quick decisions are both right and wrong. The main point is that they spend time after the decision critically examining whether they need to change course. Hallowell and Ratey point out that "one definition of insanity is doing the same deed over and over again, hoping for a different outcome." Omitting the crucial post-hoc examination means that potential seekers won't be experimenting; they'll be either wandering aimlessly or making a beeline toward insanity.

## 2. The Need for Speed

While traveling through Europe in the mid-1950s, a middle-aged American couple came across a "Bild Lilli" doll in a Swiss novelty store. Bild Lilli was a popular German comic book character. The voluptuous figurine was not intended for young readers of the comic book, however, but was instead an adult gag gift. Despite the Lilli doll's intended adult audience, Ruth Handler thought that a derivation of Lilli would be a nice enhancement to her young daughter Barbara's paper doll collection. She had noticed that Barbara spent more time playing with grown-up paper dolls than with infant or child cutouts. Handler believed that Barbara was interested in pretending that she was a future version of herself, such as a teenaged girl or a woman. She wasn't playing much with dolls similar to her preadolescent self. Handler imagined that Barbara wasn't the only little girl who fantasized about being a grown-up. When she arrived home in Los Angeles, Handler gave Lilli a bit of plastic surgery and a new name in honor of Barbara's inspiration: Barbie.[3]

No toy in recent history has achieved more fame and infamy than Mattel's anatomically contentious icon of girls' play. Ruth Handler denied knowing about the Lilli doll's adult audience before transforming Lilli into Barbie, but she was well aware of the Lilli doll's eye-popping adult dimensions. In fact, a curvaceous doll was exactly what Handler had in mind. She thought it "was important to a girl's self esteem that she play with a doll with breasts." When you consider that the whole premise of playing house is that children get to pretend that they are the parents, Handler's realization that girls want to play with older dolls seems pretty sensible. Children often want to fantasize the adult versions of themselves. Still no toy maker in postwar America had ever created a children's doll with the express desire to accent her breasts.

Ruth Handler's decision to create a doll with curves was a gamble. Attaching the name of a children's toy manufacturer to a doll with these adult features could have been disastrous for her company's image. Some of Handler's top staff expressed that very concern. In the end, it was the furthest thing from disaster for Mattel. Whatever else they may have been, Barbie and her creator were hugely successful.

But Barbie wasn't the first or the biggest gamble that Ruth Handler ever took. Barbie and her boyfriend Ken, named after the Handlers' son, is almost the story of the toy empire that never was. (The fact that the most romanticized couple in American toy history is based on a brother and sister is a topic for another time.) In 1955 Ruth received a call from an ABC executive asking if the Handlers' ten-year-old company, Mattel, would be interested in sponsoring a new television show soon to air on the network. The cost for the one-year sponsorship was no less than the sum of Mattel's entire net worth. To further complicate matters, the unknown factors in the decision facing the Handlers far outweighed the known. First, television was relatively new. The number of households with televisions was multiplying rapidly in the United States, but exploiting the boob tube for advertising was still a very new concept. Within the toy industry in particular, TV advertising was virtually nonexistent at the time. Second, toy sales rarely occurred outside of the six weeks preceding Christmas, so there was no reason to believe that extensive spending throughout the year had much promise. Yet ABC asked the Handlers to pay the enormous sum to advertise on their network every week of the year. The Handlers were asked to bet it all on an unproven medium airing an unproven show, consoled only by the knowledge that it might pay off through revenue from a sales cycle that contradicted everything they knew about the buying trends for their products. Mattel's chief financial officer, Yas Yoshida, informed Ruth Handler that, if the plan failed, Mattel probably would not be broke but certainly would be "badly bent." The decision facing the Handlers would have been akin to betting a company's future existence on an aggressive Internet campaign during that medium's infancy in 1995. If Mattel passed on the deal, sales would have likely continued at their modest growth rate. They would have always had the option to pay for TV advertising once it had been better tested. Or they could go for broke, which we know always carries with it the real possibility of making people go broke, or at least "badly bent."

After deliberating for all of about forty-five minutes, Ruth and her husband, Mattel cofounder Elliot, called ABC to inform them that they would love to bet their personal and professional livelihood on sponsoring ABC's new show, *The Mickey Mouse Club*. It worked. In 1956, sales of Mattel's burp guns soared and the company's revenue tripled over the next three years. And it would still be another three years before Barbie hit the runway at the 1959 Toy Fair in Manhattan.

Ruth Handler's gamble clearly paid off. In 1967 she took the reigns of Mattel as president and led her company to annual revenues of $300 million by the early 1970s. The turning point for Ruth Handler and Mattel was clearly the decision to go "all in" and commit to ABC's unprecedented terms to sponsor *The Mickey Mouse Club*. And Handler made that decision in less time than it takes many of us to decide where to go for dinner. She didn't have to call ABC within the hour; she wanted to, and that is an example of potential seeking at its peak—making a quick decision when it's not even required.

Or was it necessary?

It turns out that many potential seekers are convinced that they make the best decisions under time pressure. Doris J., a potential-seeking health-care executive that TalentSmart surveyed, commented fittingly, "I actually have a harder time making decisions when I have a long period of time to deliberate." Not only do potential seekers tend to make decisions faster, but they feel that time pressure enhances those decisions. This instinct stands in stark contrast to the risk managers we'll discuss in Chapter 8 who say that *not* being pressed for time is when they work best. We surveyed more than 1,000 people and asked them what conditions led to their best decisions. Most risk managers surveyed believed that they make good

decisions when they have enough time and enough informa
tion. But potential seekers overwhelmingly said that their
best decisions are made when they have to be made quickly.
Whether or not potential seekers actually make good decisions
under time pressure, or just *feel* like they do, is hard to know
for sure. But we do know that the belief is pervasive among
them. Nearly forty percent of potential seekers responded
that they make good decisions under time pressure, compared
to less than ten percent of risk managers. Perhaps even more
telling, only seven percent of potential seekers listed having enough time as a condition for good decision making. By
contrast, it was the most important factor for risk managers.
Potential seekers' belief in the virtue of pressure probably has
something to do with the flood of dopamine received under
intense deadlines. Time pressure quite literally gets our juices
flowing. The difference is in the way that rush makes potential
seekers or risk managers feel. Most risk managers feel perfectly
fine without the extra juice, so pressure does nothing more
than boost anxiety and discomfort. The opposite holds true
for potential seekers.

I was anxious to uncover why potential seekers believe
that time pressure is a catalyst for good decisions. My quest
took me to the fertile soil of America's heartland.

## 3. Pressure Drop

Don R. has spent most of his adult life scouring the midwestern plains for opportunity. He grew up the third of eight
children on a rural, midwestern family farm. After finishing
high school, he elected to leave the farm in favor of the business world, although he never veered far from agribusiness in
one form or another. Throughout Don's thirty-six-year career,
he and his high school sweetheart and their four children

have lived in no less than fourteen different homes in eleven different towns. They've owned more than forty family vehicles. That's at least one traded vehicle per year, a different domicile every two-and-a-half years, and a new neighborhood in a new town every three-years—all by choice.

Despite Don's early stints in insurance sales, door-to-door smoke detector sales, and a dry-cleaning business, by his early thirties he had settled into what had always been his calling—agriculture. Don spent the next twenty years managing grain elevators, or farmers' cooperatives. Co-ops, as they are called, are the linchpin of the farm industry, and they are operated exactly as the name implies. Every year at harvest, farmers need a place where they can deposit their grain so that it can be sold and then transported to buyers. To do this, farmers form a co-op that is managed as its own commercial entity. A board of directors consisting of elected local farmers guides the co-op in its business affairs. The co-op's forty-story cement silos—the closest thing farming communities have to skyscrapers—accommodate the storage, and an onsite office conducts the transactions that turn grain into revenue. The farmers sell their grain to the local co-op, at which point the co-op then turns around and sells it to buyers from coast to coast. Similar to a corporation, most co-ops have various branches in different towns, managers, and a board of directors. In most farm communities the co-op is the biggest business in town.

One of the challenges the co-op faces during a banner harvest is that it simply doesn't have enough storage space to accommodate all of the grain. At these times, the co-op is forced to close the door on incoming grain. No more grain means no more revenue. As grain is perishable, there is usually only a limited window of time in which cultivated crops can be sold at their highest value, free of defects. If grain isn't sold after harvest, there are no guarantees that it won't rot before it can be sold, and that is assuming that the farmer even owns adequate storage for the grain. Refusing grain during harvest is for a co-op what shutting doors on incoming inventory would be for a department store during the holiday shopping season. Not only is the co-op forced to turn away revenue, but it has to deal with the wrath of key stakeholders. The farmers—who happen to be both customers and shareholders—are understandably upset when the fruits of their harvest are ready to be transformed into profit, only to be turned away by the co-op. And they aren't afraid to voice their dismay. As you might imagine, harvest is a highly stressful period for the branch manager.

Now in his late fifties, Don has a number of memories about those tumultuous experiences. Contrary to expectation, however, the memories are some of the fondest he has about his career. The high-intensity harvest—when quick decisions are the rule of the day—were exactly the kinds of situations that most excited Don and they were the ones at which he excelled. For impulsive types like Don, quick decisions are viewed less like something to be tolerated and more as an experience that makes the rest of their job worth doing. When he speaks about harvest crunch-time, Don's stimulation is palpable. His eyes widen and he leans in a little closer to me so that he's literally on the edge of his seat. Watching the glow illuminate his face, I felt as if I could see his dopamine receptors shifting into overdrive. I asked him why he felt at his best in these situations. He replied that while other branch managers in the area panicked, "I could come up with a solution to make more room, rent storage, find space on the ground . . . just figure out a way to make it keep going."

In a response reminiscent of our Australian potential seekers Don credits his decisiveness under the gun to "not looking for approval" from his general manager. Other branch managers in his co-op were often "too afraid to risk making a bad decision, and so they did nothin' at all." One particularly memorable year, Don's branch was the only co-op in the area still taking grain until the last weeks of harvest. For an industry that lives or dies on seasonal revenues, those additional few weeks with doors open created a substantial competitive advantage.

The heart of the issue is what kept Don going so that he could effectively make the grain transactions. When Don said, "make *it* keep going," he was of course referring to his branch's ability to continue receiving and selling grain. However, "it" could also refer to the internal rush of dopamine that Don's network of receptors craved. Like many impulsive people, Don occasionally struggles to keep his attention focused. He is quick to want new experiences, as evidenced by his career moves, numerous vehicles, and practically itinerant home ownership. But during time-pressured sprints to succeed, his attention actually sharpens. His focus and his impulses do not wander far from the intended path. One of the peculiar traits often found in people with attention deficits is that they are also prone to periods of "hyperattentiveness." Instead of their minds wandering, they become intensely focused. It is as if their dopamine receptors roam aimlessly through a catalog of new experiences searching for adequate stimulation. When they find that stimulation, they fervently attack it. In Don's words, they "figure out a way to make it keep going." If the time pressure were absent, the stimulation would be missing as well.

I realized that Don and impulsive decision makers like him are effective during crunch time when there are limits to the situation. Freewheeling potential seekers seem to function best when their wheels are limited as to the direction and length of their travel. Under these high-pressure circumstances, impulsive people are free (and often encouraged) to unleash their impulses toward the singular direction of "figuring out a way to make it keep going." As long as Don remained focused on creating more storage for additional grain, he was free to let his impulses lead the way toward that goal. It seems that there is a neurological basis for a potential seeker's preference for quick decisions. This might explain why they make quick decisions even when it is not required.

Besides the excitement and stimulation of what is sometimes called "brinksmanship," potential seekers can use their style to get a leg up in business. For potential seekers used to shooting first and apologizing later, time pressure puts them into their comfort zone rather than pushing them beyond it. Their response gives them the charge their dopamine receptors crave, which reinforces the response and begs them to continue. With adequate time constraints and clear objectives in place, the situation is right for directional correctness. And since potential seekers are the minority, you can imagine the opportunity that exists if they find the right niche where the kind of highly charged environment that risk managers dislike is in fact a fertile ground for opportunity.

There is one additional element to maintaining directional correctness in these kinds of situations. Don is the first to point out that he uses his years of experience making decisions during crunch times. Without that additional piece of the puzzle, it is harder for potential seekers to keep impulsiveness functional. Don has instinctive triggers, based on each situation, that help him gauge exactly when it's the right time to jump. This doesn't mean that he is flawless in his execution—we all make mistakes. But his impulsive personality allows him to act quickly and stay hyperfocused on his goals, while referencing similar situations from the past.

## 4. Betting the Farm

A potential seeker's desire to move quickly has its fair share of consequences, but used properly, it can maximize his or her ability to obtain opportunities that others might miss. External circumstances did not compel Ruth Handler to decide to sponsor *The Mickey Mouse Club* immediately, but she did so anyway. One of Don R.'s first successes in the world of business was buying a number of feeders in a distress sale at a large discount. Don bought the feeders without actually having the money to pay for them at the time, but he still moved quickly knowing an opportunity was at hand. Don was able to turn around the feeders and realize a handsome profit, and another potential seeker's appetite for excitement was born. Much like Ruth Handler's decision to sponsor *The Mickey Mouse Club* Don gave it approximately ten minutes worth of thought before making the purchase. He told me with a chuckle that he and his friend could have waited a day and probably received the same deal. However, if they waited, they could have found a half-dozen reasons to talk themselves out of the deal. Perhaps Ruth Handler went through a similar thought process, reasoning that she and her husband would have eventually talked themselves out of a magical opportunity.

Whether Don's decision to buy the feeders or Handler's choice to invest in the *The Mickey Mouse Club* are good examples of sound decision making is debatable. In neither case were the decisions what we would typically describe as "well thought out." But in both instances, the decisions fell well within the decision maker's area of expertise. Don knew that the margin he could get on the feeders would be substantial, and he only needed to find the right buyers. For a born salesman, it was a slam dunk . . . except for the minor detail that he had to do it before his check cleared. Handler knew toys. She knew kids. She understood her customers. But she had no way of being sure that *The Mickey Mouse Club* would be a hit. There was no precedent within media or ratings history on which to base her decision. Handler simply believed that the right pieces were in place for a smashing success. Additional thinking could not have provided her with information that did not exist. Both Handler and Don saw a good opportunity for themselves and created self-imposed time restrictions for their decisions.

Putting it on the line with no backup plan is the hallmark behavior of potential seekers. It is a defining feature that consistently separates them from risk managers. Sometimes it pays off and other times . . . not. In TalentSmart's research, we found that potential seekers are more than three times as likely as risk managers to prefer a fifty-percent chance of winning $2,000 over a guaranteed payout of $1,000. It doesn't mean that they prefer the chance to lose $1,000, but they do prefer the shot at the larger sum. So, which is the logical choice? There really isn't a logical or "correct" choice here because, when analyzed according to probabilities, the outcome is going to be the same on average. A guaranteed $1,000 (1 times $1,000 equals $1,000) is equivalent to a fifty-percent chance of $2,000 (.5 times $2,000 equals $1,000). Regardless of which option you choose, if you consistently make this choice on ten separate occasions, odds are that you are going to end up with $10,000. The difference is in the path you take to arrive at that final outcome. Do you want the steady path of increase, or the one with the outside chance for high peaks?

In light of this realization, when we review our original finding that impulsive people are more likely to have incomes all over the map, the underlying reason becomes clearer. Half of the time, potential seekers are going to come out on top and get the $2,000. The other half, they end up with nothing. Over extended time and taking many people into consideration, potential seekers and risk managers will end up just about even on average income. Statistically, when we examine aggregate incomes, no difference exists between risk managers and potential seekers. At any given time, one potential seeker is probably ahead of a risk manager's average, while another potential seeker is probably well below it. On the whole, the potential-seeking gambler scores big wins and suffers big losses, and ends up coming out average, whereas the risk manager takes the average gain most times without many huge wins, but also without huge losses.

As we'll discover in Chapter 8, risk managers can and often do trek into the unknown in pursuit of opportunity. But they approach uncertainty differently than potential seekers. Successful risk managers take a much more controlled approach—taking what appears to the outsider to be a gamble, yet always making certain to mitigate possible damage by hedging their bets. A risk manager's train of thought runs something like, *If I have to go for it all right now, or lose the chance forever, the opportunity is probably too good to be true.* That line of thought is a good rule of thumb for the risk manager, but it isn't always true. There are some occasions when the opportunity—although requiring immediate, committed action—truly is a golden one. There just isn't any way of getting around that reality, or the possibility that what appears to be a golden opportunity may also severely bend you from time to time. Going "badly bent" is a consequence that risk managers usually do not deem necessary. For potential seekers, avoiding an opportunity is like cutting off the air supply. The potential seeker is more likely to just do it without the safety net. Sometimes it pays off, and other times it doesn't. For every Donald Trump there is a Donald Trump circa 1990. For every Ruth Handler, there is a Kenneth Lay—blinded to the consequences by the glow of opportunity.

After a highly successful run as president of Mattel, Ruth Handler ended up resigning. Irregularities in reporting to the Securities and Exchange Commission were cited as a contributing factor. She was never indicted on any charges, and we have no reason to question Handler's integrity. It is most likely that she simply ended up on the wrong side of a gamble when attempting to juggle her books. (Accounting is one area the potential seeker should roundly dismiss as a directionally *incorrect* path for impulsive tendencies.) Handler, who passed away in 2002, most likely would have liked the scandal erased from Mattel's history. However, the same drive behind the irregularities is probably also somewhere behind the decision to back *The Mickey Mouse Club*. Were the impulsive gambles that Handler used to build Mattel worth the fall she later took? The answer to that question might depend on whether you ask a potential seeker drawn to Handler's success, or a risk manager focused on her demise.

No strategy can eliminate the fact that as long as decision makers take gambles in their careers and personal lives, they will occasionally call "heads" only to look down and find tails staring back at them. Nor should they attempt to dampen the part of their personalities that are inclined to gamble—partly because it just isn't possible and partly because it is how they probably enjoy living. The focus should be placed on maximizing the potential of that tendency. To that end, there are two keys that potential seekers can employ. The first key has to do with developing the kind of binary thinking Bill Gates uses in order to make sure impulses are directionally correct.

Becoming binary like Gates means always questioning your judgment. Force yourself to take time to reflect and ask yourself whether an action is in line with the direction you want to travel. It won't be easy to put skepticism and restraint in front of the stimulation of acting quickly. But getting into the habit of asking key questions about the direction in which your impulses are headed can help you avoid some of the more irreparable disasters. Make sure to frame these questions in a positive way. Opportunity costs are going to resonate more than reminders of risk. For example, don't ask, *What are the risks?* Ask yourself, *Will this decision destroy future potential for me?* Instead of asking, *Could this decision damage my relationships with other people?* ask *Will this decision help me build beneficial relationships?* If you continually remind yourself to see personal relationships as beneficial to your own well-being, then your impulses will follow your lead. (Refer to the "Goal-Tracking" section of the Impulse Factor test to set up a daily e-mail reminder.)

One medical equipment salesperson I interviewed is an impulsive communicator. Tim S. was officially diagnosed with ADHD as a kid, which continues to have a marked impact on his adult behavior. He hasn't made it through more than thirty movies as a grown-up. To appease his short attention span, he spends hours a day on the phone talking with different friends, family members, or clients. Whenever his attention wanes, he picks up the phone. He uses his impulsive nature to strengthen his relationships by continually keeping other people in the forefront of his mind through constant communication. His connections act as a guide to help him remain directionally correct. Also, building up credits with the people close to him helps soften the fall when he slips. The connection that his communication forges with people causes them to be more forgiving and supportive in those moments when his self-destructive impulses accidentally get the better of him. But beyond remaining directionally correct, there's another aspect to connecting with friends and colleagues that we'll get to shortly.

The second key for potential seekers is to fully leverage the payoff from successful gambles. When I spoke with Don R., he was clear about the fact that he has made a number of mistakes over his lifetime due to his impulsive tendencies. I asked him, "If you could go back in time and talk to the Don of 25 years ago, what advice would you give him?"

He was quick to respond: "Do what you're good at and hire what you're not good at. Recognize your weaknesses."

Absent outside assistance, potential seekers too often score multiple big wins, only to have nothing to show for it later. The most skilled gamblers are bound to be left with nothing at some point if they never set aside a fraction of their winnings for the inevitable occasions when the cards just don't fall in their favor. If you don't have the discipline to put some of your winnings away for safekeeping, then hire someone who does. Edward Hallowell and John Ratey recommend hiring a "closer"—referring to the baseball pitcher who enters a game in later innings to seal a victory. At its core, the act of hiring someone to do the things you're not good at is closely related to the concept of binary thinking. Both are an admission that your judgment has its limits. Working with a closer is taking that one step further by recognizing that you need someone to help you define those limits. It requires you to recognize your weaknesses and introduces just the right amount of skepticism necessary to protect you from calamity. Our research at TalentSmart gave us essential insight into some of these ideas.

## 5. Redirection, Not Reduction

Halfway through his life, St. Francis of Assisi realized where his greatest potential lay. He then directed all of his decisions toward that goal. But he never stopped being impulsive. If you are the seeker who errs on the side of impulsivity, you've probably been told by well-intentioned teachers, parents, counselors, and friends that "you need to learn to control yourself." In other words, you need to put a damper on your impulsive tendencies. Advising more self-control has a nice ring to it, but it is doomed. A prime reason for that strategy's dismal chances of success is that you simply are impulsive, and self-control works in direct opposition to your nature. As psychologist and risk-taking expert Marvin Zuckerman[4] writes:

Simple information, reasoning, and appeals to fear of negative consequences are not enough to dissuade a high sensation seeker from trying some risky behavior that promises
an intense reward. Once established, a habit that provides
reward is difficult to extinguish because of the negative
emotional and physical state produced by withdrawal of
that reward.

Self-control mandates that you "don't do that," which is
about as effective as telling Lane McGlynn, "Don't charge
that hill," or telling Nick Wernimont, "Cage-fighting can injure
you." The advice fails to address what potential opportunities
you *can* seek, and speaks only to those you *cannot*. Potential
seekers just aren't built for that kind of stasis. If you are going
to make some behavior off-limits and therefore remove the
reward, then you have to replace it with another rewarding
behavior. Instead of beating yourself up trying to eliminate
your seeking tendencies, why not just point those active incli-
nations in a healthy direction?

Maybe your direction is one rooted in personal meaning.
Maybe your direction is the pursuit of safety for your family.
Maybe it is one pointed toward breaking ground in your profession. In the end, only you can decide what that direction should
be. But one element you may want to consider as you establish
your direction is one of connectedness. Based on his research,
Edward Hallowell recommends establishing a feeling of connectedness, whether with your family and friends, people at
work, with nature, with your heritage, etc. But that feeling of
being part of something that extends beyond your self is essential to leading a fulfilling life. As we touched on earlier, it helps
foster the functional strengths of your binary character.

St. Francis is a prime example of this connectedness with
people, with nature, and with one's heritage. His uncommon
compassion for everyone—the destitute *and* the rich; the

heretics *and* the hypocritically holy; the Christian *and* the Muslim—revealed his deep connection with people. In his relationship with the natural world, he went green way before it was cool to drive a hybrid and his kinship with wild animals is the stuff of legend. He reveled in his French heritage throughout his life, while also feeling an intense bond with the ancient church, displaying a deep connection to those who came before him.

But personal and professional connections are sometimes a struggle for the potential seeker. In one phase of TalentSmart's research, we conducted a 360-degree feedback survey on the different kinds of decision makers. As in a typical 360-degree survey, we asked supervisors, direct reports, peers, and other acquaintances to comment on a coworker's performance. They rated the coworker on an assortment of categories, and then provided answers to general questions about what the coworker was good at and what they thought was holding that person back. TalentSmart's team simply wanted to know from an outsider's perspective what certain employees were doing right and where their colleagues thought they were coming up a little short. While we asked for raters to answer a number of questions about an employee's performance, only those of us at TalentSmart knew where that employee fell on the impulse scale. Although impulsivity was not an explicit factor, we clearly saw a trend emerge in potential seekers' appraisals. We were able to conclude that connectedness not only impacts your personal happiness, but also plays a large role in your professional performance.

As we compiled the results of our survey, it was clear that potential seekers were generally regarded as passionate visionaries. Raters commented that seekers were "great with people leadership," they "challenge you to think bigger," and "see a bigger picture." On the flip side, they were also found lagging in their connections. They were often perceived as being cold, isolated, or devoid of empathy. The seekers' failure to connect can manifest itself in several negative ways in the office. Two common problems that kept popping up were an aversion to delegation and a perceived distrust in colleagues. Raters commented that "you get the feeling that if he could do it all himself, he would" or she "has a great sense of ownership and work ethic which sometimes inhibits her from delegating." Independence can be a great thing, but too much of it breaks bonds between you and coworkers or prevents them from forming in the first place. Without the strong bonds to call on when you need them, your colleagues don't feel as committed and are less likely to pitch in when you need help. In the case of one vibrant public relations director, Isabel A., her drive to squeeze the most potential out of every situation has a significant drawback. On the one hand, she is nothing short of "a breath of fresh air" to her organization. "Her intuition is very keen and accurate," and "she never fails to exude that level of confidence that make people want to support her in whatever cause she is involved in." Both comments address the enthusiasm essential to a person in Isabel's position. Paradoxically, however, her sincere passion to connect with clients and supporters in the public sphere tends to prevent her from fully realizing the connections with her colleagues. One peer said that Isabel "has a great sense of ownership and work ethic which sometimes inhibits her from delegating and allowing other people to help share the load." Isabel is a typical example of how in the midst of a potential seeker's quest for potential, she can unintentionally leave behind those that she counts on—rendering them unable to help when she needs them most.

When asked how potential seekers could improve, raters responded that the potential seeker should "relax and get to know the peers you work with as friends, a little more casually than always being on a mission," "come up for air once in a while," "enlist your coworkers . . . treat them as equals," or more plainly "learn to trust people."

Time and again, we saw that potential seekers have "a great talent for motivating" yet need better "delegation skills." Though friends, family members, and coworkers often view an aversion to delegation as a lack of trust, it has more to do with a potential seeker's lack of patience. The seeker is always on the move and dislikes being slowed down by anything— including the input of colleagues and acquaintances. Gerard C. is a guest services manager at a large resort hotel. He inherited a department with low morale among the employees that some concerned staff members felt was beginning to take its toll on the care their customers were receiving. Gerard didn't waste any time shaking things up and rallying the troops. His colleagues believed he was "light-years ahead of his time" and "has a great talent for motivating personnel." However, "at times he can become irritated with people who just don't get it." Delegation can be frustrating, especially when it involves providing instruction. But failing to delegate leaves you without support. You are also depriving your coworkers, especially direct reports or subordinates, of their own opportunity to learn and advance. Seekers' colleagues suggested "you cannot solve everyone's problems" and you could improve a little on "letting people fail for a learning opportunity vs. stepping in." Just as potential seekers learn from failure, it is important to give others that opportunity as well.

Creating connections with the people around you requires the very patience that potential seekers tend to lack. Even in the case of one savvy leader at a major beverage maker steeped in management experience, Stephen W.'s forced effort to include others was often transparent. "He actively seeks input into decisions, but you get the feeling he really already had his mind made up, and he's just asking so you feel 'included.'" Oops, strike one. Most people are much more perceptive than we give them credit for. Your spouse, your children, and your coworkers are going to see right through a thinly veiled attempt at inclusion. The effort has to be sincere.

So how can it be sincere if sincerity requires patience the potential seeker doesn't have?

Getting people's suggestions before you make a decision will always be challenging for the fast acting. Potential seekers rarely allow time for their own thoughtful input, let alone the input of others, before making a decision. Based on our extensive research at TalentSmart, our Impulse Factor test, and interviews with hundreds of workers with seeker colleagues, we determined that potential seekers should forgo a fake effort at connecting if they are eager to jump. But then it is vital that immediately after jumping, they reach out to colleagues or those who are close and analyze the decision together. Invite coworkers or family members to participate in the analysis of recent decisions. The reflection period is usually less time sensitive, since you have already made the decision, which should remove some of the pressure to keep moving and further aggravate any disconnect with those around you.

Involving the people around you in your reflection time is not just a gesture. Getting a little help from a calculating observer will not only create a sincere connection with colleagues, it will also enhance your learning. Getting their objective input on the most recent decision can help guide you the next time you need to make a similar decision.

## 6. "We Can Help"

Historian Kenneth Scott Latourette[5] noted in his classic text *A History of Christianity*, "Francis was not an organizer or an administrator. He was too impulsive, too subject to changes of mood, too unpredictable, to carry the load of running a great organization." Ironically, that "great organization" of the Franciscan monks existed not in spite of its leader's impulsivity, but because of it. However, Latourette's assessment of Francis's lackluster organizational skills does tap into a common frailty of the potential seeker. In our work at TalentSmart, we saw over and over that planning and organization can be the potential seeker's downfall. Our good friend Stephen W. was told that he should "balance the need for strategic conversation . . . with [employees'] need to have specific direction and clarity." He has "too many big ideas which sends the organization chasing after them. A bit more focus and carry through is needed before moving on to the next big thing." One middle manager, Rebecca A., was told that "organizing her time" was preventing her from rising to the next level. Other seekers were told that they could get further by "following up with work that should have been done," and that they should "come up with a plan to make his department more productive." Organizing and planning are two skills that are unlikely to put the potential seeker on top. But there is hope.

A well-intending colleague offered one of the most useful remedies for potential seekers' planning issues. She wanted to tell her boss quite simply, "We can help." A weakness in planning does not mean that potential seekers do not have great ideas, or cannot create the master strokes for a brilliant strategy. It means only that follow-through and detailed execution might be better left in a more calculating pair of hands. The potential seeker has a tendency to pounce on the immediate potential, without regard for the long term. Revealing this weakness, the famously impulsive architect, Frank Lloyd Wright, once said, "Nothing is more important than right now." That is a liberating motto that might be captured beautifully by a refrigerator magnet hanging in your kitchen. In practice, however, even though the future is not *more* important than right now, to most people and organizations the future is at least *equally* as important.

In the year after Jacques de Vitry wrote his letters of admiration about the Franciscans, Francis of Assisi reluctantly solicited the guidance of Cardinal Ugolino dei Conti di Segni, who would later become Pope Gregory IX. As Francis's following grew from a small flock to a significant religious movement, it became harder and harder for him to manage his affairs. Many of the issues facing Francis were remarkably similar to those facing key players in today's fast-growing organizations. One of these issues is how to preserve and maintain the culture and values of an organization as hordes of new members join. As a rule, Francis despised complex rules and rigid social structures. He resisted top-down efforts by church leaders as well as bottom-up requests from fellow monks to impose an organizational hierarchy for his order. He responded to each of these requests in characteristic clarity and simplicity: "Let them remember what the Lord says, 'I have not come to be served, but to serve.'" In other words, the Franciscan structure would remain as flat as humanly possible.

Yet despite his eccentricities, Francis maintained a strong sense of reality and understanding of the world in which he lived. He came to the same crucial realization at which all idealistic revolutionaries eventually arrive: A movement's long-term success depends on how effectively its followers understand the fundamental purpose of its existence. He also realized that there was not enough of him to go around. Inevitably he saw his message get lost in translation or changed as it passed from mouth to mouth. His organization needed managers and policies if it was to survive. As much as it pained him to do it, Francis willingly sacrificed some of his control over his organization. Ugolino was perfect for the job. Within the church, he was regarded as highly competent, a vital attribute for his new role as mediator between Franciscan monks and church authorities. Yet at the same time, the cardinal was sincerely committed to Francis's reform efforts. In practice,

Ugolino infused structure and insisted on the creation of policies for the Franciscans, but he left Francis with sole "creative control" of these policies. Ugolino essentially assumed the role of the driver who kept the bus on the road while Francis remained the navigator. Ugolino stepped in only when the bus began to veer off the road. With the help of Ugolino's objective guidance and diplomatic savvy, Francis was able to establish the longevity of the Franciscan movement that still exists today. Ugolino was Francis's closer.

Delegating to a closer is a sign of trust in other people, which in turn helps to foster connectedness. It also allows potential seekers to get back to their mission of building Rome by the close of business today. The primary closer will be the go-to person, so it has to be someone whom the potential seeker knows he or she can trust—someone with a strong track record of detailed execution. It also needs to be someone with whom the potential seeker gets along. While Francis did not enjoy compromising on his original intentions for the Franciscan movement, the mutual respect and friendship he built with Ugolino made the compromise an easier pill to swallow. Like most people who experienced its force, Ugolino was deeply impressed with the direction of Francis's movement. He did all that he could to preserve its potential by making the long-sighted decisions regarding organization and structure that Francis typically neglected. As a result the Franciscans grew faster and further than any other monastic order in the church.

The less critical issues faced by potential seekers are a great opportunity to explore the depth of their bull pen. They are the opportunities that allow others to get involved and share responsibility without the risk of pulling everyone into a quagmire. Before Ugolino entered the picture, Francis made it part of his standard practice to let others lead their daily excursions. Potential seekers may not be in a position to hand over the decision-making authority, but that does not mean they cannot integrate others into the process. Others can provide needed assistance, while showing off what they are good at. This advice applies to spouses and friends as much as it does to coworkers. As you read this, you might ask what you do if you do not have the authority or seniority to involve colleagues in this manner. Just because an issue might be work related, don't limit your closers to those within the company's walls. Professional colleagues, friends, and family can all be rich sources for the kind of strategizing you'll look for in a closer. Indeed, rule number one in Hallowell and Ratey's "Top Tips for Adults with ADD" is "Marry the right person."

## 7. Selecting, Connecting, and Correcting

For potential seekers, impulsivity is the proverbial sword that cuts both ways. If handled with care and given direction, the sword can be your key to victory in whichever battles you face. It is a sword, however, that doesn't lend itself to being sheathed. And if you ignore it, you might find yourself falling on it at a most inopportune time. Perhaps it will be in the midst of closing a big deal, or in irreparably severing an important relationship, or badly bending yourself when circumstances demand operating on a tight budget. Without proper direction, Neal Cassady's twilight revelation that "I'm a danger to everyone—to myself most of all" will ring eerily true for you as well.

But then again, avoiding danger is not what the potential seeker is all about. The more potent consideration for the potential seeker is that without checks on your directional correctness, the full potential that you seek will elude you. Cheap thrills will grow increasingly more expensive to your pursuit of potential, and they will become steadily less thrilling.

The success of your strategy rests largely on the efficiency with which you align your impulsivity in the direction of your choice. Maintaining directional correctness requires a habitual, constant questioning of whether the action you just took, or the decision you are about to make is in line with your chosen direction. It should be clear by now that there is no single right direction. Selecting your direction is entirely your choice. However, once you have selected your direction, you need to be mindful of the signposts. If you have selected a direction of professional success, yet you are skimming off the top of your allotted budget, refusing to acknowledge your own limitations or the authority of your superiors, or constantly undercutting the people in your career upon whom you rely, then those short-term gains are not in line with your overall direction. Similarly, if your direction is one of personal freedom, then engaging in activities that can strip you of your driver's license or land you behind bars are not in line with your direction either. While the choice of your overall direction is likely one that you will have to make only a few times during your lifetime, it should inform every decision. Your decisions should undergo a line of questioning that begins and ends with the questions *Is this [or was that] decision in line with the direction I've chosen for myself? and If not, do I need to make a correction?*

The good news is that you do not have to, nor should you elect to, do this alone. Your peers, your subordinates, and oftentimes even your superiors will help you. To reiterate an earlier point, one of the best ways to keep your daily decisions aligned with your direction is to stay connected with those around you. Actively seek input from trusted sources either before you make a decision or immediately afterward. Setting up a network of people or conditions that can be your checkpoints will prevent you from going too far astray in those moments when you forget to check yourself. This doesn't mean setting up a network of brown-nosers nor does it mean enlisting feedback from those who jump on every opportunity to degrade you. You are looking for people with whom you can have frank conversations, and who won't dismiss you for acknowledging your shortcomings.

More of these people probably surround you than you think. For instance, the exact same manager who jumped on your case for defying her or for doing something without permission could very easily be the same manager who is willing to be your partner in reflection. The difference is that, in the former instance, you behaved in a way that your manager didn't understand, and she was therefore frustrated by your actions. You might have had a perfectly reasonable explanation, but it just won't sound very good if you have to share that explanation while backtracking after being called out—that's when an *explanation* looks remarkably similar to an *excuse*. However, if you have shared your tendency with your manager, then you have provided her with a more positive frame of reference in which to view your actions. Your manager still may not approve of the outcome or of your approach, but that discussion you had *before* the event prevents her from using her imagination to find an explanation. In the latter case, you are simply managing the expectations and perceptions of your manager.

But don't expect your manager to suggest a discussion about your tendencies. It is an exceptional breed of manager who will first come to you with regular feedback. Though managers probably should be the ones to initiate such feedback, the reality is that most managers (even the good ones) are just too wrapped up with their own tasks. It is your responsibility to at least partially shape the way you are managed by reaching out and staying connected with your boss. If you take the initiative to stay connected (with your manager, partner, board members, colleague, or spouse) and have a frank discussion about the way you make decisions and the direction in which you would like those decisions to take you, you might be surprised at how much they appreciate your willingness to ask for guidance in refining your skills. Not only will they be a valuable source of feedback, but they are also likely to be much more forgiving the next time you slip up. Instead of seeing your mistakes as an act of defiance or incompetence, they are more likely to see it as a chance to offer feedback to an otherwise competent, self-aware leader with high potential. Granted, this conversation might be a little uncomfortable. But if you are afraid that airing some of the possible weaknesses of your tendency (as well as its strengths) might be a bad political move for your career, it might be time for a reality check. If you think that you can keep your susceptibility to occasional errors a secret that nobody else will notice, *you* are mismanaging yourself. Not only are people still aware of your weaknesses, but since you have chosen not to address them, the people around you also get to attribute your weaknesses to whatever source they choose— things like ignorance, arrogance, or plain old incompetence.

Think of your network of closers as lane bumpers at a bowling alley. Most bowling alleys have now installed removable rail systems in the gutters on either side of the lane. It used to be that when novices first learned to bowl, their balls would spend more time in the gutters than on the lane. Thanks to the nifty invention of bumper rails, a beginner can have the satisfaction of watching his or her ball hit the pins, while still practicing to roll it straight without mom and dad intervening. Staying connected and enlisting closers is similar to using bumper rails. Your manager or closer can facilitate your ability to roll strikes without trying to do it for you but it also prevents you from winding up in the gutter.

Ensuring directional correctness is the goal of everyone surrounding the potential seeker but is primarily the potential seekers' own responsibility. Questioning your impulses, reflecting on your past decisions, and employing a network of supporters are the best ways to make sure that your sword stays sharp on all the right edges.

# CHAPTER EIGHT

# Risk Managers:

## Conquering the Fear of Big Cats

At the 2006 Buick Invitational in La Jolla, California, I watched golf prodigy Tiger Woods add one more win to his stunning list of professional victories. What made this event a little different is that Woods actually trailed the leaders until the very last hole. On the final day of the four-day event, Australian Nathan Green appeared to have the championship locked up. Winning at the Buick Invitational promised to be a big step for Green. It would have been the first Majors Championship of his eight-year professional golf career. And he could have done it by knocking off living legend Tiger Woods, to boot.

Woods had already won this tournament three of the six preceding years. He is also an official spokesman for Buick, so beating him at the Buick Invitational was almost akin to beating him on his home turf. Green needed only a par on the final two holes to seal his triumph. Instead, he flubbed a chip shot, which let Tiger back into the hunt. Of course Woods lived up to his reputation and finished almost flawlessly. By the end of the round, there was a three-way tie for the lead. Technically

the three front-runners had to play two tie-breaker holes to determine the winner. But it was basically a foregone conclusion
at that point. Woods came out on top and claimed his fourth
Buick championship. Performances like that are probably why
*Golf Today* predicts that Woods will be a billionaire by 2010.

Tiger Woods's story is not a new one. He started swinging
golf clubs at age two, putted against Bob Hope the next year
on national television, and then went on to dominate almost
every golf circuit in which he has ever played. But underneath
the praise heaped on his phenomenal ability lies a different
story. This forgotten story carries lessons that are far more
important to the rest of us than the tales of Woods's innate
talents. The lesson lies in how other golfers deal with the approaching Tiger. Golf pundit Tim McDonald[1] wrote that "it's
as if no one feels they have a right to win with Woods in the
field. Woods seems to win quite a few tournaments, not due
to thrilling heroics of his own, but because of nervous break-
downs by his competitors." Golf is one of the solo sports, like
tennis, that demands as much, if not more, mental prowess as
physical prowess. As many muscle-bound divot-diggers can at-
test, raw speed and strength are useless without a good handle
on that mushy gray matter inside their skulls. When golfers
see a chance to beat a living legend like Woods, it is as if the
motivation to hit well dissolves into a quaking fear of hitting
poorly. Like many of us do when we detect a predator nipping
at our heels, Nathan Green lost it.

Just over a year after Nathan Green's collapse, Tiger Woods
was on the familiar road to victory in Augusta, Georgia, in the
fabled Masters Golf Tournament. Up until the 2007 Masters,
Woods had won every major tournament in which he held the
lead going into the final round. Once he took the lead, there
was no stopping him.

But history began writing a new chapter on that clear
Easter Sunday in Augusta. A little-known golfer named Zach

Johnson[2] showed the golf world what can happen when calculation meets execution. Early in the final round, Johnson tied Woods for the lead. By midday, Johnson separated himself from the pack and took an outright lead. With five holes remaining, all Johnson needed to do was hold steady. His caddie knew it. A captive national television audience knew it. Woods knew it. The rest of the golfers posted on the leader board that day certainly knew it. Johnson, however, was quite oblivious. "I really didn't know what was going on. I did what I was doing—staying in the present," Johnson said afterward. "My caddie, Damon Green, was keeping an eye on the lead. I guess ignorance is bliss sometimes."

Perhaps even more blissful was Johnson's historic come-from-behind victory over Woods. Raised in Cedar Rapids, Iowa, the thirty-one-year-old Johnson insisted after his victory, "I'm as normal as they come." That is not false modesty speaking either. It is this focus on the work at hand without a thought of magic or heroism that makes this Cinderella story significant for the less-impulsive majority—those of you who fall on the risk manager side of the Impulse Factor test. Johnson's victory represents one ordinary person strategizing his way to defeating the fear of an approaching Tiger. Most of us have heard about visualization or being "in the zone." But Johnson's accomplishment manifests something more than those catch phrases capture.

So what is the secret? What made Zach Johnson able to come through in the clutch where Nathan Green and so many other great golfers have failed?

## 1. The Flip Side of Fear

When TalentSmart surveyed the colleagues of cautious decision makers, we noticed they were often viewed as "very good at foreseeing problems." They "keep on top of changes" and tend to excel at long-term planning. Cautious thinkers were acutely aware of problems brewing on the horizon or approaching in the rearview mirror. Importantly, this ability to detect oncoming threats is an essential part of the risk manager's ability to plan ahead. Occasionally, however, that awareness compromises the risk manager's best interests. If the awareness becomes simple fear, it can lead you to vote for a politician you don't really care for, simply because you fail to keep a threat in perspective. That fear instinct may cause you to spend more money than you intended on an entrée or a mortgage. Last but not least, your golf game may suffer because of it.

To understand the origins of this sometimes crippling fear, we need to leave the golf greens for the mating scenes and explore how humans were built to love. The indie rock band Death Cab for Cutie (the origin of the name is anyone's guess) tells a lyrical tale in which a Catholic school nun preaches that "fear is the heart of love." The song's protagonist is apparently so put off by the suggestion that he decides never to return to school. Fear might not be the *heart* of love, but fear and love do share a common neurological ancestor. According to the author of *Why We Love*, Rutgers anthropologist Helen Fisher,[3] when we experience romantic love, our brains are flooded by dopamine. Fisher defines romantic love above the drive to reproduce or engage in a little puppy love. Romantic love is of the everlasting variety, whether or not it turns out to be everlasting. That chemical rush often translates to the excitement we feel every time the object of our affection waltzes into sight. And it all starts with the release of dopamine.

I stumbled into the relationship between love and fear when I began sharing TalentSmart's research on impulsivity with our clients. For some of our cautious individuals, the daring decisions that they had made for love seemed to fly in the face of everything we were telling them about risk-managing instincts. They wanted to know, for instance, how someone who is supposedly cautious could be so risky as to uproot a comfortable life just to chase an unpredictable romance. Many of us know someone, not necessarily an impulsive person, who has fallen in love and made major life changes in a very short time. I already knew from my research on historical manias, such as investment bubbles and witch hunts, that under the right conditions, people are absolutely capable of behaving out of character. But it wasn't until I learned about Helen Fisher's research on the chemical cocktail that intoxicates lovers that I had the neurological answer for the spontaneity we see in risk-managing people. In one experiment, Fisher and her colleagues scanned subjects' brains to see what happens to the human brain in the throes of an almost love affair. Using a functional MRI machine, Fisher watched as her subjects showed an increase of dopamine, the chemical that makes us excited, and a decrease of serotonin the chemical that makes us feel at ease. Specifically, the caudate nucleus—a part of what is called the reptilian brain because of its evolution dating back sixty-five million years—flooded with dopamine. If you were to look at a brain scan with that combination of elevated dopamine and suppressed serotonin, and you had no information about the circumstances, you wouldn't know whether that person was deeply in love or just about ready to impulsively pour their life's savings into a sports car.

Dopamine is one of the brains' more volatile chemicals. As we explored in earlier chapters, the need for pleasure-pumping dopamine can make a potential seeker pursue a wild thrill just to feel normal again. A shortage makes it difficult to concentrate, and a surplus of dopamine can cause just about anyone to do wild and crazy things, like pursue a lifetime bond of marriage just to feel "right" again. But the chemical concoction that gives you nature's high can do more than stir up giddy feelings. Similar to its narcotic relatives like cocaine and heroin, excess dopamine can quickly turn fun into fear and anxiety if the reward eludes you. Some people refer to this experience as a "bad trip." The object of your desire could be a love interest, a tulip bulb, or just about anything your heart passionately desires. Whatever the prize, when it eludes you, dopamine takes that delay as a cue to keep on pumping. Before long, the surging dopamine can make any personality downright obsessive.

In general, a healthy supply of dopamine causes people to engage in what psychologists refer to as "goal-directed behavior." In the realm of love, a little too much goal-directed behavior becomes what the rest of the world refers to as "stalking." Dopamine fights for what it wants. Unfortunately, when the catalyst for that surge of dopamine fixes his or her gaze on another, dopamine doesn't just throw in the towel. In *Why We Love*, Fisher explains that when people came back to her lab months after they had been left by a lover, their brains produced the same or even more dopamine than they did at the relationship's height. According to Fisher, "The brain's Reward System becomes triggered when you want something. And if the reward is delayed in coming, the Reward System just keeps firing impulses—driving you to work harder to get what you can't yet attain." The dopamine-induced glee the lovers felt before now manifests itself in a love hangover characterized by intense fear, and still more goal-directed behavior.

However, Fisher believes it is precisely that fear of losing your love forever that makes dopamine production adaptive. The same surplus of dopamine that makes you run away from the threat of a tiger makes you reluctant to give up the pursuit of a lover. In both cases, the history of humanity has proven that primal brain function can be pretty effective in achieving its goals. While fear might not be the heart of love, from time to time fear can give love an emergency bypass, which is probably why the feeling of fear is as universal as the desire for love.

The question that seemed to baffle golf fans and analysts alike was, What changes when a golfer takes the lead over Tiger Woods? Barring any supernatural talents, he truly seemed unbeatable in certain situations. With Fisher's research in mind, it seems likely that the most significant change is a physiological one in the challenger's mind. The reward of winning is there, right from the beginning of a tournament. But for lesser known golfers like Zach Johnson or Nathan Green, that reward is not exactly expected until they take the lead. Even the most confident and seasoned golfers show the same trouble coping with Tiger on their tail at the end of a tournament. The crucial period of time appears to start when the golfer begins to truly believe—to expect—that he can claim victory. This is precisely when a golfer's mind starts playing "mine" games with his endowed victory. Despite what his heart desires and his mind expects, that victory cannot truly be claimed until after the eighteenth hole. In that little window of time between when he begins to expect victory and when he can obtain it, his brain's chemical cocktail gets spiked with another shot of dopamine. Suddenly victory is no longer something for the underdog to dream about but something that he feels has been endowed to him. And when the golfer recognizes it is his to lose, all too often that's right about the time when that golfer loses it and becomes a prime candidate for impulsive action.

That feeling of possibly losing their endowment is what creates the intense goal-directed behavior even in the most cautious people. In the more rough-and-tumble endurance sports, the dopamine boost can provide the necessary surge where athletes dig down deep inside themselves for the last set, or for those hard-fought yards needed in the waning moments of the game. Golf, however, is different. So, too, is business. When you are getting to the end of a round in golf, closing a big deal, or embarking on a new venture, that dopamine surge can be counterproductive. Whereas in a sport like football a surge of dopamine might add a helpful burst to the end of a run, in golf the burst does little more than throw off your swing and cause you to make bad decisions. In the mental game of business, those surges manifest in the form of impulsivity. More often than not, the clear-headed choices that put you in this favorable position to start with are also most likely to finish the job for you.

But there are differences in the way risk managers can use that excess dopamine. While risk managers are less likely to be impulsive than potential seekers, certain conditions can clearly cause them to mimic their potential-seeking opposites. So, in these moments, risk managers can benefit by applying the same principle of directional correctness that guides their impulsive counterparts. The effectiveness of goal-directed behavior depends in large part on where exactly that behavior is directed. If your impulses are unguided, then they are likely to lead you to acts of desperation and irrational overprotectiveness.

## 2. Focus on Targets

A few years ago a sports psychologist at Arizona State University named Debbie Crews[4] gathered a group of amateur golfers to conduct a little experiment. Crews asked each golfer to hit twenty average-length putts. Then she asked them to hit another twenty putts, only the second time she told the golfers their strokes would be filmed by *Dateline*. Then she upped the ante even more for the final twenty shots. In the third round, she told them they would win $300 if, on the final twenty shots, they did the same as, or better than, they did in earlier rounds. If they failed, they would have to pay $100. In effect, Crews simulated the kind of situation in which a golfer is in the lead and needs only to maintain that level of performance in order to win.

Throughout the study, Crews monitored the golfers' stress levels. All of the golfers' heart rates, brain activity, and self-reported anxiety jumped significantly as the stakes rose in the second and again in the third rounds. However, half the golfers were still able to match or beat their earlier performances while the other half choked. According to Crews, "It's not the level of anxiety that determines performance, but how the brain processes the increase in activity. The successful golfers had comparable increases in brain activity, but that activity was spread evenly throughout both sides of the brain." The winners were the ones who were able to exercise the entirety of their mental muscle. They paid attention to the target they wanted to hit (that is, the hole) and then let their skill and prior preparation take care of the rest.

It appears that what allowed Zach Johnson to overcome his fear was not a lack of anxiety. Rather it was his sharp focus that increased his attention on nothing but the shot in front of him. When asked how he dealt with the pressure of leading Tiger Woods, Johnson replied, "Nothing changes from week-to-week. It could be a Thursday at a random tournament; it could be a Sunday obviously at Augusta. I say the same things to myself, just how to approach each shot, how to approach each hole." As Johnson played, his focus was never on Woods, nor on the final outcome of the tournament. Although remaining aware of the surroundings and changes in the landscape is essential for success, certain elements matter more than others. How Woods—or any other golfer that day—was performing did not have any bearing on the lay of the ground, the wind speed, or Johnson's skill as a golfer. Focusing on what Woods was doing would have served no purpose other than to trigger conditional impulsivity. This goal-directed behavior applied by Johnson is more than just what sports psychologists call being "in the zone." While the competitive nirvana of the zone also manifests a lack of focus on anything other than the effort at hand, Johnson's goal-directed behavior is something a little different, as it is strongly tied to events that came well before and *might come well after* each moment.

Elements of the zone were probably at work during Johnson's performance at Augusta. However, his relentless focus on targets is really much more fundamental (and applicable for the rest of us) than the somewhat magical concept of the zone. It is more about adequate preparation and then discipline in the moment. The zone is undoubtedly a fantastic place to be, but the zone is also just a short vacation. A star like Michael Jordan is famous for his memorable trips to the zone, but his impact on his team (and history) had much more to do with his consistently high-quality performance than with those few extraordinary performances when it seemed that he couldn't miss. Great teams like the 2004 U.S. women's soccer team, or the 2007 New England Patriots, are not great because they figured out how to stay in the zone. Their greatness results from the combination of talent and discipline. Even on down days, their focus seems to be unwavering. How to get in the zone and stay there remains largely a mystery. It is a place that even the most accomplished competitors drift in and out of rather haphazardly, which makes trying to find your way into the zone a terrifically unstable strategy for decision making. What we are really talking about here is much more basic. It is about training your brain to stay focused over the short and long terms rather than trying to attain some exalted state of consciousness.

Zach Johnson's performance on the longest holes at Augusta demonstrates his focus. When a golfer faces a par 5 hole, he has to make a decision. He can shoot to place the ball near the hole in two shots or three. Tiger Woods is known for having one of the more powerful drives in golf, which means that on any given hole he stands a better chance than most golfers of getting to the green in fewer strokes. The danger in going for two shots instead of three is that you might be sacrificing accuracy for distance. In 2007 Johnson's driving distance was ranked right around 150th out of PGA golfers, but his accuracy was in the top 10. The smart move for Johnson was usually the three-shot approach. But when the pressure is on and the anxiety of possibly falling behind kicks in, people don't always make the smart choice. They sometimes shoot for that pie-in-the-sky goal of staying on par with the group, even if the group is leading them toward personal disaster. What Johnson realized that eludes many of us in tense situations is that his best chance of staying on par (or a few strokes better than par, in this case) was to remain true to his own game.

Johnson played golf at the Masters Tournament in much the same way that David Dreman invests. Both operate on their own proven strategy of measured gains, disregarding the hype created by what everyone else is doing. Late in the round, when the crowd's roar from a few holes back tipped Johnson off that Woods had just done something spectacular, Johnson's caddie let him know the score. But Johnson was simply too focused on his own targets to pay Woods much attention. Keep in mind that the group is not always wrong. Occasionally your target is the same as everyone else's. After reading about tulip-mania, investment bubbles, and dinner-check sharing, it is tempting to conclude that avoiding conditional impulsivity is the same thing as avoiding conformity. Merely resisting conformity, however, can undermine the underlying strength of calculation. Sometimes the reason that everyone else is doing something is because it is clearly the best way to do it. Nonconformity for the sake of being different misses the point. Whether or not other people are making the decision that you are is usually irrelevant—maybe they are, and maybe they aren't. The risk manager's goal should be to determine the best target for his or her own specific needs, regardless of whether other people are aiming for the same target, and then sticking to it.

What makes focusing on your targets difficult is that when risk managers become too conscious of a threat, the natural inclination is to run away from it. We know from our capuchin cousins and our own voting behavior that the average person's tendency is to protect himself or herself from bad outcomes. But avoiding a bad target is not the same as focusing on a good one. Part of this has to do with the lack of specificity that comes from the act of avoidance. For example, when a potential predator is hot on your tracks, you focus on being anywhere but here. "Anywhere" is an awfully vague destination. When you place your focus on who you *don't* want to vote for, which shot you *don't* want to hit, or what you *don't* want to happen to your business, you fail to see the target that you *do* want. The "anywhere but here" strategy might be effective in the jungle, but is not up to par on the golf course or in the voting booth. Based on her work with golfers, Debbie Crews explains that when they face a long shot, rather than telling themselves, "I want to keep it out of the water," they should instead be thinking, "I want to hit a fade that starts in the left rough and cuts to that brown spot in the middle of the fairway." In other words, don't worry so much about the goal of what you don't want, and get specific about the one you do. The same practice applies for decisions off the course. To really get where you want to go, your target destination needs to be specific as to where exactly "here" is, instead of where "there" is not. This strategy is still more fundamental than the much talked about power of visualization or about "the secret" of tapping into the forces of the universe to get what you want. Focusing on targets doesn't require meditation or heightened consciousness. It just requires a plain old conscious effort to direct your impulses.

If you're beginning to think that all of this direction sounds awfully similar to the principle of directional correctness applied to potential seekers, you are right. That's because impulsive behavior is impulsive behavior regardless of whether the decision maker has a potential-seeking or risk-managing tendency. While it is true that potential seekers tend to behave impulsively more frequently than do risk managers, we know that certain conditions turn cautious individuals impulsive. Under those select conditions in which risk managers are apt to behave impulsively, the same rules of directional correctness apply. When their brains flood with dopamine, trying to remain focused on the correct direction or preset target is the best way to ensure it is the functional kind of impulsivity that overpowers the dysfunctional.

Similar to the way potential seekers cannot just eliminate impulsive behavior without replacing the reward, risk managers will find it exceedingly difficult to simply *not* focus on possible threats. Completely clearing your mind is a virtual impossibility for all but a few highly practiced Zen monks. Your mind is always busy thinking about something, and for risk-managing people, that something often defaults to possible threats. When the emotion of fear creeps in, you have to recognize it and then manage it by redirecting your sharp focus on the proper target or goal. Otherwise, thoughts of creeping predators start to take hold of your senses. Wrap your thoughts tightly around something productive—preferably something like your original game plan.

## 3. Making Effective Decisions Quickly

One respectful colleague commented about corporate executive Jim P. that he has a "large body of knowledge . . . which he uses to make effective decisions quickly." This statement adequately sums up what the risk-managing decision maker should strive for. The ability to arrive at and execute a decision quickly separates the indecisively cautious from the effectively risk-managing decision maker. There are three critical elements worth noting in that comment about Jim. First and foremost, his decisions are effective. Second, cautious decision makers can overlook the fact that effectiveness depends a lot on timing. A fantastic decision made too late can be rendered as ineffective as an inaccurate decision made on time.

And last, Jim's knowledge of his field plays a critical role in the execution of decisions. Experience counts because it provides a solid baseline of information while providing necessary confidence. Experience can be measured by time spent on the job, but more important, it should be measured by situation-specific experience. Days before the Masters began, Zach Johnson and his psychologist spent hours at Augusta practicing situational shots on or around the greens. When faced with similar shots in the actual tournament, Johnson could more easily recall (and therefore focus on) the desired targets. He had experience to draw from in that particular situation, which probably helped to keep his mind focused and confident. This confidence that comes from experience acts like ear plugs that block out the crowd's roar as your competitor gains on you. A consistent trend we see at TalentSmart is that risk managers are being held back by not having "the ability to make hard decisions"—or, more precisely, the inability to make a decision, period. We've heard time and again that risk managers need to "become more confident." This telling comment uncovers the heart of indecision. He is "always reluctant to make a stand. He frequently refers questions to others in the group, sidestepping the possibility of being accountable for the eventual outcome." Above all else, indecision equals a fear of making the wrong decision. It is the kind of ineffective strategy that focuses on arriving anywhere but at the wrong choice instead of arriving at the right choice. If your test results showed that you are a risk manager, perhaps you can remember times when you were gripped by this kind of indecision.

One way to hide from making a decision is to use both overanalysis as well as the ruse of gathering input from others when neither is really necessary. Where potential seekers often have the exact opposite problem—they fail to involve people enough—risk managers have a tendency to gather too much irrelevant input. It is not that gathering information or opinions is wrong. You have to ask yourself whether you are doing this for the sake of data collection, or whether you are attempting to avoid accountability and running from the inevitable decision.

Becoming more decisive is a matter of practice and discipline. There is no secret formula or quick trick that can compensate for good old-fashioned experience. However, there are some things you can do to gain experience faster.

## 4. Learning Decisiveness through Failure

In the late 1990s I joined a mail-order movie club, ignoring warnings from friends that VHS tapes were headed down the path of their audio counterparts, the cassette tape. I already owned a VCR and really didn't want to try one of those newfangled DVD players. The reward for my unwillingness to change is a dusty pile of plastic relics in the corner of my basement that remind me never again to ignore Moore's Law. In 1965 Gordon Moore spotted a trend in computer hardware. He noted that about every two years the number of transistors (the tiny little devices that power your computer) that could be placed on an integrated circuit board doubled. In the last few decades Moore's Law has been popularized well beyond semiconductors and even technology. Moore's Law is a rallying cry for the Information Age, warning modern citizens that accepting change is essential not just for thriving but for surviving.

Nobody understands this ever-evolving landscape better than marketing guru and high-tech entrepreneur Seth Godin.[5] Called the "Ultimate Entrepreneur for the Information Age" by *BusinessWeek*, Godin knows a lot about what it takes to succeed in fast-paced environments. When I spoke to Godin, he explained that not all of the best and brightest people are cut out for blazing new paths. In situations that demand decisive moves into the unknown, the more cautious might need a little bit of a jumpstart. Godin encourages decisive behavior in his cutting-edge companies by making failure an accepted part of the culture, practically writing it into the job description. He told me that in one of his start-ups, he went as far as bringing a group of employees into his office and telling them "bring me three failures by the end of the week or you're fired." This is Godin's version of tough love for more cautious employees. "Now, of course, safe is risky," he wrote to his loyal blog readership. In his opinion, for those people intent on avoiding fear, the "safest thing they can do, it turns out, is become a thrill seeker."

It's unlikely to think we can each reverse our natural tendencies. Nor should we spend too much energy becoming what we are not. I never did ask Godin if he actually fired anyone for *not* failing. But the point remains: Failure happens, so get used to the possibility and don't let it interfere with your decisions. The risk manager can learn something from Godin's challenge to go out and boldly face failure. Out of the three failures Godin challenged his employees to find, who knows how many, if any, panned out. The point is to prove to the cautious person that life continues after one failed decision or even after a string of failed decisions. The world won't stop turning after a failure, so you can't let that fear paralyze you.

Despite the risks it poses for investing when you shouldn't, or spending more on dinner than you wanted, conditional impulsivity brings to light the fact that a risk-taking decisive person exists inside everyone. Conditional impulsivity is dangerous if people exercise their decisiveness only in moments of desperation without a target in sight. Godin's ultimatum gave people the opportunity to practice decisiveness before it really counted. They gained the experience of decisiveness—experience they could again call on when faced with coming to a quick decision. Every failure actually instills a little more confidence.

Decision making is a habit. If you are indecisive buying groceries, you will probably be indecisive at work. Start small in your quest for decisiveness by forcing yourself to make inconsequential decisions within a time limit. Time constraints are probably the most effective tools for forcing decisiveness. Play around with it. For example, the next time you go out to eat, assign a time limit from when you open your menu until you order. You can even try the same thing at the grocery store. Then the next time you go back to the restaurant or the market, try to beat your last time. The goal is not to go darting through the store like you're playing a round of *Supermarket Sweep*, but rather to avoid the unnecessary hemming and hawing at every item on the shelves or on the menu.

Time constraints are a good way to force quick decisions, but they don't fully address the need for effective decisions. For that, you need targets. Take Debbie Crews's golf advice and get specific. It might seem counterintuitive, but leaving your options open with only a vague idea of what you want will likely waste more time than it saves. So before heading to the supermarket or the restaurant (or the negotiation or car dealership), have in mind the target you want to attain. Don't fall victim to even the smallest pulses of dopamine that threaten to drive you off your course.

This strategy helps foster decisiveness free of impulsivity. Targets and time limits are designed to maximize your inherent risk-managing style. They teach you to become confident in your preparation, without getting bogged down by over-analysis when finally faced with a decision, large or small.

## 5. Embracing the Unknown

The other advantage to this strategy is that by going directly for the specific item on your list, you won't even know that you're missing another. As Zach Johnson said, "I guess ignorance is bliss, sometimes." I am not advocating burying your head in the sand. But being too aware of every possibility is often more distracting than helpful when a decision needs to be reached. In the end, regardless of the amount of research you do, every decision is going to involve factors that are out of your control and beyond your knowledge. The key is to remember that the purpose of planning is not for the sake of planning, but to prepare you for action. Planning and research are useful only if they lead to decisions that are executed efficiently and in a timely manner.

Planning is a skill that reveals itself time and again as something that successful risk managers do well. Jim P. was said to be great at "finding resources and information for comparative data." Effective planning is about thinking ahead and planning for contingencies that prepare you for action. To most calculating decision makers, the planning part may come naturally. The key is making the leap from planning to execution. That requires confidence in your readiness for the unknown future.

Obtaining prior experience is a great way to gain decision-making confidence for similar situations in which you might find yourself in the future. But what about those situations for which there is no precedent? Presently, no industry seems to be beyond the reach of Moore's Law. That means that virtually every business today is facing the necessity of playing in innovative spaces that have yet to be born but that are exceedingly quick to mature. How can someone acquire decision-making experience in something that doesn't yet exist?

## 6. Inside-the-Box Learning

If all Americans were to close their eyes for a moment and imagine themselves driving through the nearest metropolitan area, they will likely conjure up at least one common image regardless of where they live. Somewhere along the ride, a section of the horizon will be blotted out by the contours of a building that bears a striking resemblance to a big box. Whether it's Wal-Mart, Target, Best Buy, Home Depot, or any number of other massive retail outlets, the big-box store is a ubiquitous part of our landscape. We have one man to thank for that and, contrary to what you might be thinking, it's not Sam Walton. Although Walton revolutionized the process by which the big-box outlets supply and distribute goods, through his obsessive attention to numbers, it was another fact-crazed thinker who was responsible for carving the first big box out of the national landscape.

In 1921 West Point graduate and retired general Robert E. Wood was the new vice president of merchandising at mail-order retailer Montgomery Ward. While coordinating the construction of the Panama Canal as an army officer, Wood had developed an intense fondness for the *Statistical Abstract of the United States*. After World War I, Wood picked up on an important shift in the numbers he found in the *Abstract*. He saw that agriculture was on the decline while automobile registrations were rising rapidly. At the same time, chain department stores like those belonging to James C. Penney were sprouting

up around the country. These clear trends led Wood to conclude that the American mail-order business was showing the
first signs that it had run its course.

But when Robert Wood presented the idea of the big-box
retail store (although Wood didn't use the term *big box*) to
his bosses at Montgomery Ward, they assigned the idea little
merit. Ward's new president, Theodore Merseles, was in the
midst of dealing with the economic crisis of 1921. That year's
finances saw an operating loss of $1 million for Montgomery
Ward. Fresh off of an outstanding eighteen-year run at the
National Cloak and Suit Company, which had grown from
a $1 million business to $50 million under his leadership,
Merseles seems to have viewed Wood's analysis as little more
than statistic-laden tarot card reading. Merseles was steadfast
in his conviction that the future of the mail-order catalog
giant would not be gambled away by his merchandising V.P.'s
guesswork on census data. Montgomery Ward would focus on
improving what it had done so successfully in the past, and
that would be that. After butting heads for the next three
years, Merseles ended up giving Wood the boot.

Undeterred in his faith in the numbers, Wood took his new
idea over to Chicago-based Montgomery Ward's hometown
competitor, Sears, Roebuck and Company. Although not
initially completely sold on Wood's radical suggestion, Sears
head Julius Rosenwald saw something in the plan that he was
willing to test. Rosenwald created a position for Wood, and
he immediately went to work on implementing his strategy.
In his first year, Wood opened eight Sears retail stores. Within
four years, Wood was promoted to president of Sears, and in
1933 Sears opened the first windowless department store on
Chicago's south side, thus giving birth to the first store resem-
bling a big box.

In the story of Sears's transformation from mail-order
house to big-box retail chain, the benefits and pitfalls of a

risk-managing tendency are clearly illustrated. Sears, too, felt the pinch of the economic downturn in the early 1920s, so management at both Sears and Montgomery Ward were looking to minimize their losses. Wood's idea was a radical one to those unfamiliar with the research behind the innovation. When Sears first opened its retail stores, it might have even looked like a desperate stroke of impulsivity. However, the regimented and methodical ex-military man, Wood, was not prone to act on impulse or gut instinct. Unlike other notable business titans, such as former General Electric CEO Jack Welch who says in his aptly titled autobiography *Jack: Straight from the Gut* that many of his best ideas have come to him while in the shower (a contemporary variation of the original *Eureka!* moment in which Archimedes discovered the concept of buoyancy by hopping into the bathtub), Robert Wood's strategy derived straight from the numbers.

Unfortunately for Wood's ex-boss, Theodore Merseles, he dismissed the statistical evidence. He maintained business as usual at Montgomery Ward until he too departed from the ailing catalog merchandiser in 1927. In fairness to Merseles, however, Sears also failed to comprehend the root cause of their business's misfortunes in the early 1920s, at least until Wood entered the picture. According to former Sears vice president and Kellogg Business School professor James Worthy,[6] both companies "sought to deal with [their troubles] by trying to do better what they were already doing: opening new plants to be closer to customers, tightening operating procedures, stepping up advertising, and so on." The difference between Theodore Merseles and Julius Rosenwald is that when Wood showed up on Sears's doorstep with his compelling case, Rosenwald did not turn him away. He created a position for Wood that allowed Sears to experiment with retail stores. Although untested, Wood's plan was not plucked from the ether, nor was it the product of a starry-eyed dream born of an impulsive rebel. It was a plan founded on sound census data collected by impartial observers. Rosenwald didn't give Wood free reign to turn the company on its head, but he was supportive of Wood's efforts to carefully experiment with a new course.

Robert Wood's revolutionary retail strategy proves that a risk-managing, meticulous nature is perfectly capable of yielding innovation. His realization that the nation's shift toward centralized urban locations posed at once a threat to established mail-order enterprises, as well as an opportunity to the company that addressed it, is testimony to the risk manager's ability to adapt. Conversely, Theodore Merseles's refusal to acknowledge the statistical data and Wood's strategy in favor of maintaining the status quo is an example of how an unchecked risk-managing tendency can stifle innovation. Merseles opted to stick with past successes, but his cardinal mistake was not that he decided to stay the course. Rather, his mistake was that he refused to test other courses, even courses that were supported by solid data.

In the Information Age, the refusal to test alternative courses of action is the kiss of death. But there is an important distinction to be made between testing new courses and gambling on hunches—new ways of doing things need not run contrary to a risk-managing tendency. Most new ideas can be well tested and understood before they require any risky, let's-cross-the-Rubicon-now commitment. Many times the risk can be managed by containing the variables in a controlled setting while observing and measuring them.

## 7. Evidence-Based Management

In their 2006 *Harvard Business Review* article "Evidence-Based Management," Stanford professors Jeffrey Pfeffer and Robert Sutton[7] wrote that a "big barrier to using experiments to build management knowledge is that companies tend to adopt practices in an all-or-nothing way—either the CEO is behind the practice, so everyone does it or at least claims to, or it isn't tried at all." Theodore Merseles chose the latter. He opted not to get behind Wood's idea, and the retail outlets never had a chance. Pfeffer and Sutton found that many of today's managers fall into the same trap, with decisions too often driven by dogma or belief when concrete evidence is readily available. If managers would only take the time to carry out some experimentation they would be on their way to uncovering the right information.

Given the enthusiasm that Sears's chief Julius Rosenwald had for Wood, Sears could have easily landed on the *all* side of Pfeffer and Sutton's all-or-nothing warning. Fortunately for Sears, Rosenwald had bet on the right horse, but he did so in a tempered fashion.

The all-or-nothing approach is perhaps the greatest enemy of effective risk managing. The decision to go all-in is the one that leads to conditional impulsivity. It prompts people to overreact to risk by jumping on a burning bandwagon or buying their way into a speculative bubble. On the other hand, the nothing approach involves doing, well, *nothing*. It is about sitting at the bottom of a hill watching the approaching avalanche bear down and hoping that if you close your eyes it will all disappear when you open them. Effective risk managers identify the threat (urbanization, automobiles) and seek to find its core solution. They don't apply the anywhere but here strategy by turning tail and running, nor do they freeze and ignore the threat's existence.

After waiting so long for his strategy to be given a chance, it would have been easy for Robert Wood to approach the venture with reckless abandon. His idea had already languished for three years as he watched the demographics grow less and less favorable to the mail-order business. With the support of Sears's top executive, it isn't hard to imagine Wood setting up retail outlets in every Sears distribution plant as quickly as cash registers could be installed. But that's not the way that the data-driven general operated. Instead, Wood established a sound, closely monitored experiment to test his hypothesis. He created three different kinds of outlets that would allow Sears to evaluate different aspects of a retail business's viability.

Although his plan was carefully controlled and well thought out, Wood did not waste any time. Within two months of starting his position at Sears, Wood opened the first retail store on the ground level of the downtown Chicago mail-order plant. Through the next ten months, Sears opened four additional stores at existing mail-order plants, where they already had the people, the physical space, and the necessary inventory. Wood opened two more stores in detached locations in Chicago and opened a third store in the southern Indiana city of Evansville. Even though the new stores were opened quickly, Wood took great care in selecting those first eight sites. The first five were easy choices, but the three detached locations posed a larger risk. The offsite stores required more of a commitment in terms of resources since Sears did not already own the space or have the staff. They were more vulnerable to operational glitches since they were miles away from the fine-tuned systems at the distribution plants. The Evansville store presented still another challenge. In his book *Shaping an American Institution: Robert E. Wood and Sears, Roebuck*, James Worthy described how Wood selected Evansville "precisely to provide experience with operating a store far removed from the central buying organization and the protective proximity of the mail-order plant."

Wood resisted the temptation to open up as many stores as quickly as possible. According to Pfeffer and Sutton, this tactic can corrupt management's learning process in an experimental situation. In multisite organizations, such as convenience stores, retailers, restaurants, or manufacturing plants, management can gain valuable wisdom comparing new strategies to what Pfeffer and Sutton call "control locations." Creating a control is experimental research 101. Without it, adequate comparisons are extremely tough. Had Wood dotted the landscape with stores, he very well might have corrupted his analytical process. The relationship of stores to the existing mail-order business, local economies, and competitors are just a few of the factors that Wood needed to understand to gauge his plan's success or failure. For Sears, a legitimate classic control location was close to impossible because Sears retail stores did not yet exist. But Wood did the next best thing, which was to establish the five relatively low-risk stores at existing mail-order plants. If they began to fail, Sears stood to lose little. The facility and the people operating it would simply go back to doing what they did before—mail-order distribution. In this way, even an entirely novel process was given a control group. Still, if these stores succeeded, it wouldn't prove that Wood's strategy was effective. The stores outside of the plants are where the real learning happened. For Wood's big-box strategy to prove itself, the stores outside of the Chicago area needed to succeed. Only by measuring their gains against those of the Chicago locations could Sears evaluate his strategy's potential. As it turns out, it was one that saved Sears.

James Worthy wrote that "a salient characteristic of the Sears organization at this stage of internal evolution was an openness to learning in light of experience unhampered by too many preconceptions of how things 'ought' to be done. Wood himself did much to set this learning mode." Wood adopted—or perhaps was born with—what Pfeffer and Sutton call "the attitude of wisdom." He never forgot that he always had more to learn. A harbinger of the next generation's Sam Walton, Wood spent the majority of his time either inside of, or traveling to and from, the fledgling stores. He talked to employees, jotting notes and relaying what he learned back to the corporate headquarters in Chicago, where information was then disseminated throughout the company. Despite the learning process that Wood put into place, the self-analysis never ended under his reign as Sears chairman from 1939 to 1954. It took Sears ten years to learn how to operate a retail system effectively, during which time Wood recalled "we had a 100% record of mistakes."

Despite remaining keenly aware of his lack of knowledge in certain subjects, Wood never used his ignorance as a crutch for indecision. Nor did he cite any lack of available information as an excuse to act impulsively. He knew well that he was taking his company—even his industry—into uncharted waters. Chain stores already existed, but the diversity of their merchandise was limited compared to that of Sears and Montgomery Ward. Sears offered customers everything *including* the kitchen sink. What Wood and his executives did know was the socioeconomic status of their customers. Even though no company had done what Wood was doing at Sears, his venture into new territory did not keep him from acting decisively. It was this combination of the ongoing pursuit of information, experience, and decisive action that helped the organization create the controlled situation that would ultimately lead to its salvation.

But what about the *risk* in risk management? The concept of risk and its place in work and life are frequently misunderstood. Without fail, whenever a group takes the Impulse Factor test and the test reveals to some that they have a risk-managing tendency, a number of those people are dismayed with their categorization. They respond defensively: "I'm not always cautious, you know" or "sometimes I can be awfully risky." It's as if the evaluation of "risk manager" is some kind of insult, suggesting that the test taker was barely able to make it out the door that morning, afraid the sky might fall. That kind of reaction truly is a shame. A distaste for exposure can be detrimental if it hinders appropriate action or triggers conditional impulsivity. But recognizing and efficiently managing risk is not a character flaw. Somewhere along the way the risky renegade became the only hero in town, and the implication to all the nonrenegades was that they were bound to a life of mediocrity. "Willingness to take risks" has become the gold standard by which leaders and entrepreneurs are commonly judged.

When we talk about the merits of risk taking, it is often in the context of our willingness to experiment. We want someone who isn't afraid to go against the grain and try something new without total certainty of the outcome. But risk is not a necessary component of that kind of experimentation. Innovative thinking can still occur without significant exposure to risk. To echo Seth Godin's comment, the real risk is *not* seeking out new methods and strategies because you are too averse to adaptation—or too afraid to fail. In a rapidly changing world, risk managers cannot afford to back themselves into a self-fashioned security trap by sitting still.

In short, proper risk managing is not the same as complacency or stagnation. Conversely, a change maker or innovator is not always required to be a risk taker. Robert Wood was far more of a risk *manager* than he was a risk *taker.* Sure, he led the charge into the new world of retailing empires, but he closely managed the risks every step of the way—the biggest risk of all being the risk of maintaining status quo at the troubled catalog merchandiser. As Pfeffer and Sutton put it, people like Robert Wood "aren't frozen into inaction by ignorance; rather they act on the best of their knowledge while questioning what they know."

So how can a person effectively manage risk instead of indecisively, or irrationally, avoid risk?

## 8. Think, Analyze, and React

One highly effective risk manager at a midsize law firm shared that his decision-making technique begins with "honing in on what's important." Carl D. credits his legal training for his now second-nature strategy. "In law school, you're trained to think, analyze, and react" in a limited amount of time. Thanks to ongoing practice, he's able to do this efficiently in most situations. In instances like these, thinking and analyzing are not one and the same. The first step, "think," pertains to identifying the factors that are most critical—honing in on what's important. In TalentSmart's work with clients, we refer to these situational variables as "key factors" and "distracters." Only after you've determined what you should (key factors) and should not (distracters) pay attention to, is it time to begin the analysis. If you were to dig right into your analysis by scrutinizing any and all factors in a given situation, you would run the risk of paralysis. If you take the time to sort through key factors before beginning, your analysis will more likely lead to "effective decisions quickly."

"Think, analyze, and react" is also used by successful golfers. In deciding which club to use, golfers like our friend Zach Johnson hone in on key factors like wind speed and distance, while ignoring distracters such as what the crouching Tiger Woods might be doing elsewhere on the course. Once your mind is focused on the key factors, you can get to work on analysis. *How strong is the wind blowing? How far away am I? Is the hole at the bottom of a slope or near the top?* For business decisions such as pricing, the questions might be, *What is the market used to paying for our product? What are the relevant comparison products? What are the trends we're seeing in buying behavior?* The distracters might be, *What are the cool companies doing?*

Pfeffer and Sutton cite "casual benchmarking" as a notable

strategic distracter. In one example, they point out the failure of other businesses to mimic General Electric's infamous employee evaluation system. At GE, managers are compelled to categorize employees as A, B, or C performers. The system creates noticeable pay differences between people in the same position depending on their rating. Employees in the C group are usually given the choice to either shape up or ship out. GE has experienced enough success with the system that just like Dutch tulip speculators of yore, many other businesses have taken note of the bright green grass sprouting up in Croton-ville. They've implemented the system, or an adaptation of it, in their own organizations. Unfortunately, most imitators neglect to adequately research the program. They fail to discover that a key criterion for an "A" ranking in GE's system is what one does to make colleagues—not only oneself—better. Needless to say, cutthroat cultures that have adopted GE's system through casual benchmarking have met with moderate success at best. Pfeffer and Sutton believe that without a careful examination of the logic behind the system, GE's apples are the benchmarking company's oranges. Further, these companies should have sought evidence that the system was the cause of GE's success before trying to adopt it. What everyone else is doing is often a distracter if the practices are only accepted at face value.

When you find yourself making a choice about new territory, the difference between the key factors and the distracters may not be well known. In these situations, you can point to a third categorization of factors—the untested. But the absence of information cannot prevent the final step from being taken. When faced with the untested as a key factor in a decision, you might want to look for ways to structure the decision more as an experiment, as Wood did, than as an unalterable course of action. Think about what your "outs" might be if unknown factors begin to interfere with a final goal.

Unfortunately my research has revealed that novel situations in which the untested plays such a vital role can be the biggest challenge to the untrained risk manager. At TalentSmart we surveyed more than 600 people with the risk-managing tendency and asked them what conditions separate a good decision from a bad decision. "Time" and "knowledge" topped the list. People commonly responded that they make good decisions "when I have enough information, time, and experience." Conversely, they feel most uncomfortable making decisions when "I am not given time to think and go through [my] options." In many situations, enough time and knowledge are luxuries that might not be available. Dealing effectively with these limitations requires first accepting them and then being comfortable with the fact that you are going to make a decision anyway. And, yes, it might ultimately be the wrong one. With all but a few rare exceptions, however, making the wrong decision is okay. You need to remind yourself often that if you have paid due attention to the key factors, life will not end even if you make the wrong decision.

Perhaps this is where Robert Wood's military experience played a role in his time at Sears. For example, Marines have what they call the "seventy-percent solution." Marines are instructed that when they have completed seventy percent of the analysis and feel seventy percent sure of the right choice, they should act. Of course, this isn't precise, because one could never know for certain when seventy percent of the analysis has been conducted. But it is a good reminder that perfection is not the goal of decision making. Aiming for perfection is not only unnecessarily time-consuming, it's not the goal. Variables can never be removed entirely from a decision because they always include the uncertainties of the future. The objective is to improve your odds of getting the outcome you seek.

For a risk manager to feel comfortable with uncertainty and possible failure, there is no substitute for experience. This is where Seth Godin's challenge to "bring me three failures by the end of the week or you're fired" applies. Of course, failure is not what Godin wants. But by failing and realizing that life has barely skipped a beat, his people gain comfort with uncertainty. It allows them to experience (as opposed to just being paid lip service about) the truth that most significant innovations are bound to start with a "100% record of mistakes." Robert Wood excelled by making all of those mistakes in a controlled experimental environment. He and his fellow executives could learn from every mistake in their unblemished record of wrong decisions without bankrupting the company. Requiring failure with the goal of gained experience and learning is a great way to instill Pfeffer and Sutton's "attitude of wisdom." It allows people to recognize that incomplete knowledge and failure are ever-present, and action is the only way to address them. The cardinal sin of decision making is *not* making the wrong choice; it is allowing your *fear* of making the wrong choice to lead you into a security trap.

"Think, analyze, and react" can be an effective formula for both short- and long-term decisions. What changes between the near and future term is often the emphasis on which steps deserve the most attention. For example, Carl D. applies the same procedure to buying a car, planning a vacation, hiring or promoting employees, and determining how to spend the firm's marketing budget. For familiar short-term decisions, the first step will often be less important. As long as you apply thorough experimentation to your prior experiences, you should already be aware of the key factors. (One note of caution: Just because you've "always done it that way" doesn't mean that you've tested to make sure "that way" is the right way. In certain circumstances, all of us are guilty of habitually focusing on distracters.)

For example, Carl has a hiring process that he has experimented with over the years in order to identify his key factors.

When faced with a hiring decision, he is able to skip directly to analyzing and reacting. When it comes to making marketing decisions designed to attract new clients, Carl's firm continues using its proven techniques while simultaneously experimenting with new ones. Even though Carl has a high degree of confidence in these proven methods, he understands that what worked last year may not be as effective today or tomorrow. So his company approaches new avenues for marketing experimentally, not with an all-or-nothing approach. He says that "every couple of years, we try new ways of marketing" in the form of select print and online ads. They don't scrap the old techniques unless the new method proves it deserves more attention. In most cases, they end up discontinuing the new methods in favor of the tried and true. But it never prevents them from experimenting with how to reach potential customers, and it teaches them what does work about their existing methods. That knowledge helps them to identify the key factors when scouting for new marketing methods to experiment with again. This ensures that no experiment is ever really a failure. If the experiment is designed properly, there will always be valuable, inside-of-the-box learning taking place.

## 9. Managing Risk without Running from Opportunity

Improvement and innovation are among the positive forces that are high on our list of priorities. At any given moment, opportunity and potential will be a more cautious individual's primary focus. But for the cautious majority the top spot on the priority list is always reserved for one thing: security. Only when they feel that security is covered adequately will risk managers allow themselves to refocus their sights on gain. The possibility of thriving is just not worth it if it means they have to risk their chances of surviving. Survival is the most basic driving force in the natural world—a force to which all others trail in importance. The dominant tendency among the majority of people, to tune in to risk when making even the smallest choice, is likely rooted in our fundamental drive to survive. This inclination is not without good reason, either. As a testament to the importance of being risk attentive, Intel's innovative front man and cofounder Andy Grove titled his autobiography *Only the Paranoid Survive*. As you can imagine, Grove's motto refers to his belief in the necessity of an almost pathological obsession with threats. Grove's is a well-made point. A little paranoia can indeed be healthy so long as cautiousness is a catalyst for decisive and targeted action. However, managers today generally don't want for paranoia. Unchecked, it does nothing more than make you choke when you need to keep a clear head. Paranoia as fear will lead you backpedaling into a security trap. In the context of a risk-managing tendency, perhaps a more fitting (albeit less attention-grabbing) way to state Grove's thesis is that only those who respond appropriately to risks survive.

Decision makers with a risk-managing tendency are equipped with an innate cautiousness that can be healthy. To become truly effective decision makers, cautious individuals must take an active approach to managing risk. It is not by accident that we elected to label the less-impulsive tendency "risk *managing*" instead of something like "risk focused" or "risk averse." Those might have been adequate descriptors of the cautious individual's outlook, but risk managing is both a descriptor and a call to action. It is a reminder of what the cautious decision makers need to do in addition to what they already do. To maintain security and perhaps even prosper, it simply isn't enough to be aware of risks. You have to actively manage them.

The trick for risk managers is to apply effective risk-managing techniques without letting unmanaged fear cripple their decision making. If you are a risk manager, the goal is not to train yourself to ignore legitimate threats but rather to shift your attention away from distracting threats. For example, your long-term investment decisions should not depend on your neighbor's fly-by-night gains any more than your golf or business strategy should be abandoned because a competitor makes one or two good shots. Nor should you bury your head in the sand and deny that any risks are present. Pay attention to risks, but make sure they are the right risks and then manage them. The real danger for cautious decision makers is letting fear make your decisions for you.

The best way to manage an emotion like fear is to anticipate it and prepare for it. Zach Johnson's performance at the Masters illustrate how remaining focused on appropriate targets in the moment can prevent fear from distracting you. Targets are also beneficial for longer-term strategic decisions because in order to focus on targets, you first need to set them. The act of establishing targets requires you to anticipate what the future might have in store. It involves studying both the present conditions and future trends that will allow you to make predictions. For Johnson, it meant going to Augusta early to study the course and determine which holes and which scenarios might challenge him. For Robert Wood, it meant poring over the *Statistical Abstract of the United States* and studying the nation's changing demographic makeup in order to determine what challenges threatened catalog merchandisers. For investor David Dreman, it meant analyzing how investors' psychological responses contradicted some of the assumptions of the more popular paradigms in stock-market investing. But Johnson, Wood, and Dreman didn't stop after only identifying the threat—that is what cautious decision makers do. Responding to threats with disciplined action is what risk-managing decision makers do.

Effectively determining the appropriate targets requires more than thought experiments. The process of identifying targets in an unknown future often requires outside-the-box thinking to generate hypotheses and then follow-up with inside-the-box learning. Especially for the larger, longer-term decisions, we usually have some cushion of time that can be used to our advantage. How we choose to use that time is where the active risk-managing approach differs significantly from the standard cautious approach. Instead of using that extra cushion to fret and stew until the clock runs out and you are forced to make an all-or-nothing decision, the risk manager will quickly come up with a working hypothesis and set out to test it in the way Robert Wood tested his retail store hypothesis within two months of starting at Sears. Maybe your hypothesis will be right on the money, or maybe it will turn out to be off the mark. Who knows? What you can be sure of is that sitting around worrying about the decision won't provide any of the answers you're looking for. Being decisive about experimenting does not mean that you have to put all of your eggs into an untested basket in the way a potential seeker like Ruth Handler might have. It does involve a willingness to experiment with a couple of your eggs with the complete understanding that some of those eggs will break in the process. But if you put a few of those eggs into a few different baskets and keep them all *inside the walls of the box*, you can closely monitor how well each egg is incubating and learn why some are faring better than others. It is in the act of experimenting and, yes, frequently failing that the real learning happens.

Staying ahead of the curve even in the Information Age need not involve extensive risk, especially when you consider that taking no action is often the biggest risk of all. Nevertheless, if the experimentation process lasts for months or years, it is very possible that your predisposition toward caution and certainty might make wading through uncertainty for long stretches taxing on your mental and physical health. Defying the natural order of things can be seriously stressful. Not to fear, however, because nature has already done a marvelous job of providing a solution for you. And that solution might be sitting next to you right this very moment. Just as potential seekers can use the help of a risk-managing closer, risk managers can enlist the assistance of a potential-seeking starter to carry out the frontline activities of the experimentation process. The concluding chapter of *The Impulse Factor* illustrates how potential seekers and risk managers are the key ingredients to Mother Nature's recipe for successful survival and expansion of her species, as well as how successful organizations are using that recipe to foster innovation.

# CHAPTER NINE

# Striking a Balance

In the summer of 1859 Swiss entrepreneur Henry Dunant led his horse-drawn carriage through northern Italy on his way to make the acquaintance of the French Emperor Napoleon III. At thirty-four, Dunant had set his sights on the pursuit of riches in the timeless game of real estate development. His plan was to turn a large plot of dry land in North Africa into a suburban oasis, but he needed to obtain the land's water rights, which happened to belong to the emperor. Eager to take care of the matter as quickly as possible and move on with his development, Dunant planned a personal visit. Unfortunately the emperor was preoccupied helping his Italian allies drive Austrian invaders from their borders. Ambitious as he was, Dunant traveled east across the Alps' southern foothills to settle the issue directly with Napoleon at his command post.[1]

Dunant arrived at his destination on the eve of a more or less accidental meeting of the Austrian and Franco-Italian armies. Neither side had intended to attack the strength of its enemy's army. But when the morning sun appeared that day in late June it illuminated well over 200,000 soldiers suddenly facing each other. What Dunant witnessed in the coming hours and days not only drastically altered his own future, but the events also profoundly impacted the way humanity would handle such large-scale human loss and suffering. Before Dunant's eyes, death cast a long shadow over the grassy plane. Nine hours of fighting left more than 20,000 wounded men strewn across the blood-stained pasture. The heaps of tattered soldiers torn apart by bayonet and musket-fire were all that remained of the bloodiest battle in the Austro-Sardinian War.

Dunant was horrified that so many of the wounded survivors continued to litter the countryside long after the battle ended. Soldiers lay in anguish wherever they had fallen—left for dead as the limited number of medical professionals were too overwhelmed to handle care and transportation. Most of the wounded soldiers were meant to do what generations of fighters had done before them—lay still for hours or days listening to anguished cries until their last torturous breath escaped them. It was an image Dunant never forgot. His reaction was immediate and decisive. He quickly mobilized women at a nearby church in Castiglione to administer food and water to as many men as possible.

Upon returning to Geneva, Dunant devoted his attention to writing an account of the events he saw. In *Un Souvenir de Solferino* (*A Memory of Solferino*),[2] Dunant described both the day's horrors as well as the humanity displayed by soldiers after the battle. He concluded that it was not the viciousness of human nature that was responsible for the terrible aftermath, but simply the lack of organization on the part of the two armies. Toward the end of his graphic account, he asked the question: "Last of all—in an age when we hear so much of progress and civilization, is it not a matter of urgency, since unhappily we cannot always avoid wars, to press forward in a human and truly civilized spirit the attempt to prevent, or at least to alleviate, the horrors of war?"

Europe's heads of state answered Dunant's question with a resounding "yes." One year after *Un Souvenir* was published, Dunant organized an international conference that established the "Geneva Convention for the Amelioration of the Condition of the Wounded in Armies in the Field," known more commonly now as "the Geneva Convention." Shortly after, the International Red Cross and later the United Nations grew out of the same conference. Although neither of these organizations have an unblemished history of effectiveness, it is difficult to name an institution that has had more of a positive impact on humanity.

Ironically, despite his well-organized vision for tending to the wounded, Henry Dunant was not much of an organizer. It was a deficiency that did not go unnoticed by Dunant's contemporaries. Of the five men who joined together to form what would later become the International Committee, it was Dunant's closest peer (at least in age) Gustave Moynier who provided the clear yang to Dunant's yin. British writer and author of *Dunant's Dream*, Caroline Moorehead described Moynier as "cautious, shrewd and a superb organizer," in stark contrast to Dunant, who was "impetuous and imprudent." Their tendencies clashed immediately. In late October of 1863, Moynier suggested that the committee host a conference in Geneva where all of the crowned heads of Europe could send delegates to discuss the idea of an international volunteer corps of wartime nurses and doctors. Shortly before Dunant departed on a whirlwind tour of Europe in order to garner support for the event, he had a revelation that this volunteer corps should be made neutral. As Moorehead explains, the very next day "with characteristic impetuousness, Dunant wrote a supplement on neutrality to add to the International Committee's original proposals, and sent it off to everyone who had been invited to the October meeting in Geneva." In typical shoot-first-apologize-later fashion, he failed to consult the other committee members about his amendment. Dunant later felt a twinge of guilt for his impulsive amendment and asked Moynier and the committee's president, Henry Dufour, for their opinions about neutrality. Moynier bluntly told Dunant that he "was asking the impossible" from the militaristic European leaders. The much older and more even-tempered Dufour chose not to respond at all. Dunant's more cautious colleagues seemed to have felt that a neutrality stipulation posed a threat to the whole endeavor. But they were wrong. The heads of Europe whole-heartedly embraced Dunant's bold idea of neutrality.

In 1901 Henry Dunant received the first Nobel Peace Prize. Yet by that time Dunant was financially bankrupt and no longer had anything to do with the operations of the committee that he began thirty-eight years earlier. Dunant had failed to do his homework on his big plans for real estate riches in North Africa. He was so enthralled by the exotic land and the seemingly unlimited potential in Algiers that he seemed not to notice that all of the fertile plots of land next to the river had already been taken. Furthermore, he neglected to account for how long it would take to acquire the property. By the time Dunant entered the market, acquiring any land worth buying took an extraordinarily long time. Eventually the procurement process outlasted Dunant's limited capital. Right after the successful October convention, at which all of the foreign delegates signed on to support the International Committee's bold proposal, Dunant turned his attention back to his personal affairs. In an attempt to stay afloat, he started playing the Paris stock market and became a director of the failing Credit Genevois bank. Months after assuming his directorship role, the bank went under and the court ordered the directors to personally reconcile with the creditors. Dunant was not the only defaulting director, but according to Caroline Moorehead, Dunant took the cake for worst management of his own case—failing to attend significant meetings and poorly defending himself on the occasions that he did attend. He subsequently bore the public brunt for the bank's demise. The court ruled that Dunant had "knowingly swindled" his fellow investors. He left Geneva for good and lived in relative obscurity for his last forty-three years.

The impulsive Dunant gave birth to a revolution in humanitarianism, but without the other calculating committee members who continued to carry the torch, that movement seemed destined to languish in the obscurity of the zealous dreamer who imagined it.

## 1. Intermediate Strategies

Helen Fisher, our expert on the science of love, is putting her extensive academic research to practical use. A few years ago, representatives from the popular online dating site Match. com contacted her to glean some wisdom on what really constitutes lasting love. Fisher's scientific conclusion that love is "a chemical high" sparked such a reaction that a new affiliate site, Chemistry.com, was launched.[3] According to Fisher, the traditional approach to matchmaking focuses on finding common interests and personality traits. Fisher doesn't deny the approach's value, but she thinks it overlooks a key component of compatibility. She believes that successful dating begins with the premise that "we fall in love with someone who has a different chemical profile for dopamine, serotonin, estrogen and testosterone that complements our own." It seems that some similarity is important for trudging through first-date small talk, but balance creates true and lasting chemistry. Apparently, if opposites fail to attract initially, they should probably reconsider for the sake of their mutual long-term benefit.

So why is it that opposites work so well together?

If we step outside the human world for a moment, we can find a clue hiding in the behavior of insects. Peter Abrams,[4] an ecologist at the University of Toronto, has been infatuated with insects since he was six years old. Although in his professional career he strives to understand biology through mathematics, he frequently looks to his first love for assistance with research. In the early 1990s, Abrams discovered that red ants—the little pests that pack a potent sting—may have met their match. It turns out that a creature known as the scuttle fly likes to use fire ant corpses as a nest. This is why scuttle flies have the nasty nickname "ant-decapitating flies." Scuttle flies are heroes for people in the American Southwest, where fire ants have been a problem since the 1930s when fire ants managed to smuggle themselves over to the land of the free along with some Brazilian cargo. Since then they've proven to be virtually unstoppable. However, an entire colony of fire ants may completely stop gathering food in the presence of a lone scuttle fly.

But just like tenacious human explorers, fire ants don't quit without a fight. Abrams discovered that nature's long-term solution for ants to the trade-off between seeking and becoming food favors the development of "intermediate strategies." By employing these intermediate strategies, the successful ant colonies find a middle ground that's neither too explorative nor too cautious. It is the same way in which the Venezuelan capuchin monkeys strive to balance their need to eat with their equally pressing need *not* to be eaten. In some situations, Abrams has found that an ant colony's reaction to the presence of predators is so effective that their population actually grows. But in other situations the reaction is too extreme. Some insects can become so timid that they drive themselves to extinction as every successive generation focuses more and more on avoiding predators, and less and less on finding food.[5] In response, nature deals the successful species a set of intermediate traits that allow them to adequately compete for food without making them overly vulnerable to becoming another creature's dinner.

Over at the University of Utah, biologist and mathematician Fred Adler[6] believes that these strategies develop depending on both predators and same-species competitors. For instance, fire ants have to worry not only about scuttle flies but also about invading ants encroaching on resources. Looking at the world of business, the process is similar to the way music producers have to protect themselves from competing production companies, as well as free music download sites that threaten to devour both them and their competitors. Usually the native and invading insects converge on a shared strategy that allows them to coexist while adequately avoiding predators. They strike what Adler calls the "balance of terror." Through a mathematical formula, Adler concluded that the shared intermediate strategy causes species to "remain in balance in response to their terror of being eaten." The less terror from predatory free download sites, the bolder the competition between the rival producers, and vice versa.

However, in 2007, a group of researchers led by theoretical biologist Max Wolf[7] at the University of Groningen in the Netherlands made an intriguing discovery that offers yet a new perspective of the ongoing struggle between risk and caution in the animal kingdom. In a study that received widespread attention, Wolf and his team found that people might not actually have a monopoly on personality. Ants, apes, fish, birds, and sixty or so other species exhibit distinct and stable personality traits. These characteristics manifest themselves in relation to expectations for future survival. For instance, individuals that take more care and caution in their search for food tend to be less bold in confrontations with predators and less aggressive when competing with their own species. Thanks to a more thorough approach, these less aggressive individuals have acquired more high-quality food sources. This security tends to make them less willing to risk their future. So when a predator approaches, the thorough risk managers shy away from the threat because they have more to lose. In other words, their personality is somewhat reserved.

But other animals are less thorough in their food collection and that makes them react boldly to predators. This group ends up producing even more aggressive offspring in successive generations. Sure these go-getters may wind up dead (or "badly bent," like Ruth Handler) but they also might come away with the forbidden fruit that their neighbors (that is competitors) were too timid to approach. More important, since they have been less thorough in their resource collection, they have less to lose by dying. These guys who live and die by their boldness are the animal kingdom's answer to the ice road trucker, futures trader, street-corner crack dealer, and the occasional secretary of defense. Good luck convincing their offspring to be timid and cautious.

Max Wolf's team saw the same results when they pitted same-species individuals against each other in competition for resources. In this experiment they called the aggressive personalities "hawks" and the less aggressive personalities "doves," mimicking the designations assigned to warring humans. Due to their aggressive tactics, the hawks usually came away with a bigger payout when they squared off against doves. However, doves always managed to survive even when they walked away from the encounter with less food. In contrast, the hawks' aggressive behavior doesn't know when to quit. When a hawk butted heads with another hawk, they often battled to the death of one or both of them.

It appears that one of the ways in which a group might achieve the balance of terror is by each individual evolving adaptive intermediate traits. In this model, everyone strives to meet in the middle—the cautious individuals become bolder and the bold become more cautious. But Wolf and his colleagues offer an alternative route to achieving group harmony. Wolf's study revealed that two opposing tendencies based on two separate expectations for the future can, and often do, coexist within the same group. So when we put these tendencies together, we can create a collective balance for the whole group. As Peter Abrams explained to me in e-mail exchanges about his work, the advantage of one trait "depends on the frequency of both—being bold is more advantageous when no one else is bold." The individual members of the group are not actually evolving more similar traits, but at the group level they are still achieving balance. "While this results in an intermediate average 'boldness,' no individual actually uses this." The view from 10,000 feet makes it appear that the group has developed a successful intermediate strategy, even though no individual within that group employs an intermediate strategy.

Wolf and his team's research is a fitting representation of human decision makers. As we've explored, individuals differ in a meaningful way regarding how they approach decisions. We are unlikely to ever converge into one decision-making tendency—and a universal tendency might actually do our species harm. Over time both hawks and doves tend to survive, but each survives for different reasons. Hawks need to be bold and aggressive because of their less thorough approach to resource collection. Hawks can't afford not to go for the jugular when they encounter a chance to pick up necessary resources. Doves, on the other hand, risk destroying the advantage of their thorough approach by being too bold and aggressive for no good reason. Both styles have developed the traits that best complement their resource collection.

One of the primary reasons opposites attract in love might very well be so that future generations can acquire the more adaptive intermediate traits. But it is just as important for people to seek out their chemical opposite to most effectively balance potential seeking with risk management within their own lifetime. Even beyond the realm of mating, if your companion's, your best friend's, or your business partner's traits complement your own, then you might not have to wait for the next generation in order to benefit from that intermediate strategy. Any union can itself create that balance for those involved.

Nature appears to be doing its part by providing us with a healthy mix of seekers and calculators in the general population. The rest is up to us.

## 2. Balanced Selection

Remember our friend the novelty-seeking gene from Chapter 1? The novelty-seeking gene arrived on our doorstep only by tagging along with its successor, the older and more level-headed four-repeat variation. The seven-repeat mutation has made rapid strides and spread its seed over the last 50,000 years. However, the geneticists and psychologists at UC Irvine doubt that we are in the middle of a genetic coup in which the novelty-seeking gene will eventually overtake its predecessor. Instead, they believe that the novelty-seeking gene has expanded its reach through generations of a back-and-forth process known as "balanced selection."[8]

Balanced selection means that even though a particular trait may be helpful in some cases, it can be damaging when too many people have it. For example, if there are too many hawks, then the doves live on cautiously but happily while the hawks fight each other into extinction. In the case of dopamine-related genes, the more cautious and popular variation (four-repeat) is like the older sister, while the novelty-seeking gene is the antsy, runny-nosed younger sister (seven-repeat). Big sis is usually the more responsible and makes sure that the basics are taken care of. Mom, dad, and even big sis herself occasionally appreciate how little sis keeps things interesting with her inspired bursts of creative ideas and energy. But if all the kids in the family shared little sister's impulsive personality, society would likely end up chasing its collective tail. The bold moves that might have felt rejuvenating coming from little sis could turn into unrelenting chaos if everybody joined in.

The Irvine researchers say that "the evolutionary payoff for a particular kind of personality will depend on the existing distribution of personality types." In essence, if everybody were impulsive, then humans might have hiked out of Africa and continued trekking aimlessly for eternity. They may have regularly stumbled onto something good, but never sat still long enough to exploit it. Even if those impulsive seekers had planted the first seeds of agriculture, farming probably would not exist without the thorough risk managers, because it takes way too long to see the leafy return on a crop. If we all became seekers, the Pincher Creek avalanche might have produced eight deaths instead of two, cage fighting would become the national pastime, and the International Red Cross would have remained nothing but the fleeting thought of a dreamer.

Even advocates for quick movers in the Information Age like Seth Godin agree that balance is essential. As Godin told me, "My CFO doesn't need to be a thrill seeker. His job is to keep the IRS from auditing." Harvard Business School professor David Garvin and strategy consultant Lynne Levesque[9] preach a similar message to large corporations that seek to keep pace with market innovations. Large corporations have a reputation for being slow responders, which has become a significant hurdle for them in the rapidly changing Information Age. Similar to the thorough-collecting doves in Max Wolf's experiments, large corporations have acquired a lot of resources over the years, which has made them less bold and less aggressive. They simply have more to lose than a small upstart.

That usually equates to the corporation playing the cautious, protective role of the dove. The result has been a number of start-up entrepreneurs successfully invading markets that used to belong exclusively to large corporations. Smart corporations have taken note of this trend and attempted to counter.

Garvin and Levesque explain that most innovative new ventures within a corporation fail because they fail to take a balanced approach. Businesses either charge every manager with the task of creating bold new innovations, or they isolate innovative efforts in a peripheral division of the company that lacks commitment from the core business (another variation of Pfeffer and Suttons's all-or-nothing approach). Garvin and Levesque write that, to be successful, "corporate entrepreneurship" efforts require balance. It is a balance between bold trial-and-error experimentation and thorough calculation, as well as combining the experience of the past, with an innovative outlook on the future. One without the other rarely works.

## 3. Putting It to Work

In the fall of 1999, senior executives at IBM received an alarming wake-up call. Their chief executive officer, Louis V. Gerstner, Jr., caught wind that IBM had missed out on an opportunity in the lucrative biotech industry. Gerstner wasn't happy about it, and he didn't waste any time letting his top team know. Gerstner wanted to know why IBM so often seemed to be the late bloomer in emerging industries. Being an early supporter of emerging technologies has been increasingly vital for growth in the high-tech industry. However, for the biggest players like IBM, their enduring stronghold on the market seems to have gone hand in hand with a slow response to these opportunities.

But as times change, innovation isn't a requirement for just

Silicon Valley start-ups anymore. With the warp speed onset of globalization and the unprecedented speed of information transfer, innovation is no longer the way for cutting-edge businesses to get ahead. In fact it has become essential for virtually all businesses just hoping to keep up with the pack. As General Electric CEO Jeffrey Immelt was quoted in *Fortune*, saying, "Innovation is the 'central necessity' of modern business." Traditional corporate powerhouses are confronting the challenges of an empowered customer base that can access products and information from around the world with just a few key strokes.

According to a case study conducted by Garvin and Levesque, Louis Gerstner's message was necessary to galvanize IBM's executive leadership. The result was IBM's Emerging Business Opportunity management system. This task force, which is still in place, concluded that one of the primary hindrances to IBM's innovation was that the company's culture was geared to reward steady financial growth. That's not a bad goal for a publicly traded company, but it created an environment where nobody swung for the fences. Managers throughout the organization had too much to lose by striking out, so nobody dared bet their career on something like Ruth Handler's "Mickey Mouse" venture. Large corporations are the quintessential "thorough gatherers" of the business world. They have gained substantial resources of market share and revenue streams and they aren't willing to risk losing them. Instead of swinging for the fences, they hold back and try to find the shallow outfield gaps that can give them a safe base hit. Despite the noise about encouraging failure and risk taking, IBM's task force found that its culture operated in stark contrast to the lip service paid to trying and failing. Gerstner was determined to change all that.

Garvin and Levesque concluded that a key step to promote a corporation's successful entrepreneurial activities is to get specific players onboard. They call these individuals "mature turks." A mature turk is that special breed of maverick manager who has built a solid corporate career while showing a penchant for bucking the system when necessary. But "turks" also know their limits. They aren't just unfettered cowboys. They are veteran leaders with a proven track record of challenging the conventions of the larger structure and succeeding— proving their ability to remain directionally correct. Turks are the people who are comfortable playing in an ambiguous market space, where it is not always possible to distinguish between the key factors and the distracters that risk managers use to make decisions. Turks are excited by the thrill of new opportunities, as opposed to being anxious about the dangers of the unknown. Though it may not have come as naturally for them as it did for Bill Gates, time and experience have taught mature turks the merits of binary thinking. They know that their impulses are fallible, because they have a full catalog of experienced failures to remind them, yet their failures don't change the fact that they are still very much in tune with where their impulses direct them.

## 4. Defining Boundaries

Marie O., a risk manager, runs a midsize, online business-to-business product supply company that launched in the mid-1990s. Her business partner and cofounder, Leon P., is an avowed potential seeker. When I interviewed Marie, she described the challenges and opportunities that their conflicting tendencies created for their business. Determining which (if any) new products to pursue occupies the majority of strategic debates at Marie and Leon's company, in much the same way that emerging business opportunities have become the hot topic inside large corporations. By their nature, new products offer the most potential and the most risk, so it isn't surprising that decisions regarding new products can be some of the most polarizing. Marie confesses that in the early days these types of decisions and their consequences put her partnership in jeopardy. Like most new businesses, Marie's lost far more money in the first couple of years than it made. As the debt continued to grow, so did Leon's spending on new product development and marketing. Since they opted not to pursue venture capital, they each had a very personal connection to the company's balance sheet.

Small hints and subtle reminders did little to curb Leon's spending. After his third project in a year went three times over the agreed-upon budget, the issue came to a head. On a long flight home after a client meeting, Marie told Leon she was shocked by his careless spending and that something would have to change if their partnership was to continue. It was a turning point for them. Marie told me, "If he would have just said 'sorry, but can we just work with it and move on' then our partnership would have imploded." Marie needed him to recognize that the situation was not acceptable and could not be easily dismissed. He had shot first, and now she needed him to be sorry enough to correct his direction. Leon confessed that he recognized his impulsive tendency and that it manifested itself elsewhere in his life. "He wanted me to know that he was aware of it and he was going to prove that he could manage it." He also identified a short-term cost-cutting plan that would help recover the losses. Leon's responsiveness was an important signal to Marie that his apology was not hollow. Leon is guided by the potential-seeking principle of shooting first and apologizing later, and his apologies are more than an empty exercise in pacification. As Marie puts it, "He does recognize his mistakes, and *actually tries to fix them*."

In hindsight, Marie admits that much of the money Leon had spent turned out be a good long-term investment, even though it made Marie very uncomfortable at the time. His marketing expenditures ended up scoring some valuable recognition in the marketplace for their burgeoning business, in spite of their failure to produce immediate returns. (As we'll see later, many companies are now finding that new ventures often need a little wider berth and an extended time frame to realize their potential.) If Leon had asked for consensus before shooting, there is a good chance that Marie's risk-managing tendency would have halted the spending before it began. What Marie felt was the "right amount" would have been very close to zero until some revenue started pouring in. Her concern was grounded in reality, but the catch is that, without spending, hardly anyone would have known about their business, and so there was no telling when revenue would have come in. The correct amount of spending probably sat somewhere in the nether region of more than what Marie was comfortable with, and less than what Leon wanted. Together they arrived at an intermediate strategy that neither would have likely found on their own.

It was a watershed moment for their company. That kind of self-awareness proved to Marie that Leon—although he probably would never change his potential-seeking ways—had the ability and the willingness to be directionally correct. For his part, the devout potential seeker Leon recognized that he would never be able to convert Marie to the way of impulsivity. It showed them both that their partnership still held potential. They embraced the fact that their business would forge ahead through a constant push-pull between protecting their assets and attacking new opportunities. This strategy is less about compromise than it is about balance. The point is not to dilute either tendency but to balance them. For example, if impulsive decisions were red and cautious decisions were blue, then compromise would suggest that every decision be a purple one. Balance, however, is about some decisions being blue and an equivalent amount being red. Now, if you made a mosaic using a year's worth of those red and blue decisions and then looked at your masterpiece from a distance, it would appear as though you had a very purple year when in fact you had a collection of red and blue choices that forged an aggregate intermediate strategy. In contrast, if you tried to make every decision purple, at the best you would eventually get out of balance as one style would inevitably be less willing to compromise and slowly gain influence. At the worst you would create crippling stalemates in which neither side budged. Essentially, the goal is to let the blues be the best blues they can be, and let the reds do likewise.

In Marie and Leon's case, the problem was a situation that was a long way from perfect harmony, but Marie recognized that as long as Leon was capable of questioning himself she could deal with some discomfort. That ability to question oneself is a critical difference between Garvin and Levesque's "mature turk" and an insubordinate renegade who refuses to adhere to guidelines. Years later, Marie says that she still gets frustrated from time to time. The company's leadership still disagrees on how to invest resources, but it has grown into a more comfortable balance.

Marie has become more open to Leon's new product ideas. She sees that her clients respond positively to these ideas even if they ultimately fail to produce a new revenue stream. "People like seeing what's new," she said. Perhaps more important, Marie has grown open to the possibility of failure. Whereas Marie still feels more comfortable with the pursuit of only those ventures with a well-known chance of succeeding, she now recognizes the value of taking leaps into the unknown. She knows that Leon "is going to pursue five failed opportunities for every one that works." The epiphany for Marie came when she realized that customers don't necessarily hold failures against them. "I thought the four that didn't work were going to be black marks on our record, and they just aren't. I thought that the failures would have bad consequences, and that's why you're supposed to avoid them." Without Leon's predilection for pushing boundaries, it is hard to know if the company would have become profitable so quickly. Without Marie's efforts to set boundaries, it is hard to know if the company would still exist.

Like all potential seekers, Leon needed guidance and direction. Garvin and Levesque wisely point out that "novelty for novelty's sake is seldom a source of competitive advantage." Letting brazen potential seekers run roughshod through the marketplace without direction is going to leave a company without productive innovation, and just plain old impulsive behavior. As former Home Depot CEO Robert Nardelli told Garvin and Levesque, "There's only a fine line between entrepreneurship and insubordination." What lies on either side of that fine line should be two clearly marked road signs. It is up to the top brass (or the partner in Marie and Leon's case) to determine which sign points in the direction of entrepreneurship and productive innovation, and which sign reads "Insurbordination—Next 3 Exits." A company's leadership needs to identify which direction is correct, but leave it to the potential seeker to make progress in that direction. Marie keeps an eye out for those of Leon's ideas that tend to be "tangential and unrelated" to the business. When she spots such an idea she will intervene and suggest Leon pursue it either outside of their business or not at all. Leon has taken both routes from time to time, and he has also pushed back and attempted to plead his case. Again, this could cause problems for their partnership if Leon were unwilling to check his impulses, or if Marie were forever attempting to derail Leon's actions. But over the years their push-pull relationship has built a certain degree of trust. Leon says that because Marie usually allows him freedom to explore new opportunities, when she does take a hard line on something, he forces himself to reconsider the potential risks accompanying an opportunity.

Most of the time, however, Marie is happy to let Leon take a chance. Marie is able to do this because she has set boundaries in advance. Instead of saying no, she simply limits the investment. "Whatever commitments we've made financially, he has to stick to them." Leon has a natural aversion to budgets because of the restrictions they place on his impulses, but he now accepts their importance.

Marie has also discovered that repetition works best when it comes to getting Leon to acknowledge consequences. Instead of making one forceful argument hoping to create a dramatic impact, she constantly reminds him of the risks. Repetition can come in the form of multiple in-person reminders, as well as pulling in reminders from external sources. For instance, she might have a face-to-face conversation, followed up by an e-mail of the current state of the budget, or she might get other key personnel to voice their opinions and reinforce her point. Conversely, if the budget isn't in real danger of being exceeded despite Marie's discomfort with the spending, and other key personnel don't have a contrary opinion, then Marie is forced to rethink whether there is significant risk that Leon needs to be reminded of. If she can't make a valid case, then she has to recognize that it might just be the primal corners of her mind crying "predator" when in fact no real threat exists. In this way the reminder process itself helps to maintain the balance.

The necessity to plant reminders speaks to Leon's tendency to become consumed with potential and to dismiss risk. One stern warning that "hammer-heading is out of the question" doesn't go far enough to stave off the impulsiveness that can cause any company an avalanche of fiscal woe. Multiple reminders, however, start to penetrate the potential seeker's consciousness. When he hears the same message from different sources or the same message repeated from a single trustworthy source, he begins to pay closer attention. This condition probably has a physiological component to it. For most people, one salient risk is enough to invoke a fear response to avoid danger. However, risks and consequences just don't make as potent an impact on someone like Leon that the potential dopamine rush of a new opportunity does. Leon's thirsty dopamine receptors have very little recollection of being satisfied by risk avoidance, so they encourage him to pursue the reward despite the risks. Since his sensitivity to the fear response is somewhat muted in comparison to his reward-seeking mechanism, the quality of a threat warning is lower. His muted sensitivity means that the threat *quantity* is going to be more important than threat *quality*. Instead of waiting for one supposedly powerful threat warning, Marie is more effective at getting Leon to acknowledge risks when she orchestrates a series of risk reminders for him.

## 5. Setting Targets

As we've learned, the impulsive potential seeker is focused largely on the immediate—making a decision about what seems best either right now or in the near future. Plotting a long-term strategy can be too farsighted to affect moment-to-moment behavior. The difference between the long and short term distinguishes a direction from a goal—at least a long-term goal, which is the kind with the most value to a person or an organization. Potential seekers are predisposed to live in the now without paying much attention to whatever might be around the corner and down the road. It is not that the long-term consequences are irrelevant; it is just that potential seekers are not wired to focus on them. Compelling cases for staying focused on where a company should be in five or ten years will be largely a wasted effort if there isn't a more immediate potential for reward. Even if the goal is personal paradise in the form of early retirement via stock options, and the potential seeker fully believes in the vision, the goal will still have little impact on the decisions made the very next day and every day thereafter. That kind of distant but powerful promise will not change the fact that the person's impulses are shortsighted. If the long-term strategy cannot translate into some kind of a gain in the here and now, it will be ineffective in guiding the small decisions necessary to execute long-term strategy.

Leon illustrates this mindset when he pursues opportunities that he sees as the "low-hanging fruit." Along with the tendency to pull the trigger quickly and set aside potential pitfalls, he is also distracted by the opportunities that can be seized upon quickly. The problem with this strategy is that low-hanging fruit can usually only be grabbed one at a time. There is no effort to build a structure over time, which might yield less satisfaction in the short run but an abundance of reward down the road. Aesop would have seen Leon as the cricket to Marie's ant. Marie isn't opposed to grabbing the low-hanging fruit, but she is farsighted enough to see that if they can just be patient they could have a tenfold payoff. Just like the animal behavior in Max Wolf's study, some members of the group are thorough food gatherers—patiently sniffing out the richest sources of food, while the "superficial" gatherers are plucking every piece of low-hanging fruit that meets their eye. Even worse, the pursuit of low-hanging fruit can have ethical as well as strategic implications. Is it better to perhaps bend the rules a little in the short term, in order to receive a greater return in the long run? The danger of going for the quick buck is that it can risk damaging a prosperous long-term relationship.

In addition to the potential ethical issues, the more

prevalent threat is that the emphasis on the low-hanging fruit can be a source of misdirection for the potential seeker. Maintaining directional correctness in daily decisions made by potential seekers requires action followed by reflection. As discussed in Chapter 7, the reflective process is best carried out with the assistance of other people—preferably those who naturally tend to be more careful. Let's look at the structure of IBM's Emerging Business Opportunity task force as the kind of framework a company should put in place to balance impulsive and cautious personalities. As they explored opportunities, IBM's team looked at short-term, preset targets at defined points throughout the change process. In those early stages the goal was simply to make forward progress as opposed to running in circles. The initial goal was not to become immediately profitable or even revenue generating—those goals would come later on down the road. So, the targets were essentially checkpoints to identify if and when management needed to pull the plug on a particular project. Targets are critical for keeping the rest of a company's leadership informed, but they also act as an excellent series of low-hanging fruits that hold the potential seeker's attention, while maintaining the pursuit of the longer term goal. Monthly targets create the necessary time pressure to keep the potential seeker's impulses from straying off course in a way that an annual, or even quarterly, goal cannot.

One of the stated purposes of IBM's targets was to get their Emerging Business Opportunity teams to acknowledge ahead of time that failure was a possible outcome. Recognizing this before they began—that the venture has preset milestones that must be met if the project is to continue—creates a system of binary thinking for any turks that might lean toward the potential-seeking end of the spectrum. A more ambiguous "let's try it for a few months and see how it works" type of a milestone fails to capture the very real possibility of failure and also fails to create the necessary time pressure to stay focused. As Marie and Leon learned, a target-free approach leaves too many directionally incorrect possibilities open to the impulsive thinker and too much open-ended time within which to pursue the wrong course of action.

These targets can very well be financial, but Garvin and Levesque recommend broadening the scope of targets to include nonfinancial measures, especially in the early phases. They reason that most financial measures are inadequate in the uncharted territory of an emerging business. Emerging businesses are often "opportunities" for the very reason that nobody else has already mastered them. Early financial expectations for a business are often little more than guesses. Judging only by financial indicators may put an unwarranted halt to a business that is starting to gain momentum.

Like any good target, nonfinancial milestones need to be clear and measurable even if the path to get there is not. For example, the golfer's longer term target is invariably the hole. In business, the overall target for an innovative venture is invariably revenue. But just because you didn't put the ball in the hole on your tee shot doesn't mean that it's going to be a wasted venture. If your ball is still in the middle of the fairway, you are in a good position for success. Similarly, even though your venture might not be generating new revenue right away, if you have met some of the nonfinancial targets you might not want to pull the plug just yet. Garvin and Levesque cite examples of nonfinancial targets such as, "we will receive three positive mentions in trade journals in the next two months," or "we will conduct five customer trials in these two industries in the next three months."

At some point in the future, you will eventually need to hit the hole. If your eighth shot on a par-3 hole lands in the middle of the fairway, you need to reevaluate your potential for success. Sooner or later the innovative venture needs to make money in order to sustain itself and realize its potential. It is at this point that the targets become financial.

## 6. The Role of the Risk Manager

Both financial and nonfinancial targets are a company's source of information to decide whether to continue with a venture or to pull the plug and conduct a postmortem. The monthly sessions that IBM held were not limited to task force members, thereby expanding the potential for risk managers and potential seekers to share in execution. Division heads and key people from the finance and research departments attended the meetings to make sure the directional focus was intact. These additional attendees provided objectivity as well as the kind of analysis necessary to dissect what was working and what was not. The process facilitated the kind of inside-the-box learning that Robert Wood applied in the first Sears retail stores.

Garvin and Levesque write that one of the central issues for IBM's Emerging Business Opportunity system was that "the teams needed help defining their strategic intent; they found it difficult to set boundaries around what they wanted to accomplish." This challenge should come as no surprise. For a company, large or small, considering a venture like IBM's to create essential opportunities, you'd target the mature turks, or potential seekers, to bend the system without breaking it. For decision makers with defining features like boundary blindness, impatience with long-term planning, and a primary focus on potential reward, setting limits will always be a challenge. Garvin and Levesque noted that "assumptions about market needs and the business's ability to deliver were often wildly optimistic." This isn't to say that turks are not the right people to lead teams like IBM's Emerging Business

Opportunity teams; its just that they needed guidance from their colleagues. Establishing boundaries serves a dual purpose of keeping potential-seeking managers directionally correct, as well as satisfying the need for data points. Along the way, managers should be required to provide the evidence that risk-managing executives rightly demand. Preset boundaries open the door for new opportunities while still allowing for inside-the-box learning.

These same principles for using risk managers to balance potential seekers apply to existing operations as much as they do to new ventures. Even if you consider your business to be one that has somehow been able to insulate itself from the rapid changes induced by globalization and the Information Age, you are still charged with the task of adapting and making decisions regarding an uncertain future. Your choice might involve deciding whether to keep more bread on hand at the sandwich shop you manage or to run a radio ad for the big event you have coming up. It might be which employees you should assign to which tasks on the shift you supervise. Or it might be deciding whether your corporation should dabble in biotech or stay the course in device manufacturing. In any case, the balance struck between risk management and potential seeking has proven to be one of nature's most successful strategies for group adaptation in general.

Risk managers are the necessary foil to potential seekers in business and life, especially when uncharted territories lie ahead. And the future of anything, by its very nature, will always involve some uncharted territory. Risk managers can structure the contours of an effort, within which potential seekers take their chances. This counterbalance between the two camps of impulsivity is an essential part of the connectivity we discussed earlier. One group without the other can steer the ship in the wrong direction: either aground, or adrift without opportunity-seeking wind in the sails.

One question you might be asking yourself is, *Can a risk manager assume the leadership of an innovative business?* The answer is yes. Robert Wood is one example. Despite her risk managing tendency, Marie is another. She made a significant personal investment into an unproven business. People with low impulse factor scores are very capable of innovation, and of exploring new territory. They will explore under the right conditions. Great new ideas don't always pose great new risks, and everyone enjoys novel experiences. In the earlier phases of TalentSmart's testing, we asked people to choose what they thought better described them: "I like sticking to what I know best" or "I like new experiences." It turned out that nearly eighty percent of all people "like new experiences." Out of those who had an otherwise risk-managing tendency, only one-third preferred to stick with what they know as opposed to testing new waters. In hindsight, these results elicited a "duh" from those of us conducting the test. Of course most people like novel experiences! Exploration is ingrained in our DNA. One hour spent with an insatiably curious child (which includes pretty much all children) is evidence that our attraction to novelty starts from day one. To a certain extent, we all have an inner novelty-seeker . . . just as long as that novel experience isn't too risky.

There is a marked difference between being curious and acting on one's curiosity despite the risks. When an element of danger is involved, the difference between impulsive and cautious individuals is once again firmly drawn. When we asked survey subjects about whether they like doing things that "I already know I enjoy" versus "trying new things, even if they might be dangerous," the answers fell back in line with the results we would expect. It seems that we all like novel experiences, but only a fraction of us still prefer to pursue novelty when it might pose a risk to our well being.

Risk managers are keenly aware of the dangers that might

accompany a novel experience. This awareness makes them more apprehensive than potential seekers when pursuing many novel opportunities. It might be possible to train risk managers to take more risks, and maybe even to make risk managers more comfortable with risk in general. But practically, you would have to ask yourself *why*? Why spend a significant amount of time and resources trying to reprogram people into something they are not, when what they are is perfectly healthy and valuable? Why try to defy people's biological composition through behavioral conditioning, when one out of four people naturally behaves in the way you might want them to in a given situation? Chances are that you already have the potential seekers that you need on board. So take your talented risk managers and partner them with potential seekers instead of trying to impose a new and conflicting personality trait on them.

## 7. The Final Act

The story of humanity's need to seek out new opportunities and to protect those it already has can be thought of like a classic three-act play. The first act devotes itself to laying the foundation for the inevitable conflict that will ensue in Act Two. Traditionally, Act Three sees the conflict resolved in some way, depending on the nature of the story. In a tragedy's third act the heroes fall shortly after they are filled with irony and despair after recognizing too little too late that they have made a mistake that has irreparably reversed their fortune. In a comedy, Meg Ryan and Tom Hanks meet and fall in love, then they drift apart, and then they fall back in love for all eternity . . . or at least until the credits start rolling.

Act One of humanity's impulsive drama kicked off with the introduction of a mutated dopamine gene around 50,000 years ago on the dry plains of Africa. The mutation led to the first steps of humanity's round-the-world road trip (minus the roads). Act Two looked promising at the outset. Our ancestors continued their wild ride across the planet. They began painting, playing music, farming, and crafting some nifty tools, increasingly picking up momentum as they went. Before the curtain fell on Act Two, humanity started moving at light speed just when Einstein discovered that the speed of light was all relative.

Enter the conflict. All of a sudden the gift that allowed our rapid progress and expansion began revealing its dangerous shortcomings. Unlike the nifty tools we had created earlier, the new tools turned out to be a bit more destructive and operated on a more massive scale than we would have preferred. Our children started losing their focus, and my VHS tapes became obsolete overnight. Without warning, our magic carpet appeared to be getting yanked out from under us.

Now, Act Three begins. We are all there on stage, and the spotlight shines down on our glistening brows, making it hard to see. We have no script, and we have not been told yet whether this is a tragedy or a comedy. It is entirely up to us to determine whether Act Three will go the way of *Oedipus Rex* or *You've Got Mail*. A captive audience filled with infinite future generations of our children, our neighbors, and our shareholders waits for us to point the way for the finale. Succumbing to stage fright is not an option. This is at once the challenge and the opportunity offered by *The Impulse Factor*: for each individual to take the first step on a courageous new path toward surviving and thriving.

# Afterword

## Putting Big Ideas to the Test

The Impulse Factor began as a question: *What causes human beings to make choices that seemingly betray their best interests in such a universally predictable manner?* The question began years ago as nothing more than a curious psychology student's fascination with some of the quirkier artifacts of human judgment. More than anything else, I got a kick out of my real-life observations of so many people—including myself from time to time—falling prey to these ingrained behaviors. But the question took on a life of its own after two of the most significant events of my generation. These were the rise of the Internet and its subsequent effect on the economy, and September 11 and its political aftermath. Perhaps it was the proximity in time of the bursting of the tech bubble in 2000 and the September 11 terrorist attacks the next year that turned my longtime fascination with impulsive behavior into a more serious study. Immediately following the question *Why do we do what we do?* came the more pragmatic *And what can we do about it?* I used to believe that one shouldn't raise a question like the first one without being prepared to answer a question like the second. After all, what good is it to understand impulsivity if you can't do anything with that understanding? But over time I came to understand the value of the process of discovery.

One thing that psychology proves time and again is that people's subjective understanding of why they do the things they do has limitations. But if I were to guess what drew me to TalentSmart, it has something to do with the company's emphasis on addressing the two questions *Why do people do what they do?* and *What can we do about improving the way people do those things?* TalentSmart is an organization founded on both the descriptive and the prescriptive elements of behavior. Already a world leader in applied emotional intelligence research and skill development before I arrived, TalentSmart was also leading the field in addressing a pervasive misunderstanding about human behavior. Specifically, it was addressing the misconception that emotional reactions are the exclusive result of weak or inferior minds. In his autobiography, Nobel laureate Daniel Kahneman, of whom I wrote earlier, illustrates this fallacy in an encounter he had with a prominent American philosopher. The two met at a party of mutual friends shortly after Kahneman began his work on some of the curious mental shortcuts people use when making decisions. He wrote, "Almost as soon as I began my story [the philosopher] turned away, saying, 'I am not really interested in the psychology of stupidity.'" Apparently the unnamed philosopher was not too keen on the psychology of humility, either.

In our quest to glorify the superiority of the human animal's capacity for reason, we sometimes lose sight of the fact that one [situation's] rational conclusion is another's irrational impulse. We have emotions and instincts that have done a remarkable job at making humans fit for survival. Simply because, every now and then, circumstances align to make our impulses betray our best interest doesn't mean that the people acting on those impulses are stupid or weak minded. Rather, they are simply human, sometimes for better and sometimes for worse. But neither does it mean that we are helpless to limit the potentially harmful effects of our impulsivity. It is the balance of impulse and caution that makes humans function efficiently. After the turn of the millennium, I believed that somewhere in that balance was the answer to my questions about how world events influenced business and society.

When I began TalentSmart's research on impulsivity, I sought to provide answers for our clients who wanted to get a better handle on the decisions made within their organizations. But throughout the process I began to see a curious overlap—the convergence of my personal questions with the answers we were finding in our applied research. I saw that our results at TalentSmart, designed to help our clients deal with the rapidly changing business environment, could also be applied to the way people drive, vote, conduct foreign relations, approach religion, and make investment decisions. Although these other lines of research would take TalentSmart into new territory, I was free and, in fact, encouraged to explore these broader aspects.

Shortly after my arrival at TalentSmart, our core leadership team was gathered around the conference room table engaged in fairly typical business conversation. Ostensibly it was strategic planning that at some point took a decidedly existential turn. We started asking questions about where our vision was taking us, and how the organization's direction aligned with the world's events. In today's business age, this sort of identity-defining discussion really has become rather standard. In fact, the very notion of redefining oneself or one's company—once deemed as visionary—has become something of a cliché (try Googling "change management" and see how many million hits you get). However, I also suspect that all management thinkers agree on this point precisely because it is such an obvious truth: Preparing for adaptation has become the safest bet in a world filled with people who love nothing more than a safe bet. Adaptation itself is nothing new. It has always been crucial to survival for individuals and organizations. But what is relatively new is that the cycle of adaptation has been compressed dramatically. We no longer have the luxury of time to get comfortable with our new surroundings.

It was against this backdrop that we debated TalentSmart's future. In particular, we wanted to make sure we fulfilled our mission to maximize the talent available to the organizations we worked with—whether this talent was already within the company's structure or ready to be brought in from the outside. Our discussion involved not just warm, but also some downright heated exchanges, which are actually encouraged at TalentSmart when we are constructively talking about a subject that elicits passion. At one point, I remember the president searching the tabletop for one of those James Bond buttons that might launch me into shark-infested waters. I think he was joking. Thankfully, for me, our technological sophistication is limited to the online world and does not include trap doors. Eventually we reached consensus that TalentSmart is the company that "puts big ideas to the test." More than just a slogan, putting big ideas to the test was our operating principle. It applies to our core offerings of psychological tests and training programs based on leading ideas in the field of human development and performance. The statement also captures TalentSmart's desire to both welcome and challenge the plethora of "big ideas" circulating in individual and organizational behavior.

Our goal is to identify the best of those big ideas and then test their validity and practicality. A big idea without both doesn't pass the test. We give all concepts their due attention, but until they can feasibly and meaningfully benefit people they remain beyond the scope of our company's offerings. Finding and sharing ideas that can maintain that delicate balance between empirical validity and real-world practicality is not only TalentSmart's niche but also our responsibility to our customers and newsletter subscribers.

The Impulse Factor is one big idea that we continue to test. There are few, if any, concepts in psychology that allow for an open and shut investigation into a behavior's origin and its full range of impact. Like all rules, psychology's were made to be broken, and we are constantly looking at new data that trump or contradict the old. The process of understanding is ongoing based on science, research, individual discovery, and the ever-shifting world in which we live. The field of decision making is no exception and, by extension, so too is the Impulse Factor. One of the reasons psychological principles are so prone to inconsistency is that they are applied to the most complex creatures—humans. How a person will behave in a given situation has an infinite number of variables that concern not only what the person does, says, or believes, but also what that person does, says, or believes while the decision is being made, and then again after the choice is made. When you throw in situational variables, the formula becomes exponentially more complex. My hope is that *The Impulse Factor* has made a significant contribution to the field of decision making, and that it might help to pave the way for more research aimed at creating a deeper understanding of the issues caused (and solved) by our impulsive tendencies.

Much of psychology's ongoing research will be bolstered by technological advances in science. Already the advances in brain scanning and imaging techniques—such as the functional MRI—have given behavioral research a significant boost. For the first time, psychologists are able to go a step beyond the theoretical and take a precise look at what happens inside the brain alongside a particular behavior. The behaviorist school of thought championed by such famous researchers as E. L. Thorndike, Ivan Pavlov, and B. F. Skinner dominated much of psychological research in the twentieth century largely because of our inability to peer inside the mind. Behaviorism's basic premise is that psychology should be studied on the basis of observable behaviors instead of the more traditional Freudian views that required digging into a person's "psyche." Behaviorism sees the human mind as a black box that can be understood only when we can identify everything that goes into the mind and then comes out of it. Rather than embark on what they believed to be the fool's errand of trying to identify all of those inputs and outputs, behaviorists chose to study only the resulting behaviors rather than how the mind directed those behaviors. Because of the success of behaviorism's pragmatic approach to psychology, many researchers and practitioners concluded that behaviorism was a more suitable scientific framework for improving psychological functioning.

Toward the turn of the millennium, sophisticated brain imaging techniques allowed researchers to peek inside the black box. Rather than discrediting behaviorism, however, the brain imaging seems to be providing more evidence about why many behaviorist developmental techniques are effective. Suddenly, researchers were able to match long-observed behaviors with specific regions of the brain. The ultimatum game you read about in Chapter 4, for example, has been a mainstay in behavioral research for decades. The reaction to reject or accept trades was well known by researchers, but there was no concrete explanation as to *why* people behaved that way. Not until Alan Sanfey's incorporation of the functional MRI were researchers able to see the regions in the brain that were activated in response to an unfair deal. Knowing that this region is an ancient one was a clue that this response is rooted more in primal instinct than in rational thought. That information reveals a lot about how we might address a departure from rational behavior. Logical arguments aimed at correcting that type of flawed reaction will be about as effective as kicking the tires on your car when it refuses to start, because the logical part of the brain isn't causing the problem. Using similar techniques, researchers came to understand the root of emotional intelligence—the way in which our brains give precedence to our feelings over our logic, unless trained to do otherwise. Based on this knowledge, applied research organizations like TalentSmart have been able not only to add a layer of depth to their study of the topic, but also to apply more effective prescriptions for improving one's mastery of emotions and behavior. But the potential of brain imaging to improve our understanding of behavior has a long way to go before it is fully realized. In the meantime, the next major advances in behavioral research are already on the horizon.

We have only just begun to scratch the surface of the exciting field of genetic research. It undoubtedly holds answers still unknown and critical to the human puzzle. Although immensely valuable for clueing us in to what is happening neurologically, the functional MRI stops short of telling us *why* a certain behavior happens. Exactly why a person's brain responds to a given situation remains a mystery unless we also have knowledge of that person's genetic code. Knowing the full genetic basis for a behavior is almost like a trip back in time to uncover the origin of that behavior (or at least a pattern of behavior). And if we can know how a person's DNA influences behavior, we have yet another piece of information that we can apply to a targeted development effort. For example, if we know that you have a genetic predisposition toward impulsivity, that helps us to further target any advice we offer you.

It is very likely that we have only begun to outline the complete genetic picture of the behaviors discussed in *The Impulse Factor*. Any single behavior or pattern of behavior results from a complex interaction of genes and environmental influences on the individual carrying those genes. Nevertheless, researchers have begun to uncover fascinating relationships between genes and behaviors, and those relationships can provide us with information that no other source can. So while we should be careful not to overstate a single gene's influence, some genes are certainly more influential than others. The gene corresponding to dopamine receptor D4 is quickly revealing itself as one of those influential genes for impulsivity.

In keeping with the spirit of putting big ideas to the test, TalentSmart has embarked on its own research project to investigate the genetic underpinnings of the Impulse Factor. Despite the unanswered questions, DRD4 has proven to be an exceedingly fruitful source of information. This gene's relationship to impulsive behaviors will most certainly provide our investigation into impulsivity with important data. If it is in fact only one of many parts of the puzzle of genetic impulsivity, we believe it is a corner piece. TalentSmart's research team has already started to examine the relationship of DRD4 to the impulsive tendencies present in the working population. In our pilot study, we collected and analyzed DNA samples from a group of experimental subjects composed of a cross-section of the population, in order to determine exactly which variation of DRD4 each subject possessed. We are now comparing the genetic results to scores on the Impulse Factor test to see what type of relationship exists. In doing so, we expect to shed more light on the ideas you have just read about. In the coming years, we will continue collecting genetic data and comparing them to our Impulse Factor test results, as well as stacking up the genetic data against a battery of outcome variables and demographic data.

The very notion of genetic testing has proven to be a lightning rod for emotional reactions in the people I've spoken with—some rooted in excitement, and some stemming from paranoia about what the data will be used for and how they will be stored. Much of the skepticism is soothed when we explain that the kind of DNA sample we collect from our research subjects becomes contaminated after just a few weeks or months if stored in a refrigeration unit. And

the results of our studies are stored with an anonymous coding system thereafter so that no connection can be made to
an individual's identity. Regardless of any of our individual
viewpoints—for or against genetic research—the one thing
that we can all be sure of is that the frequency and precision
of genetic testing is going to increase exponentially. DNA se-
quencing could quite possibly be the biggest "idea" available
to the study of human behavior. We have the choice to either
embrace or hide from it. While ethical considerations exist, we
have specifically designed our research methods in such a way
as to make those risks negligible.

Our study is an ambitious undertaking that brings us to
the edge of a new frontier in science, where the questions far
outnumber the answers. Although we remain duly respectful
of the doubters, and firmly renounce any misuse of genetic
testing, we believe the potential reward to be much greater
than the minimal risks. It is important to acknowledge that it
is largely the potential *misuse* of genetic testing that spawns
most of the naysaying. I suspect that some skepticism is based
on the philosophical debate that pits free will versus deter-
minism, in which case genetics appears to side with determin-
ism. A complete treatment of that long-standing debate goes
way beyond the scope of this closing note, but it deserves
brief mention here. Suffice it to say the existence of free will
is one of the most fundamental beliefs on which "free" nations
were founded. It is not surprising then that a practice such as
genetic testing, which seems to support a deterministic view,
meets with opposition. However, genetic testing is compat-
ible with free will in that genes are simply a *guide* to potential
behaviors, as opposed to an all-inclusive *determinant* of behavior. For example, supposing that some variation of the DRD4
gene creates a reduced sensitivity to dopamine, it can only
tell us that a person has a reduced sensitivity to dopamine.
What it cannot determine is how that person will go about

compensating for that reduced dopamine sensitivity. Maybe that individual will be a crazy driver, a compulsive gambler, a sex addict, a drug addict, or a deadbeat. Or maybe he will get his dopamine fix by burying himself in scientific endeavors and revolutionizing physics or architecture in the process. Or maybe she will push the boundaries of our thinking about the way people conduct business, or revolutionize how we as humans display compassion. To a large extent these paths will always be a matter of choice. Just as the launch pad can never fully determine the destination, neither can genetic testing ever eliminate free will.

For an organization whose stated goal and responsibility is to put big ideas to the test, we see no other idea that deserves our attention more. We anticipate our examination of DRD4 to be only the beginning of our search for more answers to the questions of why people do the things they do, so that we can develop more effective ways of doing those things.

—*Nick Tasler, Minneapolis, 2008*

# Acknowledgments

This book exists because of the efforts and minds of so many people. Some of the greatest of these minds belong to my colleagues at TalentSmart. I thank all of the Smarties for their overwhelming support of me both in word and deed during the months spent writing this book. In particular, I wish to acknowledge Jean Greaves and Travis Bradberry for fostering the spirit of discovery at TalentSmart, and for more acts of support, loyalty, and guidance than I could possibly mention here; Jean H. Riley for her unrivaled competence in just about everything; Lac D. Su for his creativity and unwavering encouragement; Lexi Herrera-Hernandez for bearing the burden of my absence with a smile; Yufan Chen for being the backbone of our infrastructure; Cecilia Ngan for helping to make the Impulse Factor test what it is. For being there when we need them the most, I want to thank Isabel Peraza, Kim Malloy, Lindsey Zan, Saakshi Arora, Andee Kunsa, and Deborah Braun.

This concept was brought to life thanks to the sharp mind and equally sharp wit of my agent Harvey Klinger; the uncanny ability of my editor at Touchstone Fireside, Zachary Schisgal, to pleasantly demand perfection; the patience of his like-mannered associate, Shawna Lietzke, with procrastination; and commitment of the entire team at Simon & Schuster.

Thanks to everyone who so graciously offered their time and mental energy to fine-tune the book's ideas: Tanya Maslach for her insights, honesty and sense of humor; Mike Kelly, Rob Peterson, and Tom Vollberg for being my unofficial lifelong editors; once again the Smarties for their brilliant feedback and expansive knowledge; Steve Keller, Tony Chen, and Cheng Li for guiding me through the ins and outs of genetics; of course, my family and friends for their support of me and their understanding of my mental absence for so many months.

On behalf of TalentSmart, thank you so much to the thousands of people who took part in our testing, and to those who took the time to comment on their decision-making habits and/or be interviewed for our research.

Lastly, no idea is born out of thin air. I am greatly indebted to all the brilliant researchers, past and present, whose findings helped shape the idea of the Impulse Factor.

# Appendix A
# Technical Manual for the Impulse Factor Test

By Nick Tasler, Lac D. Su, and Jean H. Riley

## What is the Impulse Factor test?

The Impulse Factor test is the culmination of TalentSmart's applied research from the last decade on decision making, impulse control, and individual differences. To create the test, we incorporated findings from our study of hundreds of thousands of people collected from in-person consulting and coaching sessions, group discussions, self-ratings, responses to opinion surveys, and ratings of one person by knowledgeable third parties in 360-degree feedback sessions. Together this variety of sources and methods of data collection provided TalentSmart with a comprehensive view of how and why people make the choices they do. Based on these data, we deciphered the fundamental differences and similarities between human decision makers. The fact that our discoveries helped to explain the findings of other researchers from fields as diverse as neuroscience, ecology, molecular biology, and clinical psychology made it clear that we were tapping into a basic truth about how each of us makes decisions. The Impulse Factor test is the result of that discovery.

During our research we also discovered that the distinction between a "good" and a "bad" decision is often an elusive designation determined by, literally, countless variables. Most often the quality of a decision is determined in hindsight by its outcome. For instance, if one investment decision yielded a higher return than another, we might conclude that the former higher-yielding choice was the better choice. But this sort of post-hoc reasoning can be dangerous in that it discounts the role of chance in determining the outcome. One decision may have appeared better simply because chance variables created a better outcome, rather than the outcome being caused by the quality (or lack thereof) of the decision process.

The outcome-only based evaluation also fails to consider how the choice impacted the decision maker's sense of well being throughout the process of arriving at the decision and while waiting for the situation's outcome to be known. For example, in the investment scenario, the higher-yielding investment may not be worth the emotional distress and worry resulting from the decision maker's choice to select a more volatile investment. For these reasons the Impulse Factor test takes into consideration both outcomes of decisions and the feelings and processes that resulted in the eventual decision.

The Impulse Factor test is a conceptual measure of both outcomes and processes involved in decision making.

## What theory is the test based on?

The test is based on the original theory of decision making presented in *The Impulse Factor*. Human decision makers can be meaningfully separated into the two main categories of risk managing and potential seeking. The theory is derived in large part from TalentSmart's proprietary research but also owes a debt of gratitude to the abundance of psychological research leading up to and supporting the theory's premises. Much of that research is presented in *The Impulse Factor*. Notable contributions come from Lola Lopes's Security-Potential/Aspiration (S-P/A) theory. In her complex and elegant theory, which is beyond the scope of this book, Lopes identifies two different types of decision makers that can be reasonably connected to the Impulse Factor designations of risk managing and potential seeking. Her theory was in some ways a direct rebuttal to Daniel Kahneman and Amos Tversky's controversial prospect theory, which made no distinction between the differing types and preferences of decision makers. Although the comparisons and contrasts between the two theories run far deeper than presented here, it is the views on opposing individual tendencies that relate most closely to the Impulse Factor theory. Lopes's S-P/A theory asserts that choices that might first appear to be irrational are often little more than a matter of personal preference. Nevertheless, it is Kahneman and Tversky's findings about the way people behave in conditions of loss that provide much of the basis for the theory of conditional impulsivity presented here. So both theories and their primary proponents played a role in the development of the Impulse Factor theory.

In addition, Marvin Zuckerman's four decades of research on the personality trait of sensation seeking has provided a rich source of usable material on the topic of individual differences regarding impulsive behavior. Zuckerman regards impulsivity as an element of sensation seeking connected to two of Hans Eysenck's personality dimensions of extraversion and psychotisism.

## What does the Impulse Factor test measure?

Impulsivity is the psychological dimension bearing the most prominence in the Impulse Factor theory. Although the test was designed to be a broader measure of overall decision-making tendency, impulsivity is the latent psychological trait most readily measured by the test. Impulsivity has a long history in psychological research. However, psychology's major focus on impulsivity research has been in the clinical context. Given clinical psychology's foundation in medicine, it should come as no surprise that most research focuses on what is *wrong* with impulsive behavior, or the "illness" of impulsive behavior and how those behaviors might be "healed," with very little attention paid to what is *right* with impulsive behavior. Impulsivity's connection to social ailments and functional deficiencies such as compulsive gambling, criminality, and drug addiction garners the most attention from psychological researchers.

Scott Dickman's work on functional and dysfunctional impulsivity in the 1990s is a notable exception to the trend of studying impulsivity as an illness. Dickman's work sought to distinguish between the two types of impulsive person. One slight distinction between the Impulse Factor theory and Dickman's theory is that one could infer from Dickman's research that some people seem to carry the functional trait of impulsivity, whereas others carry the dysfunctional trait. The Impulse Factor theory holds that there are individual differences with regard to the trait of impulsivity, but that among the impulsive subgroup the difference between functional and dysfunctional is matter of learned behaviors—which is to say that even those with more dysfunctional habits can be trained to exhibit more of the functional habits than the dysfunctional.

This line of thought is not to deny the import of the aforementioned ailments, as they truly are damaging symptoms that may stem from a highly impulsive personality. Nevertheless, there are many impulsive individuals who lead perfectly healthy lives. So the Impulse Factor theory and the corresponding research on impulsivity do not refute these past findings. Rather we have sought merely to expose the potential benefits of the trait of impulsivity.

## Is the Impulse Factor test a personality test?

The decision-making tendency measured by the Impulse Factor test is most likely a stable trait that could be considered an element of personality. However, we have no theoretical basis to believe that this tendency is a core dimension of any prominent personality theory. It is most likely a combination of personality traits interacting with one another in a significant way when people engage in the specific behavior of decision making. Indeed, many elements of an individual's personality are not intended to be measured by the Impulse Factor test. So even though your Impulse Factor may be a personality trait, it would be misleading to label the Impulse Factor test a "personality test," as it does not provide a comprehensive measurement of your personality.

Determining which personality traits most directly correspond to your Impulse Factor could prove useful in future research. But that determination, if it is made, is unlikely to significantly improve the overall effectiveness of the decisions you make, which is why it has not been a primary focus in TalentSmart's decision-making research.

## What is the purpose of the Impulse Factor test?

Clearly stated, the purpose of this test is to help you make better decisions. As TalentSmart is an applied human performance research firm, all of our tests are designed to improve the test takers' performance— personally and professionally. We create psychometrically valid assessments that meet all of the standards required to label a psychological assessment "accurate." With an accurate assessment of some relevant dimension of your skill and your traits, we are able to provide you with customized strategies for improving your performance. In regard to the Impulse Factor test, that means we accurately assess how you make choices, and how *well* you make choices. This knowledge makes individual test takers aware of the common strengths of their tendency, as well as the common frailties and biases that they need to guard against. This awareness—in conjunction with TalentSmart's learning methodology, which includes action steps and TalentSmart's proprietary goal-tracking system—is an effective method for enhancing the overall quality of your decision making.

In describing the test's purpose, it is also important to note what its purpose *is not*. The Impulse Factor test is *not* designed to be a clinical measure used in the diagnosis of psychological disorders. This is perhaps the most crucial distinction between our approach to studying impulsivity in general—and our measure of impulsivity, specifically—compared with the approaches of most other prominent researchers who study impulsivity.

## Why does the test use this format instead of others?

The underlying difference between our decision-making tendencies can be brought to the surface in how each of us responds to particular choice scenarios. For example, we all have cautious and impulsive tendencies to certain degrees. The difference between us lies in which tendency drives our actual choices when both tendencies are at work. Almost without exception, people will choose high odds over low odds if the payout is the same in both options. Similarly, all normally functioning people will choose a higher payout over a lower payout when the odds are the same. Choices like this are more a matter of common sense than they are a distinction in preference or symptomatic of a latent psychological dimension. So to ask people, "How much do you like choices with high odds?" by itself is not an especially valuable test question for our purpose, because it will fail to make a meaningful distinction between individuals. Moreover, in real life our choices are rarely that clear-cut. We are most often faced with the difficult and complex task of choosing between two options that offer equal degrees of benefits and drawbacks. We make decisions like this all the time in choosing our homes, choosing which schools to attend, which people we become involved with in relationships, which jobs we take, and so on.

Therefore, in order to uncover those fundamental differences between individual people, we must simulate these complex choice scenarios by asking test takers to choose between two options that could be equally desirable. But each option will be desirable for a different reason than the option it is paired with. This is what is traditionally referred to as a "forced-choice" format. Both options will likely be somewhat appealing to everyone, but we want to find out which is more appealing to the test taker when he or she is "forced" to make a choice between them. This is not a true forced-choice test in that we provide test takers with a neutral option that frees them of the otherwise forced obligation to choose one option in the pair.

We also wanted to know whether test takers agonized over which choice to select or whether one option was clearly the right choice for them. As with real decisions, even though two people may make the same choice, it is valuable to know whether one person made the choice more reluctantly than the other person. For that reason, we included an intensity scale that allows test takers to select not only which option describes them but also how strongly they feel that one option describes them more than the other option in the pair.

## Can people "fake" the test?

With any self-assessment, the question of "social desirability" arises. Social desirability means that people answer questions in a way that will position them in the most favorable light, as opposed to what they believe is a truly accurate response. In other words, it addresses whether people can fake good answers to the test. While socially desirable responses will play a role to varying degrees in every self-assessment, they are unlikely to play a significant role in the Impulse Factor test for two reasons.

The first reason is that the test's design makes socially desirable responses difficult. One strength of the forced-choice format is that people are presented with two "right" answers. This makes it very difficult for the motivated test taker to figure out which is the "better" answer.

The second reason is that the test's subject matter makes socially desirable responses somewhat pointless because there is no reason to believe that one tendency is more desirable than the other. If you believe that one response is more desirable than the other, that belief is probably a manifestation of your tendency, so by responding according to your belief of what is socially desirable, you will in effect be responding exactly the way the test was designed to measure your tendency. For example, if you think that "purple" is the most socially desirable response to the question *What is your favorite color?* there is a strong chance that purple is indeed your favorite color. By responding "purple," you have answered the question the way it was meant to be answered. During the process of creating the test, we received feedback from people saying that one option in the pair for a given question or another was "obvious." However, we often received the same comment about the same question from someone with the opposite view—believing that the other choice in the pair was the "obvious" selection. Essentially, potential seekers tended to believe that options offering high potential were the clear best choice, and risk managers believed that options that mitigated risks were the right answers. So, in that regard there are right answers, but which answer is right depends on who is answering, which is the point of the assessment.

## Is this test valid?

*Validity* is a blanket term that refers to a number of different statistical indicators of a test's quality. For a test to be considered valid, it must first be proven reliable. One of the most common types of reliability refers to what is called "internal consistency." Internal consistency addresses how well the questions in a test are related to one another. If one group of people tends to answer different questions in the same general pattern, then we can assume that the set of questions is tapping into some trait that these people have in common. For example, in a typical multiple-choice survey, if the same group of people who selected "a" for question 1 also selected "c" for question 2, but a different group selected "b" for question 1 and also selected "d" for question 2, then we can assume that those two questions are *consistent* with each other. If the same consistent patterns are found for all the questions on a test, then we can conclude that this test is internally consistent.

The internal consistency measurement of reliability is calculated using a statistical procedure that produces a number called a reliability coefficient. That number falls somewhere between 0.0 and +1.0, where 1.0 indicates perfect consistency. The closer the reliability coefficient is to 1.0, the more closely that test's items are related. The rule of thumb is that an acceptable coefficient is .70 or above. The scale scores on the Impulse Factor test have reliability coefficients ranging from .79 to .87.

### How do we know that the test is measuring my impulsivity and my decision-making effectiveness, and is not measuring other things?

This is an important question for assessing the quality of a test, so we give it special attention here. The question refers to another aspect of validity called "construct validity." Construct validity can be broken down into two categories. The first category is *convergent validity*, which measures how closely people's scores on the Impulse Factor test compare to the same people's scores on a different test measuring impulsivity (that is, do the test scores seem to *converge* on the same psychological dimension?). To use an example, you can be sure that your bathroom scale is reasonably accurate if your weight at home is similar to your weight on the scale at your doctor's office or your gym. Similarly, if many people's scores on two tests are correlated, we can conclude that both tests are measuring a similar construct. To measure the convergent validity of the Impulse Factor test, we compared the tendency scale scores on the Impulse Factor test to the functional impulsivity scale pulled from Scott J. Dickman's (1990) Impulsivity Inventory. There are many tests of impulsivity; however, as mentioned earlier, Dickman's scale is one of the only other measures to approach at least some facets of impulsivity from a positive perspective. For the Impulse Factor tendency scores, we found weak to moderate correlations with Dickman's functional impulsivity scale. Specifically, we found a significant correlation of .38 between the tendency score and Dickman's functional impulsivity scale.* The risk subscale on the Impulse Factor test correlated .42 with Dickman's functional impulsivity scale, and the hastiness subscale correlated .33 with the functional impulsivity scale. All of the comparisons were statistically significant. Based on these findings, we can reasonably conclude that the Impulse Factor tendency scale is at least measuring a construct that is very similar, though not identical to the concept that Dickman labeled "functional impulsivity."

Although statistically significant and practically meaningful, the correlations we found between the functional impulsivity scale and the Impulse Factor scales were not considered to be strong. The discrepancy is probably due in part to the differing formats of the tests.

---

*All correlations mentioned in this section are statistically significant (p < .05).

The forced-choice format applied by the Impulse Factor test provides test takers with two "right" answers for every test question, whereas Dickman's scale simply asks for the level of agreement on a single statement. For example, on a test item such as "people have admired me because I can think quickly" on Dickman's functional impulsivity scale, many people are likely to select "agree" or "strongly agree" because of the positive wording of the question. In contrast, when people are faced with two options on the Impulse Factor test, such as "I am at my best when I have to make quick decisions" and "I am at my best when I have time to think through my options," the responses will be much more distinct and variable. It is easy to see how two people could have selected different choices on the Impulse Factor test question, while selecting the same level of agreement on the functional impulsivity scale. A person could easily believe that he operates best when he has ample time to make a decision, while simultaneously remembering a time that he was admired by other people for making quick decisions when he needed to. The latter question doesn't address whether or not individuals make quick decisions by choice, or avoid those decisions whenever they can and act quickly only when they absolutely must do so. We can conclude from these results that, by design, the Impulse Factor test measures both functional impulsivity and a concept such as "functional cautiousness," whereas Dickman's scale measures only functional impulsivity. Thus we should expect only a moderate correlation between the two assessments, which is what we found.

The effectiveness subscale on the Impulse Factor test presented a greater challenge for convergent validity measures, primarily because we are not aware of another validated assessment of general decision-making effectiveness. Therefore, without a similar assessment we have no scores with which we can compare our effectiveness scores. To continue the bathroom scale analogy, it is as if we have only the bathroom scale and no other scale for comparison—not at the doctor's office, at the gym, or even at a neighbor's house. So we would seem to have nothing for our scale's measurement to "converge" with. In this case, we would have to rely on more creative methods of measuring the scale's convergent validity. One way might be to round up a group of people and record their weights on the bathroom scale, and then measure each of their heights and their waistlines. We could reasonably assume that if two people shared the same height, but one had a smaller waistline, then the one with the smaller waistline should be lighter on our bathroom scale. If we observed this trend with all of the people we weighed and measured, then we could assume that the scale is in fact measuring the dimension of weight, and it is doing it fairly consistently, although possibly not perfectly. What this method won't tell us is whether the scale is measuring everyone twenty pounds too heavy or too light. We only know that if it is in fact overweighing, it is doing so consistently, which still makes comparisons between people relevant.

Fortunately, the Impulse Factor test's effectiveness scale is normatively measured, which means that we are only concerned with measuring how individuals compare to one another and not now they compare to some intangible, objective standard. So we don't have to worry about whether our scale is twenty pounds too heavy or thirteen pounds too light, as long as it is twenty pounds too heavy or thirteen pounds too light for everyone (we can be sure of that because of the internal consistency we found, as described earlier). Whereas "0" on a bathroom scale should mean that the thing being weighed literally has no weight, "0" on the effectiveness scale is arbitrary—it means something relative only to other scores on the scale. If we were to tell you that your effectiveness score is "32" or "532," neither of those scores would mean anything to you unless you knew what a "normal" score was. By themselves, the numbers are arbitrary.

But we still have the issue of how to tell whether the scale is consistently measuring the concept of effectiveness. The effectiveness scale has a reliability of .81 so we know that it is reliably measuring *something*. The question is whether or not that *something* is what we are calling the construct of "decision-making effectiveness." We define decision-making effectiveness as how well people's decisions lead them to the outcomes they strive for in their personal and professional lives. If the effectiveness scale truly is measuring what we designed it to measure, then we should see at least some kind of a significant relationship between effectiveness scores and outcome variables pertaining to people's personal and professional lives. Similar to the way we can assume that in people of a similar height, a smaller waistline should correspond to a lower weight. (This type of measurement is also referred to as *concurrent validity*.) We found statistically significant correlations between the effectiveness scale and life satisfaction (.29), job satisfaction (.27), and job performance (.21). We would not expect these to be strong correlations, mainly because decision-making effectiveness taps into only one of many variables that play a role in determining things such as satisfaction and performance, and also because these outcome variables are highly subjective. Of course this is a less precise method than the comparison between two similar, validated scales, just as a bathroom scale's comparison to waistline will be less precise than a bathroom scale's comparison to the scale at a hospital. Nevertheless, this method does provide meaningful data in the absence of a superior alternative.

The other type of construct validity is *divergent validity*. Divergent validity looks for just the opposite result as convergent validity. This means that a scale seeking to measure one thing should not strongly correlate with a scale that measures something different. For instance, a thermometer (temperature measurement device) shouldn't correlate strongly with an anemometer (wind speed measurement device) because temperature is different from wind speed—wind can be blowing fast in both warm and cold temperatures. Therefore, these two scales should have divergent validity.

To measure divergent validity, we compared the tendency scores on the Impulse Factor test to the effectiveness scores on the test. The Impulse Factor theory states that people can be effective decision makers regardless of whether they have a low or high Impulse Factor. In keeping with the theory then, this means that tendency scores on the Impulse Factor test should not correlate with effectiveness scores on the test—they should *diverge*. This is how we can tell that what we are labeling effectiveness is not simply another measure of impulsivity that is only mislabeled, or vice versa. The effectiveness scale correlated only .08 with the risk subscale, only .17 with the hastiness subscale, and .10 with the overall tendency scale. Since anything less than a .20 correlation is regarded as "no correlation," we can conclude that the tendency and effectiveness scales are sufficiently divergent.

Interestingly, we did find a moderately significant correlation of .44 between Dickman's functional impulsivity scale and the effectiveness scale on the Impulse Factor test. We were initially surprised by this finding since we found a significant correlation between tendency scores and Dickman's scale, yet we found no correlation between our effectiveness scores and our tendency scores. However, it appears that the tendency scale on the Impulse Factor test might be tapping into the impulsivity part of Dickman's functional impulsivity scale, and the effectiveness scale on the Impulse Factor test taps into the functional aspects of the functional impulsivity scale. Whereas we specifically designed the tendency scale to be free of any measurement of value or quality (that is, high or low tendency scores are not better or worse than one another), by virtue of the label *functional* that Dickman applied to his scale, we can assume that he intended to ascribe some measurement of value to it—we can assume that "high" should be somewhat better than "low" on any scale of functionality. But we can also assume that our effectiveness scale did not correlate even more strongly to the functional impulsivity scale because Dickman sought only to measure functionality as it pertains to the realm of impulsivity. We can assume that a high score on Dickman's scale means that a person is functionally impulsive. However, a low score could mean two things: It could mean that the test taker is impulsive but not *functionally* impulsive, or it could mean that the test taker is simply not impulsive, period, functionally or otherwise. That would also explain why we found no correlation between Dickman's scale and the outcome variables of satisfaction and performance.

## How did TalentSmart decide on these questions, and not others?

The TalentSmart research team is composed of graduate-trained professionals in statistics and industrial-organizational psychology. The team was integral to the development of the Impulse Factor test and its questions. They have been collecting survey data on decision making for more than a decade. In 2004 the TalentSmart research team began examining decision making through the lens of impulsivity. The Impulse Factor test is the result of more than three years of research compiled into an intuitive format that is easy to understand and follow. We attempted to capture impulsivity traits without an excessive number of questions needed to achieve statistical and face validity.

With years of subject matter expertise and applied assessment experience, the TalentSmart research team and I took a pool of items from our extensive item-index library. We used an iterative process of selecting and reworking these items to fit what is "necessary and sufficient" for the test. We used no more or no less than what covers the elements of the model and trait. The first test was completed in 2005 and consisted of twenty-five test items. After administering the test to a sample population varying in age, ethnicity, and gender, we reduced the length of the test to twenty reliable items. A factor analysis revealed that there were eight items pertaining specifically to impulsivity. Since that initial testing, thousands more people have taken the test. The current version of the Impulse Factor test was rooted in this original scale, but the subsequent research conducted at TalentSmart made the most significant contribution.

After many rounds of additional pilots and analyses, we built out the concepts from the original twenty-question scale to include fifty-nine questions. The items were then presented to subject matter experts, consisting of Ph.D.- and master's-trained industrial-organizational psychology practitioners and MBA-level business professionals with management experience. This qualified group was brought together to establish the content validity and face validity of the Impulse Factor test.

Following refinement of the pool of questions based on the expert feedback, we gathered another simple random sample of survey participants. Based on factor analysis results from this round of testing, we were able to determine that we could adequately and reliably break down the test into two primary scales or factors. One scale addressed impulsivity and the other addressed effectiveness. The impulsivity scale included twenty-three items that were closely related. Within those items, eight clustered together reliably to form the risk subscale, and the remaining fifteen items clustered together to form the hastiness subscale. The effectiveness scale consists of one tightly clustered set of twelve items. Together the Impulse Factor test consists of thirty-five questions. Once we had our final set of thirty-five questions, we collected responses from more than 1,000 people to provide further evidence of reliability, as well as to establish the construct validity, as discussed earlier.

Consistent with TalentSmart's proprietary model of developing timely, nonintrusive, and easy-to-use surveys, we eliminated all but the items that were absolutely necessary to assess the traits and skills covered by the Impulse Factor test. While the test is shorter than many psychological assessments used in the workplace, TalentSmart takes great care in ensuring that the Impulse Factor test, like all TalentSmart surveys, is an accurate and useful measurement tool.

## Is this test scored ipsatively?

Yes and no. Ipsativity is a test-scoring methodology that asks test takers to distinguish between one or more options. It is commonly applied to tests with a forced-choice format. The Impulse Factor test is ipsatively scored in that each question of the test has two statements that we ask test takers to choose between. Each statement is loaded in a way that distinguishes the test takers preference for one statement or another, and for each question the test taker must choose which of the two statements he or she tends to gravitate more toward. One of the major drawbacks to an ipsatively scored test is that it does not allow for comparisons between individual test takers. For instance, if you select that you prefer using e-mail over using the phone to communicate, then we know something about you that could be valuable. However, if one of your coworkers prefers to use the phone over using e-mail, we cannot conclude that your coworker prefers using the phone more than you do. It is very possible that you might simply like to communicate more than your coworker, so you like all forms of communication (including the phone) more than your coworker does, even though when forced to choose you prefer to use e-mail.

However, the Impulse Factor test is not a pure forced-choice assessment because test takers are given the option to select "neutral" and also to rate how strongly that statement describes his or her preference. The statements for each question are on the opposite side of a continuum in the ways a person prefers to do things. On one side of the continuum, we ask if that statement "strongly describes you," "describes you," or if you are "neutral"; and we ask the same if you lean toward the other side of the continuum. Here's an example:

## WHICH STATEMENT BEST DESCRIBES YOU?

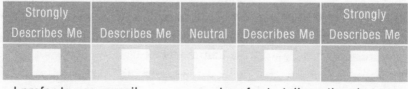

| Strongly Describes Me | Describes Me | Neutral | Describes Me | Strongly Describes Me |
|---|---|---|---|---|
| ☐ | ☐ | ☐ | ☐ | ☐ |

I prefer to use e-mail.      I prefer to talk on the phone.

Because test takers provide responses in a range, we are able to make comparisons between individuals. For example, we can reasonably conclude that if you select the option "Strongly Describes Me" for the statement "I prefer to talk on the phone" then you like to use the phone more than someone who selected "Neutral" or simply "Describes Me." In addition, the scale scores are based on normative averages to provide further basis for comparison between people.

## How are scores calculated?

Scores on the Impulse Factor test are calculated based on normative averages drawn from our database of worldwide respondents. This is another distinction from the standard ipsative scoring system. Ipsative scoring is defined by a preset sum of scores. So, for instance, if we categorized all of the statements in such a way that one statement was an indication of a cautious tendency and the other statement was an indication of an impulsive tendency (which we have, in fact, done), and if every respondent's score was 23 since there are twenty-three tendency score items (which it does not), then that would be an ipsative scoring system. The differences between test takers' scores would be only in regard to where on the scale their points were dispersed, but everyone would have a total of 23 points. For example, 10 points on the cautious statements and 13 points on the impulsive statements, or 5 in cautious and 18 in impulsive, and so on would still tell us something about the person, but something a little different than a scale that told us that one person scored only 18 points while another scored 37. This latter version would allow us to make comparisons between people.

## Can a person's Impulse Factor change over time?

People's traits, manifested in their preferences and tendencies, are generally regarded as being stable and enduring throughout the course of their adult lives. For practical purposes, we can be certain that one person's impulsivity will not change enough to make appreciable differences over the course of a lifetime. For example, through diligent practice you can learn to take a few extra minutes to think about whether or not to buy that new Rolex you saw in the store's showroom. Though your tendency is to be the first of your peers to buy the latest gadget in the market, for reasons of your own, it may be that the Omega is a better watch. A conscious effort to put your impulsivity in check over the course of years may appear to improve how you make decisions. However, it does not mean you change the way you naturally view the decision—only that you have adjusted for that natural disposition. Different situations call for different analyses of the right thing to do. With practice, it simply increases how often you consciously choose to exhibit one of the many behavioral facets that combine to lead you to make good decisions.

## Is the Impulse Factor test appropriate for non–English speakers?

The Impulse Factor test is appropriate for English speakers at the fifth-grade level. However, some of the terms and idioms present in the test are suitable for people at the high-school level and above. Translations of the test into other languages are in process.

## What feedback does a participant get with the Impulse Factor test?

Respondents receive a Feedback Report describing whether they have a risk-managing or potential-seeking tendency. They are also provided with numerical scores on the tendency subscales of risk and hastiness. Respondents are provided with a description of the decision-making effectiveness results, ranging from "very low" to "very high." Finally, the feedback report provides suggested action plans and TalentSmart's proprietary goal-tracking system to guide test-takers in their development of better decision-making skills.

## Do tendencies vary from a person's personal life to his or her work life?

The Impulse Factor is a trait-based model. A trait is a person's characteristic pattern of behavior that is relatively permanent. In such case, your tendencies, manifested through your internal and latent attributes, do not vary from your personal life to your work life. In your natural state, your tendencies and preferences are stable across time and situations. However, if you consciously monitor and modify your behaviors in different situations, your tendencies can vary, but that will require significant extra effort. Otherwise, your tendencies, preferences, and motivation are stable and relatively permanent. The Impulse Factor test is based on your natural tendency across situations. While we might expect your scores to vary slightly from work to home, the difference is not likely a large one.

If you are especially concerned about this, and believe you have special circumstances that significantly alter your behavior, a good rule of thumb would be to add 5 points to or subtract 5 points from your scores on the risk and hastiness subscales from work to home. However, if you have a high impulse factor, for example, and you believe that you are perhaps less impulsive at work, you should take a look at the situational variables. If the situation is such that it puts more limits and prohibitions on your impulses, that does not mean that your natural tendency to be impulsive has changed. It simply means that the situation is confining your natural tendency. If other impulsive people would also be less able to be impulsive in your specific work environment because the consequences are so salient that even a potential seeker cannot ignore those risks, then your tendency scores still would not be any normatively lower than if everyone were in the same situation.

To take your own online Impulse Factor™ test,
visit www.theimpulsefactor.com and key in the code
found on the inside back cover of this book.

# Appendix B
## Who Is TalentSmart?

TalentSmart® is a think tank and consultancy whose fresh ideas have assisted more than half of Fortune 500 companies. TalentSmart is the leading provider of emotional intelligence tests, products, and training. The following products, as well as free articles and a twice-monthly newsletter, are available at www.TalentSmart.com.

### The Impulse Factor Test

A precise measure of natural decision-making tendencies, as well as overall decision effectiveness based on the groundbreaking discoveries found in *The Impulse Factor.*

### The Emotional Intelligence Appraisal™

A quick and accurate assessment of all four skills from Daniel Goleman's benchmark EQ model. Available as a self, 360°, or team assessment.

### Emotional Intelligence Training

Take part in the most dynamic and engaging emotional intelligence training program available. TalentSmart trainers teach through assessment, interactive exercises, and blockbuster Hollywood movies in a blended solution that gets bottom-line results.

## Emotional Intelligence Training Certification

Come experience the laziest thermometer in the world while you learn to deliver—and are certified to own—the number1 EQ training. Certification sessions are held regularly in sunny San Diego, California.

## BRAINS! Emotional Intelligence Training Video

No more boring training videos! Brings emotional intelligence to life for your group using clips from Hollywood movies, television, and historical events.

## Emotional Intelligence PowerPoint®

A complete twenty-six-slide presentation with leader's guide and reproducible participant handouts.

For inquiries about these products, *Impulse Factor* keynotes by the author, and other solutions from TalentSmart, contact us at:

www.TalentSmart.com
1–888–818-SMART (toll-free)

# NOTES

## Introduction: Thrill Riders

1 The information regarding avalanche conditions and causes comes from *Avalanche Accidents in Canada* (Vol. 4), ed. Bruce Jamieson and Torsten Geldsetzer (British Columbia: Canadian Avalanche Association, 1996). Names, ages, and other details from the Pincher Creek avalanche that were not provided by Brian Cusack can be found in a 1994 article in the *Pincher Creek Echo* reporting the incident.

2 Daniel Kahneman and Amos Tversky's study on the European vacation problem was first published in "Prospect Theory: An Analysis of Decision under Risk," *Econometrica* 47, no. 2 (1979): 263–92. An extensive review of Kahneman and Tversky's research on prospect theory, as well as an assortment of other notable research that derived from prospect theory is contained in Kahneman and Tversky, *Choices, Values, and Frames* (New York: Cambridge University Press, 2000).

3 Lola Lopes lays out her theory in "When Time Is of the Essence: Averaging, Aspiration, and the Short Run," *Organizational Behavior and Human Decision Processes* 65, no. 3 (1996): 179–89.

4 D. L. Murphy et al. "Biogenic Amine-Related Enzymes and Personality Variations in Normals," *Psychological Medicine* 7 (1977): 149–57.

5 Marvin Zuckerman provides an excellent summary of research on the connection between MAO and various behavioral traits and psychological disorders in his book *Sensation Seeking and Risky Behavior* (Washington, DC: American Psychological Association, 2007).

## Chapter One: Origin of Seekers

1 To learn more about the National Children's Study, including center locations and other syndromes being studied, see www. nationalchildrensstudy.gov.

2 The term *attention deficit disorder* first appeared officially in DSM-III (*Diagnostic and Statistical Manual of Mental Disorders*) in 1980. Prior to that, in DSM-II, published in 1968, a syndrome described as "hyperkinetic reaction of childhood" was noted and is the precursor to what the later edition would label ADD. Whether or not ADD can exist independently of hyperactive behavior is still debated.

3 Information about Jim Swanson and the UC Irvine researchers' studies on ADHD came from personal communication with Jim Swanson and an assortment of articles summarizing their research. For statistics on the rise in the number of medical visits to treat ADHD, see Swanson et al., "Etiological Subtypes of Attention-Deficit/Hyperactivity Disorder: Brain Imaging, Molecular Genetic and Environmental Factors and the Dopamine Hypothesis," *Neuropsychology Review* 17 (2007): 39–59.

4 The original UC Irvine research on the relationship between the novelty-seeking gene and ADHD can be found in Swanson et al., "Attention Deficit/Hyperactivity Disorder Children with a 7-Repeat Allele of the Dopamine Receptor D4 Gene Have Extreme Behavior but Normal Performance on Critical Neuropsychological Tests of Attention," *Proceedings of the National Academy of Sciences* 97 (2000): 4754–59.

5 Richard Ebstein published his findings about the connection between the DRD4 gene and novelty-seeking in Ebstein et al., "Dopamine D4 Receptor (DRD4): Exon III Polymorphism Associated with the Human Personality Trait of Novelty Seeking," *Nature Genetics* 12 (1996): 78–80.

6 David W. Cameron and Colin P. Groves's *Bones, Stones and Molecules: "Out of Africa" and Human Origins* (Burlington, MA Elsevier, 2004) is a very accessible review of the research surrounding human evolution and the Out of Africa hypothesis.

7 The origin of the novelty-seeking gene's mutation, positive selection, and suggested relationship to early human migration and technological advances can be found in Y.-C. Ding et al., "Evidence of Positive Selection Acting at the Human Dopamine

Receptor D4 Gene Locus," *Proceedings of the National Academy of Sciences* 99 (2002): 309–14.

8 The state of the UC Irvine research program on the DRD4 gene is summed up in D. Grady, R. Moyzis, and J. Swanson, "Molecular Genetics and Attention in ADHD," *Clinical Neuroscience Research* 5 (2005): 265–72.

9 Information on the life of Stephen Siller, his heroic efforts on September 11, and the annual charity run to commemorate him can be found on www.tunneltotowersrun.org.

10 Tom Brokaw, *Boom! Voices of the Sixties* (New York: Random House, 2007).

## Chapter Two: Impulsivity's Hidden Side

1 An overview of the origin and subsequent development of Jack Kerouac's writing process, as well as the text of *On the Road* can be found in the Penguin Classic edition *On the Road* (New York: Penguin Putnam, 2000), which includes an introduction from noted Kerouac biographer Ann Charters.

2 The details of Neal Cassady's life were taken from David Sandison and Graham Vickers, *Neal Cassady: The Fast Life of a Beat Hero* (Chicago: Chicago Review Press, 2006).

3 Stephen Manes and Paul Andrews, *Gates: How Microsoft's Mogul Reinvented an Industry—and Made Himself the Richest Man in America* (New York: Touchstone, 1993).

4 Solomon Asch's classic conformity studies took place throughout the 1950s. His first publication on the topic was "Effects of Group Pressure upon the Modification and Distortion of Judgments" in *Groups, Leadership, and Men*, ed. H. Guetzkow (Pittsburgh: Carnegie, 1951). The reversal of the situation in which one person was an actor instructed to give the wrong answer comes from Asch's book *Social Psychology* (New York: Prentice-Hall, 1952).

5 Gary A. Williams and Robert B. Miller, "Change the Way You Persuade," *Harvard Business Review* (May 2002).

6 Scott J. Dickman, "Functional and Dysfunctional Impulsivity: Personality and Cognitive Correlates," *Journal of Personality and Social Psychology* 58 (1990): 95–102.

7 Marika Paaver, Diva Eensoo, Aleksander Pulver, and Jaanus Harro, "Adaptive and Maladaptive Impulsivity, Platelet Monamine Oxidase

(MAO) Activity and Risk-Admitting in Different Types of Risky Drivers," *Psychopharmacology* 186 (2006): 32–40.

8 Information on drunk-driving statistics can be found in *Traffic Safety Facts 2004*, issued by the National Highway Traffic Safety Administration. Retrieved from www-nrd.nhtsa.dot.gov/Pubs/TSF2004.pdf

9 M. A. Luengo, M. T. Carillo-de-la-Pena, J. M. Otero, and E. Romero, "A Short-Term Longitudinal Study of Impulsivity and Antisocial Behavior," *Journal of Personality and Social Psychology* 66 (1994): 542–48.

10 *Forbes's* annual list of the world's richest people can be found at www.forbes.com/lists.

## Chapter Three: Eat or Be Eaten

1 The information on how capuchin monkeys deal with jaguar predators came from an interview that Lynne Miller did with Jim Metzger (www.pulseplanet.com/archive/Feb99/1814.html).

2 More information on primate "freezing" and other responses to predators can be found in Lynne E. Miller (ed.), *Eat or Be Eaten* (New York: Cambridge University Press, 2002).

3 "Era of Good Feelings" was a quote by Benjamin Russell in the *Columbian Centinel* (July 1817).

4 A brief biography of James Monroe can be found at www.whitehouse.gov/history/presidents/jm5.html.

5 Information on the conditions surrounding the election of 1828 come from H. W. Brands's biography *Andrew Jackson: His Life and Times* (New York: Doubleday, 2005).

6 Other mudslinging accounts come from, "The Myth of America's Genteel Political History," author Kenneth C. Davis's audio commentary on National Public Radio (www.npr.org/templates/story/story.php?storyId=4129492).

7 The election scenario between "Jane Candidate" and "Mary Nominee" is my adaptation of experiments conducted by George A. Quattrone and Amos Tversky in "Contrasting Rational and Psychological Analyses of Political Choice," *American Political Science Review* 82, no. 3 (1988): 19–36.

8 Lola Lopes, "When Time is of the Essence: Averaging, Aspiration, and the Short Run," *Organizational Behavior and Human Decision Processes* 65, no. 3 (1996): 179–89.

## Chapter Four: Bubblology

1 Personal details about Conrad Gessner come from Konrad Gessner (n.d.) *Encyclopedia of the Early Modern World*. Retrieved October 1, 2007, from www.answers.com/topic/conrad-gessner.

2 Charles Mackay's classic text originally titled *Memoirs of Extraordinarily Popular Delusions* was first published in 1841 in London. Mackay's book is still the most thorough treatment available on "tulip-mania" and a fascinating review of the historical phenomenon of popular delusions. The edition used here was edited by Andrew Tobias, *Extraordinary Popular Delusions & the Madness of Crowds* (New York: Three Rivers Press, 1980).

3 The tulip's estimated worth in U.S. currency is found on the Web site "Stock Market Crash: The History of Financial Train Wrecks." Retrieved from www.stock-market-crash.net/tulip-mania.htm.

4 Daniel Kahneman's portrayal of his working relationship and friendship with Amos Tversky are found in Kahneman's autobiography on the Nobel Foundation Web site (http://nobelprize.org/nobel_prizes/economics/laureates/2002/kahneman-autobio.html).

5 Daniel Kahneman and Amos Tversky, "Prospect Theory: An Analysis of Decision Under Risk," *Econometrica* 47, no. 2 (1979): 263–91.

6 Hiroyuki Sasaki and Michihiko Kanachi, "The Effects of Trial Repetition and Individual Characteristics on Decision Making under Uncertainty," *The Journal of Psychology* 139, no. 3 (2005): 233–46.

7 Uri Gneezy, Ernan Haruvy, and Hadas Yafe, "The Inefficiency of Splitting the Bill: A Lesson in Institution Design," *Economic Journal* 114 (2004): 265–80.

8 Details about the rise and fall of the tech stock market can be found in John Cassidy, *Dot.con: How America Lost Its Mind and Money in the Internet Era* (New York: Harper Perennial, 2003).

9 Henry Blodget's quote comes from his "Internet/Electronic Commerce Report" from March 9, 1999.

10 Paula Horvath and Marvin Zuckerman, "Sensation Seeking, Risk Appraisal, and Risky Behavior. *Personality and Individual Differences* 14 (1993): 41–52.

11 Alan G. Sanfey et al., "The Neural Basis of Economic Decision-Making in the Ultimatum Game," *Science* 300 (2003): 1755–58.

12 David Dreman's first research and theories on overreaction can be found in his book *Contrarian Investment Strategy* (New York: Random House, 1979). His more recent thoughts on the topic are found in *Contrarian Investment Strategies: The Next Generation* (New York: Simon & Schuster, 1998) as well as in David N. Dreman and Eric A. Lufkin, "Investor Overreaction: Evidence That Its Basis Is Psychological," *The Journal of Psychology and Financial Markets* 1, no. 1 (2000): 61–75.

## Chapter Five: Common Sense of Ownership

1 Richard H. Thaler, "Toward a Positive Theory of Consumer Choice," *Journal of Economic Behavior and Organization* 1 (1980): 39–60.

2 Jack L. Knetsch, "The Endowment Effect and Evidence of Nonreversible Indifference Curves," *The American Economic Review* 79, no. 5 (1989): 1277–84.

3 Phil Taylor's article "Manning Mania" comes from his April 26, 2004, posting on SportsIllustrated.com. Retrieved from sportsillustrated .cnn.com/2004/writers/phil_taylor/04/26/taylor.manning.

4 Oliver Wendell Holmes's quote comes from his essay "The Path of Law," *Harvard Law Review*, 10 (1897): 455–77, as cited in David Cohen and Jack L. Knetsch, "Judicial Choice and Disparities between Measures of Economic Values," *Osgoode Hall Law Journal* 30, no. 3 (1992): 737–70.

5 M. Keith Chen, "How Basic Are Behavioral Biases? Evidence from Capuchin-Monkey Trading Behavior," *Journal of Political Economy* 114, no. 3 (2006): 517–37.

6 Daniel Gilbert, *Stumbling on Happiness* (New York: Knopf, 2006).

## Chapter Seven: Potential Seekers

1 A number of biographies are devoted to the life of St. Francis of Assisi. The details cited here come mostly from Donald Spoto, *Reluctant Saint: The Life of Francis of Assisi* (New York: Viking Compass, 2002).

2 Edward M. Hallowell and John J. Ratey, *Delivered from Distraction* (New York: Ballantine, 2005).

3 Ruth Handler, *Dream Doll: The Ruth Handler Story* (Stamford, CT: Longmeadow Press, 1995).

4 Marvin Zuckerman has been studying the trait of sensation seeking for decades. He has written a number of books and journal articles on the topic that have inspired much of the thinking on seeking behaviors of all sorts, included some of the ideas presented here. Zuckerman's *Sensation Seeking and Risky Behavior* (Washington D.C.: American Psychological Association: 2006) is a comprehensive academic review of the latest research on the topic.

5 Kenneth Scott Latourette, *A History of Christianity* (New York: Harper & Row, 1953).


## Chapter Eight: Risk Managers

1 Tim McDonald's quote came from his blog posting "Will No One Step Up to Challenge Tiger Woods?", January 30, 2006. Retrieved from www.travelgolf.com/blogs/tim.mcdonald/2006/01/30will_no_one_step_up_to_challenge_tiger_w.

2 Numerous articles covered Zach Johnson's surprise defeat over Tiger Woods. The details referenced here came specifically from Cameron Morfit, "Ryder Tough," April 8, 2007, retrieved from www.golf.com/golf/tours_news/article/0,28136,1607982,00.html; and from a postvictory interview transcript, "Zach Johnson, 2007 Masters Champion, Talks about Beating Tiger Woods," April 19, 2007, retrieved from www.worldgolf.com/pro-talk/zach-johnson-talks-about-masters-win-pro-talk-5169.htm.

3 Helen Fisher's *Why We Love* (New York: Holt, 2004) is a fascinating scientific journey through the physiology of love.

4 Debbie Crews's research on stress and golf was presented as the cover story titled "Golf in Science—First Prize: Putting Under Stress, 2003, retrieved from cgi.cnnsi.com/golfonline/instructions/science/firstprize.html.

5 Seth Godin is the author of a number of books on marketing and operates the most popular marketing blog on the Internet. You can find more information about Godin and his most recent books at www.sethgodin.com/sg/bio.asp.

6 James C. Worthy, *Shaping an American Institution: Robert E. Wood and Sears, Roebuck* (Urbana: University of Illinois Press, 1984).

7 Jeffrey Pfeffer and Robert I. Sutton, "Evidence-Based Management," *Harvard Business Review* 84, no. 1 (2006): 63–74.

## Chapter Nine: Striking a Balance

1 Caroline Moorehead's *Dunant's Dream* (New York: Carroll & Graf, 1999) is an entertaining and comprehensive look at the foundations of the International Red Cross with special attention to the personalities that made Henry Dunant's dream a reality.

2 The complete text of Henry Dunant's *A Memory of Solferino* can be read online at the Web site of the International Committee of the Red Cross www.icrc.org/WEB/ENG/siteeng0.nsf/html/p0361.

3 Helen Fisher's work with Chemistry.com is documented in an interview available at www.chemistry.com/drhelenfisher/interview cjdrfisher.aspx.

4 Peter Abrams, "Optimal Traits When There Are Several Costs: The Interaction of Mortality and Energy Costs in Determining Foraging Behavior," *Behavioral Ecology* 4 (1993): 246–53.

5 Peter Abrams and Hiroyuki Matsuda, "The Evolution of Traits That Determine Ability in Competitive Contests," *Evolutionary Ecology* 8 (1994): 667–86.

6 Fred Adler, "The Balance of Terror: An Alternative Mechanism for Competitive Trade-Offs and Its Implication for Invading Species," *The American Naturalist* 154 (1999): 497–509.

7 Max Wolf, G. Sander van Doorn, Olof Leimar, and Franz J. Weissing, "Life-History Trade-Offs Favour the Evolution of Animal Personalities," *Nature* 447 (2007): 581–84.

8 Y.-C. Ding et al., "Evidence of Positive Selection Acting at the Human Dopamine Receptor D4 Gene Locus," *Proceedings of the National Academy of Sciences* 99 (2002): 309–14.

9 David Garvin and Lynne Levesque, "Meeting the Challenge of Corporate Entrepreneurship," *Harvard Business Review* 84, no. 10 (2006): 102–12.